EDUCATION AND THE NATIONAL ECONOMY

During the last six years the Western education system has undergone many major shocks and changes which have stemmed largely from the state of the economy. Public expenditure through local government has been cut drastically in an attempt to bring it into line with national economic performance. However, "cuts" are by no means the only effect which the state of the economy has had on education. Schools, colleges and universities are being asked to tailor their 'output' to suit the *needs* of the economy — technologically and scientifically skilled manpower being its immediate requirements.

This book is a detailed, up-to-date study of all the major past, present and foreseeable future effects of the economy on education and covers such controversial subjects as "Education Vouchers". There is also a chapter on education and the Third World which presents contrasting evidence for the effect of the economy on education.

EDUCATION AND THE NATIONAL ECONOMY

◆

J. R. Hough

CROOM HELM
London • New York • Sydney

© 1987 J.R. Hough
Croom Helm Ltd, Provident House, Burrell Row,
Beckenham, Kent, BR3 1AT

Croom Helm Australia, 44-50 Waterloo Road,
North Ryde, 2113, New South Wales

British Library Cataloguing in Publication Data

Hough, J.R.
    Education and the national economy.
    1. Education — Great Britain — Finance
    I. Title
    379.1'21'0941   LB2826.6.G7
    ISBN 0-7099-3735-0

Published in the USA by
Croom Helm
in association with Methuen, Inc.
29 West 35th Street
New York, NY 10001

Library of Congress Cataloging-in-Publication Data

Hough, J.R.
    Education and the national economy.

    Bibliography: p.
    Includes index.
    1. Education — Economic aspects. 2. Education and
state. 3. Manpower policy. I. Title.
LC65.H68 1987   338.4'737   87-9169
ISBN 0-7099-3735-0

Printed and bound in Great Britain by
Biddles Ltd, Guildford and King's Lynn

CONTENTS

TABLES

Tables

PREFACE

As an economist based in a Department of Education,
I have had to spend much of my available time in
recent years examining the various relationships
between national economic performance and the
education system. This book stems from that work
and from the encouragement I received from the
publishers to complete such a book.

My grateful thanks are due to a number of
colleagues at Loughborough University who have helped
me in various ways, including reading and commenting
on draft chapters. Professor Leonard Cantor and
Professor Lou Cohen provided support and encouragement throughout. In particular I am grateful to the
staff of the university library and especially Miss
M. McKay, for time and trouble spent tracing sources
and checking references.

I also have to thank Mrs Marjorie Salsbury and
Mrs Brenda Shaw who typed drafts of chapters and
Mrs Gloria Brentnall who typed the final typescript.
Without their ready and efficient help the book
could not have been completed.

Final responsibility for the text and for any
errors and omissions does of course lie with myself
alone.

As with my previous books, arrangements have
been made with the publishers for all author's
royalties to be remitted direct to Christian Aid.

J.R. Hough
Loughborough
November 1986

Chapter One

EDUCATION AND THE ECONOMY: AN OVERVIEW

The United Kingdom is one of the richest countries
in the world and enjoys a standard of living which
people in the world's poorer countries admire and
envy. As compared with her principal competitor
countries, however, the UK's economy has suffered
relative decline more or less continuously in the
forty-year period since the end of the Second World
War and increasingly so over the latter half of that
period. As measured by the four conventional targets of macro-economic policy, economic growth,
inflation, the balance-of-payments and unemployment,
the UK has fared worse than all of the other member
countries of the OECD which are her main trading
partners.

ECONOMIC INDICATORS

On economic growth the UK's record has been
indifferent with annual rates of growth frequently
below 2 per cent and rarely above 3 per cent, whilst
Japan has recorded between 8 and 10 per cent, France
and Germany each around 5 per cent and the USA often
between 3 and 4 per cent. For the four-year period
1974-1978 the UK's economic growth totalled less
than zero, i.e. a net *minus* figure, before the rate
improved again somewhat. Apart from the question
of the direct increase in the standard of living
which may become immediately available, a high rate
of economic growth also carries with it the
potential for higher levels of investment and modern-
isation, and so increased efficiency for future
production, all of which will tend in turn to
reinforce the growth cycle.
    Inflation was generally not seen as a serious
problem before the onset of the successive oil

1

crises from 1973 onwards but even in those earlier
years the UK frequently had annual inflation rates
between 5 and 6 per cent whilst other developed
countries tended to have figures between 4 and 5 per
cent: for one or two years such a differential
might not seem very serious but when continued over
a longer period the cumulative effects on the UK's
competitiveness and trading position became much
more noticeable. After 1974, with the quadrupling
of oil prices, inflation in the UK escalated dramatically, reaching 26 per cent in 1975 and remaining
in double figures for the next few years. All
other oil-importing countries were also seriously
affected but few of our competitors had such high
rates of inflation as did the UK.

In all industrialised countries unemployment
remained at relatively low levels for the first
thirty years or so after the ending of the Second
World War and then started to rise to reach levels
that were so serious that they would previously have
been considered socially and politically unaccept-
able: this trend occurred earlier and went further
in the UK than in other comparable countries. In
mid-1974 unemployment in the UK was around 550,000;
by mid-1978 it had trebled and by mid-1986 had
reached over 3.3 million (compared to around 2.25
million in each of France and West Germany, each
with a similar size population to the UK). Unemployment seems to have settled at its present very
high level and economists and politicians are now
increasingly of the view that the figure may not
fall significantly for many years, perhaps not before
the twenty-first century: even as some growth and
expansion does take place increasingly the trend is
for this to be via highly-automated production processes and computer-operated machinery such that very
few if any jobs are created. *Hi-Tech, robotics* and
informatics are just some examples of the vocabulary
of this new world of *machines driven by machines*.

The balance-of-payments had traditionally always
been seen as the major constraint on the operation
of economic policy in the UK. With an ever-present
deficit on foreign trade, only offset by a successful
annual surplus on 'invisibles' such as insurance,
banking and finance, and with more often than not an
overall deficit on the current account of the balance
of payments, this was a constant problem which led
all too easily and frequently to financial crisis,
speculation against the pound, monetary and fiscal
deflation of the domestic economy and devaluation.
Leading economists confidently asserted that

once Britain was receiving the full benefit of her
huge stocks of oil in the North Sea there should be
no more balance-of-payments problems for the ensuing
thirty years. It was to take only a very few years
for such forecasts to prove over-optimistic. By
the 1980s it was increasingly clear that not only
were British manufacturers finding it increasingly
difficult to sell their products in overseas markets
but foreign-produced goods were selling so well
within the UK that they were in danger of taking
over some domestic markets completely. The figure
that 60 per cent of all new cars purchased were
imported (a fairly static figure over a period of
several years) received much publicity. Rather
less dramatically anyone going to buy a new washing
machine, refrigerator, television set, hi-fi music
centre, or any other consumer durable, would
increasingly find displays dominated by imported
items which were recommended at the point of sale
as being both cheaper and more reliable.
Early in 1985 an OECD report found that of all
major new inventions in industrialised countries in
recent years, some 55 per cent originated from the
UK, a truly impressive record. In very many of
these cases, however, the inventors could not get
support for their new ideas at home and had to have
them produced and sold overseas, some returning to
the UK as imports.
It would be possible to continue this sad story
almost *ad infinitum*. A major study[1] showed that
Britain's share of world trade had fallen continuously, that her labour productivity was low, capital
investment inadequate, industrial profitability too
low and concluded,

> *Viewed both aggregatively and disaggregatively,*
> *the performance of British manufacturing*
> *industry has been disappointing.*

A companion study[2] focused on the revolution in
micro-electrics, found that this was bringing and
would continue to bring fundamental changes in
practically every industrial and service occupation,
but concluded that the UK's record in this field was
disappointing and that the UK was poorly placed to
take advantage of the new technologies. This was
in great contrast, for example, to Japan which had
'integrated design and development of products and
productive processes'.[3]
By 1986 the latest worry was the collapse in
the international price of oil. Whilst the latter

should aid the battle against inflation and favour
increased competitiveness, it was also liable to
bring worsening balance-of-payments problems for a
country that was now a net exporter of oil. At the
time of writing the effects of this latest dramatic
change are still working their way through the
economy.

LABOUR MARKET TRENDS

Throughout the period since 1945 the UK economy has
been undergoing quite rapid change, consisting in
part of the continuation of earlier trends often
extending back to the early years of this century
and in part of the influences of quite new patterns
of demand and supply and particularly technological
changes. All such changes have inevitably had
major effects on the market for labour, which is the
principal link with the education system since the
products of the latter must supply the labour needs
of the former.
      Occupational patterns in the UK have gradually
changed throughout the twentieth century, with
broadly the same trends continuing into the more
recent period of twenty years covered by Table 1.1.
As the table shows, there have been clear trends
towards employment relatively declining in *agriculture* and throughout every category of *industry*:
not one of the main industrial branches shown
escaped this trend. Approaching 4 million jobs in
industry were lost during this period of just over
20 years. Of all employees, over 50 per cent were
in the industrial categories in 1961 but by 1983
only just over one-third. Employment in services,
on the other hand, continued to expand although not
evenly so, with *transport and communication*, for
example, recording a decrease; all the other
categories of *services* recorded increases and total
employment in the services categories increased by
over 3 million.
      By 1983 over 43 per cent of all employed were
women, this percentage having increased steadily
over time; over 73 per cent of women work in the
services categories.
      It should be noted that the total number of
jobs shown fell from 22.2m to 21.1m, i.e. by 1.1m,
whilst unemployment rose by some 2.75m, over a
period of years when the size of the working population rose only slowly. Therefore at least part
of the much-publicised increase in unemployment must

Table 1.1: Employees by Industrial Category (UK), 1961-1983 (numbers in thousands)

	1961 Number	%	1971 Number	%	1981 Number	%	1983 Number	%
Agriculture, forestry and fishing	710	3.2	432	2.0	352	1.6	349	1.6
Industry								
Energy and water supply industries*			797	3.6	709	3.2	662	3.1
Extraction of minerals and ores other than fuels, manufacture of metal, mineral products, and chemicals	11,141	50.1	1,278	5.8	934	4.3	821	3.9
Metal goods, engineering, and vehicle industries			3,706	16.8	2,920	13.4	2,651	12.5
Other manufacturing industries			3,102	14.0	2,368	10.8	2,170	10.2
Construction			1,207	5.5	1,138	5.2	1,016	4.7
Total Industry	11,141	50.1	10,090	45.6	8,069	36.9	7,320	34.4
Services								
Distribution, hotels, catering and repairs			3,678	16.6	4,167	19.1	4,209	19.8
Transport and communication	10,382	46.7	1,550	7.0	1,423	6.5	1,332	6.2
Banking, finance, insurance business services and leasing			1,335	6.0	1,739	8.0	1,837	8.6
Other services			5,035	22.8	6,122	28.0	6,164	29.0
Total Services	10,382	46.7	11,598	52.4	13,451	61.5	13,542	63.6
All industries and services	22,233	100.0	22,122	100.0	21,870	100.0	21,210	100.0

Note: Totals may not add up due to rounding.

*Includes coal mining.

Source: Department of Employment.

5

relate to an increased labour participation rate and
to an increased tendency for people to 'sign on' and
thus become included in the official statistics,
rather than to a 'real' rise in unemployment. The
underlying rise in unemployment has been particularly
serious in the case of young people, in Britain as
throughout Europe: one recent estimate is that in
Britain and in other comparable countries of those
young people who have left school around 50 per cent
may not have been able to find work within the first
year.   This catastrophic rise in youth unemployment,
which by the mid-1980s shows no sign of abating, is
evidently the most important change to have over-
taken the youth labour market in recent years.
    Table 1.2 shows longer term trends by occu-
pational class of the working population.   Whereas
the statistics included in Table 1.1 are compiled on
a regular annual basis by the Department of Employment, those in Table 1.2 only become available on
the occasion of each national census, normally held
every ten years.   The manipulation of such
statistics is a minefield for the unwary and care
should be taken particularly in any attempt to draw
relationships between data derived from different
sources.   Thus it is apparent that the total number
of employment positions covered by Table 1.2 is much
greater than those covered by Table 1.1 even though
the geographical coverage of the former is limited
to Great Britain whereas the latter covers the whole
of the United Kingdom and thus includes Northern
Ireland.   The discrepancy relates to the fact that
Table 1.1 refers to employees only whereas Table 1.2
also includes employers and the self-employed.
    Table 1.2 makes clear the major trends relating
to classification by occupational class over the
period from 1931 onwards with, in every case,
uninterrupted trends continuing throughout this
period: the very significant increases in *non-manual*
employment, *professional* (the largest relative rate
of increase, up from 968,000 or 4.6 per cent of the
total to 3,735,000 or 14.7 per cent), *employers,*
administrators and managers (up from 1,479,000, 7.0
per cent, to 3,552,000, 14.0 per cent), and *clerical*
workers (up from 1,465,000, 7.0 per cent, to
3,761,000, 14.8 per cent).   In all, non-manual
forms of employment accounted for 20.1 per cent of
the total in 1931, 30.4 per cent in 1951, 46.1 per
cent in 1971 and 47.7 per cent in 1981.   The concomitant relative decline in manual working was
shared between the skilled, semi-skilled, and
unskilled categories, the sharpest relative falls

Table 1.2: Occupational Class of Working Population (GB), 1931-1971
(numbers in thousands)

	1931 Number	1931 %	1951 Number	1951 %	1971 Number	1971 %	1981 Number	1981 %
1. Professional	968	4.6	1,493	6.6	2,770	11.1	3,735	14.7
2. Employers, administrators, managers	1,479	7.0	2,364	10.5	3,110	12.4	3,552	14.0
3. Clerical workers	1,465	7.0	2,404	10.7	3,479	13.9	3,761	14.8
4. Foremen, inspectors, supervisors	323	1.5	590	2.6	968	3.9	1,072	4.2
Manual workers								
5. Skilled	5,619	26.8	5,616	25.0	5,394	21.6	4,434	17.5
6. Semi-skilled	7,360	35.0	7,338	32.6	6,312	25.2	6,163	24.2
7. Unskilled	3,115	14.8	2,709	12.0	2,987	11.9	2,699	10.6
All	21,029	100.0	22,514	100.0	25,021	100.0	25,406	100.0

Note: Totals may not add up due to rounding.

Sources: *National Censuses: 1931-71 adapted from G. Routh, Occupation and Pay in Great Britain 1906-79 (Macmillan, 1980). 1981: supplied to me by Dr. Routh.*

being in the semi-skilled category until 1971 but in the skilled category thereafter.

It is particularly striking that the number of unskilled jobs actually increased between 1951 and 1971 before declining again thereafter. A further breakdown of the Census statistics relating to manual employment reveals striking differences in this respect between men and women: the fall in semi-skilled employment related almost solely to men, the numbers of semi-skilled women in employment remaining almost constant to 1971 before some decline; skilled employment rose for men but fell for women whereas unskilled employment fell for men (2,645,000 down to 1,615,110) but rose sharply for women until 1971[4] before falling thereafter (overall 467,000 up to 1,083,790). The 1981 Census statistics for women are given in Table 6.2 in Chapter Six.

The trends indicated in Table 1.2 should be seen in conjunction with those in Table 1.1: the large loss of manual jobs largely relates to the declining industrial employment whereas much of the increased non-manual employment relates to the services categories. Expansion has taken place in those forms of employment requiring higher standards of education both at entry and in terms of subsequent qualifications whilst those forms of employment requiring least education have been declining. This leads us on directly to the question of the relationship between Britain's economy and industry and her educational system.

THE EDUCATION SYSTEM

There have been many attempts to attribute blame or responsibility for Britain's industrial decline. Scapegoats have included, perhaps not surprisingly, both trade unions and management, or the social class system has been seen to be at fault. The country's education system, too, has not escaped criticism. Over a long period of years there have developed allegations that schools and colleges, and even polytechnics and universities, were paying insufficient attention to the needs of the economy in general and of industry in particular and were even guilty of inculcating anti-industrial attitudes. Young people emerged from the education system, it was alleged, determined if at all possible not to work in industry or, as the argument was sometimes cited, '*not to get their hands dirty*'.

The notion of a direct and crucial relationship between the national economy and the output of
the education system has received much attention
over the last two years or so.   It was referred to
in the White Paper *Better Schools*[5] published in
March 1985 and was the dominant theme throughout the
Green Paper *The Development of Higher Education into
the 1990s*[6] published in May that year;   we will
revert to these later.   Commentary on such a
relationship has a long history.   It was referred
to by the early economists in the nineteenth century
and figured in publications relating to education
throughout the first half of the twentieth century.
The rapid growth of education after 1945 led on to
the perceived need for a series of official reports
covering different aspects of the education system,
and one aspect referred to in each of these reports
was the connection with the needs of industry and of
the national economy.

It has to be remembered that education in
Britain, perhaps influenced by the public school
tradition and by nineteenth-century notions of a
'Classical Education', has always sought to have a
wide focus and to educate *'the whole child'* with all
that that implied in terms of the development of
cultural, literary, and aesthetic awareness (even
leading on in more recent times to the notion of
'education for leisure'):   such emphasis needed to be
set alongside notions of the economic dimension to
the education the pupils received, as was clearly
recognised by the first of the major reports in
question, the Crowther Report:[7]

> *The task of education in the technological age
> is thus a double one.   On the one hand, there
> is a duty to set young people on the road to
> acquiring the bewildering variety of qualifi-
> cations they will need to earn their living.
> On the other hand, running through and across
> these vocational purposes, there is also a
> duty to remember those other objectives of any
> education, which have little or nothing to do
> with vocation, but are concerned with the
> development of human personality and with
> teaching the individual to see himself in due
> proportion to the world in which he has been
> set ... we have tried not to lose sight of the
> economic and vocational purposes that an
> effective educational system should serve.
> But children are not the 'supply' that meets
> any 'demand' however urgent.   They are*

9

individual human beings, and the primary
concern of the schools should not be with the
living they will earn but with the life they
will lead.

It was perhaps significant that this report covered
school pupils in the age group 15 to 18 and had much
to say about the economy and about economic change,
although as will be seen this was more from the
standpoint of the pupils than in terms of the needs
of industry:

Of all the driving forces of change in the
present day, among the strongest are those that
show up in economic form, those that bear ...
upon the living the pupils in the schools are
looking forward to being able to earn.

Since a high level of national productivity can
only be sustained by brains and skill, the
schools have a higher challenge to meet.

It is now (or should be) apparent to all that
education pays, always in the long run, and
often quite quickly.

Not only have there been plenty of jobs for the
qualified, there has been a steadily growing
list of desirable callings that cannot be
entered without a qualification.

The other great force ... that is transforming
the role of education is the rising importance
of being properly qualified.

Qualifications have always been required for
the professions.   What has been happening in
the last twenty years is that the same require-
ment has been spreading over a much larger field
of employment.

The report went on to revert to the dual theme cited
previously:

In this report, we have made no attempt to
disentangle (the) two purposes of education.
Both are worthy and compelling and we accept
them both.   Primacy must be given to the human
rights of the individual boy or girl.   But we
do not believe that the pursuit of national
efficiency can be ranked much lower ...   If

> *(education) be regarded as a social service, as
> part of the 'condition of the people', there
> seems to us to be no social injustice in our
> community at the present time more loudly cry-
> ing out for reform than the condition in which
> scores of thousands of our children are
> released into the labour market.   If it be
> regarded as an investment in national effici-
> ency, we find it difficult to conceive that
> there could be any other application of money
> giving a larger or more certain return in the
> quickening of enterprise, in the stimulation of
> invention or in the general sharpening of those
> wits by which alone a trading nation in a
> crowded island can hope to make its living.*

These extracts have been quoted at some length
because they show clearly that concern over the
relationship between education and the economy,
which has received much public attention in recent
years, is neither very new nor very original.   Over
twenty-five years ago it was articulated at length
but whereas other aspects of the Crowther Report -
such as the raising of the school leaving age - were
immediately seized on and became the focus for major
issues of educational policy, this particular aspect
passed comparatively unnoticed.   Worries over
Britain's deteriorating economic performance had
not in 1959 come to achieve such predominance as
they were to do subsequently and it is therefore
understandable that this aspect received much less
attention in the report, as the above extracts
indicate, than the future careers and livelihoods of
the young people with whom the report was concerned.
The authors of the report felt, as is clear from the
above extracts, that they should not go on to assess
whether more (or fewer) scientists and technologists
would be needed in the future but they do seem to
have suspected that if there were to be a problem
over the numbers so qualified, far from there being
a deficit there could even be a surplus.

One other question referred to in the above
extracts and developed at length elsewhere in the
Crowther Report, namely the use by employers of
educational certificates as a filtering mechanism
when recruiting staff even when the subjects studied
have no direct connection with the work to be done,
subsequently received much attention under the title
'*the screening hypothesis*' and will be considered
further in a later chapter.   This is, as we shall
see, closely related to the view of educational

qualifications as a screening or filter mechanism faciliating the task of employers in choosing young people for employment situations, even when the subjects studied have little or no direct relevance to the work in question.

Only a year and a half after Crowther the government of the day felt the need for another major study, this time of '*the education of pupils aged 13 to 16 of average and less than average ability*' and therefore overlapping considerably with it: the Newsom Report, *Half Our Future*,[8] was published in 1963 and it had no doubts as to the nation's requirements for technically qualified personnel:

> *The progress of automation and the application of other technological developments are likely to be delayed by lack of trained personnel ... 'It remains doubtful whether the number of new entrants into skilled occupations will be sufficient to match future needs.'*

(the last sentence being quoted with approval from the 1962 White Paper on Industrial Training). Newsom recommended the extension of practical work-experience and of '*Introduction to Industry*' type courses but in general concentrated on matters within schools and had rather little to say about links between education and the world of work, possibly because it did not wish to overlap with the work of Crowther.

In the same year, 1963, came the report[9] which is now seen in retrospect as the cornerstone on which the subsequent mushrooming of higher education in Britain was based. The Robbins Committee was set up not by the Minister of Education but by the Prime Minister and its report emanated not from the Ministry of Education but from the Treasury and was presented directly to Parliament as a Command paper: its status was therefore virtually assured in advance. The oft-cited main principle embodied in the Robbins Report, that:

> *courses of higher education should be available for all those who are qualified by ability and attainment to pursue them and who wish to do so*

was seen by the authors as being directly, although by no means solely, related to economic and vocational needs, whether or not the courses in question imparted specifically vocationally-relevant

or technical skills. A companion recommendation,
which has received much less subsequent publicity,
was that the future growth of degree-level education
(then concentrated almost entirely in universities)
should embrace:

> *some further increase beyond 51 per cent in*
> *the proportion of students taking science and*
> *technology.*

In reaching this conclusion the Committee was
apparently influenced partly by evidence of general
vocational trends, partly by statistics showing that
from 1958 onwards A-level passes in mathematics and
science had been increasing more slowly than those
in non-science subjects, and partly by such views as

> *developments in science are increasingly a*
> *part of daily life*
> and
> *a science course, whether pure or applied,*
> *can make as valid a contribution to general*
> *education as any other.*

The concept of a need to aid the re-direction
of students towards science and technology does not
sit easily with the UK educational system's traditional reliance, at least at the level of post-
compulsory education, on the 'Social Demand'
approach, i.e. provided students are qualified
(usually via appropriate passes at GCE A-level) to
take a degree-level course of study they should be
able to choose the subject area in which they wish
to specialise, almost without restriction.
The theme of needing to have more students in
the fields of science and technology was to be taken
up by detail by an official report commissioned just
two years after Robbins and published in 1968. Any
student of educational developments during the years
in question should have at least an outline knowledge of the place and significance of the Crowther,
Newsom and Robbins Reports. Which of them will have
even heard of the Dainton Report,[10] let alone know
anything of its content or recommendations?
Perhaps the subsequent obscurity of this report,
which was entitled *Enquiry into the Flow of Candidates*
in Science and Technology into Higher Education,
signifies the lack of public interest in what it had
to say and may therefore be taken as symptomatic of
the alleged gulf that was opening up between educational development and national economic need?

Be that as it may, the views of the small Dainton Committee, which had only six members, make powerful reading:

> *the implications of the swing from science are far-reaching. Foremost, for scientific manpower policy, is the prospect of a pause in the growth of new supply to the stock of qualified scientists and technologists ... In relation to the educational system our findings suggest a conflict between patterns of personal preferences and social aspirations (working against the traditional sciences) and published evidence as to the demand for more scientists and technologists ... Tighter competition for newly qualified manpower in the early 1970s could have restrictive effects on new developments dependent on graduates in specialised fields.*

Attempts by the Dainton Committee to diagnose the cause of the drift away from science and technology at degree level focused on reactions to the study of scientific subjects in schools, reactions summarised in unattractive terms:

> *some pupils ... are deterred by the apparent rigour and unattractiveness of science*
>
> *most young people are now able to choose apparently less rigorous alternatives*
>
> *scientific studies in schools may be suffering from the after-effects of the intense competition for university places in science and technology which characterised the 1950s*
>
> *for many young people science, engineering and technology seem out of touch with human and social affairs*
>
> *the objectivity of science and the purposefulness of technology have become identified, for some, with insensitivity and indifference*
>
> *there are indisputable signs of an acute shortage of graduate scientists in schools at present, particularly in mathematics, in the intensive use of science and mathematics graduate teachers in schools compared with those in other disciplines, and in the extent to which*

> *these subjects are taught by teachers whose*
> *main subject of qualification is in other*
> *fields.*

The fate of the Dainton Report may be summarised by
noting that its main conclusion:

> *We recommend a broad span of studies in the*
> *sixth forms of schools; and that, in*
> *consequence, irreversible decisions for or*
> *against science, engineering and technology,*
> *be postponed as late as possible*

was never acted upon, indeed was completely ignored,
before eventually being resurrected in another guise
some fifteen years later.

And finally, in this consideration of official
reports relating to education, rather briefer
reference may be made to the Russell Report.[11]   The
Russell Committee, in what now seem as curiously
restrictive terms of reference, was set up to
enquire into '*non-vocational adult education*' but
that the Committee did not feel narrowly bound by
this brief is shown, for example, by the fact that
one whole section of the report was devoted to
'*Adult Education in Relation to Industry*': here
and elsewhere the report emphasised the trends
already noted above, viz. towards more skilled working and towards regular up-dating and acquisition of
new skills during a time of rapid technological
change. Adult Education as traditionally defined
in the UK was, however, seen by implication as making
only a marginal contribution towards the fulfilment
of such needs.

CONTINUING CRITICISM AND THE 'GREAT DEBATE'

Criticism of the educational system and its economic
role has continued more or less ever since. An
early and influential critic could write:

> *So far from there being a close relationship*
> *between what the schools attempt to do and*
> *what industry requires, indeed, there have in*
> *the past been strong influences against*
> *vocational education, at any rate until after*
> *the secondary stage*[12]

and such accusations continued intermittently in
subsequent years.

With the *'Great Debate'* initiated by Prime
Minister James Callaghan in 1976 this question came
once more into prominence. Speaking at Ruskin
College, Oxford, in October, Mr Callaghan detailed
at some length the alleged shortcomings, largely
from industry's point of view, of the education that
children and young people were receiving, at all
levels:

> *I am concerned on my journeys to find complaints*
> *from industry that new recruits from the schools*
> *sometimes do not have the basic tools to do the*
> *job that is required.*
>
> *I have been concerned to find that many of our*
> *best trained students who have completed the*
> *higher levels of education at university or*
> *polytechnic have no desire or intention of*
> *joining industry. Their preferences are to*
> *stay in academic life (very pleasant, I know)*
> *or to find their way into the civil service.*
> *There seems to be a need for a more techno-*
> *logical bias in science teaching that will lead*
> *towards practical applications in industry*
> *rather than towards academic studies.*
>
> *Or, to take other examples, why is it, as I am*
> *told, that such a high proportion of girls*
> *abandon science before they leave school?*
> *Then there is concern about the standards of*
> *numeracy of school leavers. Is there not a*
> *case for a professional review of the math-*
> *ematics needed by industry at different levels?*
> *To what extent are these deficiences the result*
> *of insufficient co-ordination between schools*
> *and industry? Indeed how much of the criticism*
> *about the absence of basic skills and attitudes*
> *is due to industry's own shortcomings rather*
> *than to the educational system? Why is it that*
> *30,000 vacancies for students in science and*
> *engineering in our universities and polytechnics*
> *were not taken up last year while the humanities*
> *courses were full? ... There is no virtue in*
> *producing socially well adjusted members of*
> *society who are unemployed because they do not*
> *have the skills. Nor at the other extreme must*
> *they be technically efficient robots.*[13]

Much the same theme was repeated by the government in
the Green Paper *Education in Schools* issued the
following year:

The Prime Minister's concern about the rele-
vance of present-day education to the needs of
industry and commerce was reflected in many of
the comments about this aspect of schools
education at the regional conferences. It was
said that the school system is geared to pro-
mote the importance of academic learning and
careers with the result that pupils, especially
the more able, are prejudiced against work in
productive industry and trade; that teachers
lack experience, knowledge and understanding of
trade and industry; that curricula are not
related to the realities of most pupils' work
after leaving school; and that pupils leave
school with little or no understanding of the
workings, or importance, of the wealth-
producing sector of our economy.[14]

The 1985 Green Paper

It was, however, as indicated previously, in 1985
that the question of a crucial relationship between
economic performance and the country's education
system came once again into prominence with the
publication, within two months of each other, of the
White Paper *Better Schools* and the Green Paper *The
Development of Higher Education into the 1990s*.
The former included various references to this
relationship on the lines of: *'pupils need to have
acquired, far more than at present, the qualities
and skills required for work in a technological age'*.
Throughout the Green Paper, however, this theme
appears in every section and may be said to be the
dominant idea that the Green Paper expressed - indeed
much of the criticism subsequently directed at the
Green Paper suggested that it had gone too far in
that direction, to the neglect of other priorities.
The following extracts will serve to indicate
the flavour of the Green Paper's emphasis:

Our higher education establishments need to be
concerned with attitudes to the world outside
education, and in particular to industry and
commerce and to beware of 'anti-business'
snobbery. The entrepreneurial spirit is
essential for the maintenance and improvement
of employment, prosperity and public services.
Higher education should be alert to the hazard
of blunting it and should seek opportunities to
encourage it. More generally, higher education
needs to foster positive attitudes to work.

> *Higher education's output of able, skilled and*
> *well-motivated graduates is vital to the*
> *country's economic performance ... Although*
> *a wide range of courses is available at*
> *different levels to meet the needs of industry,*
> *commerce, the professions and the public*
> *services, there is continuing concern that*
> *higher education does not always respond*
> *sufficiently to changing economic needs.*
>
> *Institutions and academic staff have a*
> *responsibility to seek closer links with*
> *employers, which are essential if higher*
> *education is to realise its full potential in*
> *meeting the needs of the economy, in terms of*
> *highly qualified manpower and also of its*
> *contribution through research, technology*
> *transfer and consultancy.*

The Views of Industry

Evidence of such continuing concern was given at
some length in a report by the authoritative
National Economic Development Council[15] which contained detailed and wide-ranging criticisms of
education in Britain from the point of view of the
nation's industry:

> *There is widespread concern in industry that*
> *the education system does not provide a general*
> *training which adequately prepares young people*
> *for work. This is strengthened by the*
> *apparently low priority which education accords*
> *industry through its curricula, emphasis on*
> *academic attainment and very limited awareness*
> *of, or links with, industry. At the same time*
> *there has been a lack of effective means by*
> *which industry needs could be expressed other*
> *than through rather weak income and unemploy-*
> *ment signals. The education sector can easily*
> *feel therefore that industry demands have been*
> *vague, inconsistent and without real commitment.*
> *A gap exists in understanding the practical*
> *constraints under which each sector operates*
> *... At a general level there is concern in*
> *industry that negative attitudes to business*
> *and commerce are allowed to develop from school*
> *onwards; that much of the skills and knowl-*
> *edge acquired by pupils bears only a tangential*
> *relation to employment; and that exam results*
> *must be heavily relied upon in selection,*

> *despite giving no indication of some important
> industrially relevant qualities ... Repeated
> attempts have been made to make education in
> the UK more appropriate to people's working
> lives. Despite that its character remains
> predominantly that of a filtering system for
> identifying the academically most able ...
> Industry itself has found it difficult to
> articulate a clear statement of its needs and
> has no effective mechanism at its disposal for
> making its views felt. Income and employment
> signals alone have not compensated for this
> ... Many teachers are fully aware of the
> problem (but) teacher training is generally
> remote from industry ... Allocation of funds
> is heavily decentralised and little influenced
> by industry. This greatly limits the extent
> to which those outside education can bring about
> a different distribution of resources, in par-
> ticular towards more vocational and higher
> technical education.*

The above extracts make it clear that industrialists accept that by no means all the fault for the
apparent gulf between education and industry lies
with the former; industry accepts that it too must
bear its share of the blame. Nevertheless accusations against the education system have clearly
continued for many years: they gradually increased
in prominence during the 1970s and have been even
more strongly expressed in the early 1980s. Such
accusations may be summarised as follows:

(1) *The development of 'anti-industry' attitudes
by young people*: the imprecise nature of this
charge makes it difficult to quantify or assess
but there does seem to be at least some truth
in it. At least some teachers have gone into
teaching because they are not attracted by the
alternatives and the great majority of teachers
have little first-hand knowledge of industry,
except possibly that gained whilst working at
low-level summer vacation jobs when they were
students. At least some young people will be
urged by their parents to aim at the often more
attractive, socially more prestigious, and even
cleaner, forms of occupation that may come their
way as a result of educational success: the
educational system is thus often seen, in a
rather mechanistic way, as the pathway towards
wider opportunities and a better lifestyle.

Teachers may tend to encourage young people in
the same directions especially since at least
part of the job of most teachers relates
directly to helping their pupils to succeed in
external examinations.   The values of school
and home may therefore reinforce each other.
The NEDO report goes on to suggest a
variety of measures to counter this problem,
all on the lines of greater direct links
between education and industry, especially
those negotiated at local level, and focusing
perhaps on visits to factories and industrial
locations by pupils in the later years of their
secondary schooling.   It has to be admitted,
however, that such visits are not without their
problems and far from helping to overcome 'anti-
industry attitudes' may well reinforce them: a
deputy headteacher of a large comprehensive
school recently recounted to the writer at some
length that when pupils from his school were
taken on visits to industry they tended to
return disenchanted at what they saw as the
unattractive working conditions, especially in
terms of noise, cleanliness and the often
unsociable working hours.   The deputy head said
that he and his colleagues had not found any way
of overcoming this problem and he had come to
the view that there was a real danger that, in
terms of the objectives they were supposed to
achieve, such visits might do more harm than
good.

(2)   *Young people lack the basic skills industry
      requires*:   in terms particularly of the tra-
      ditional '3 Rs' industrialists are apparently
      increasingly disappointed with the educational
      standards of young people leaving school.   At
      first sight it seems easy to refute this charge
      in terms of the steady and continuous increases
      in the young people, both in numbers and as
      percentages of their respective age groups,
      emerging each year with external examination
      successes, whether at GCE A-level, GCE O-level
      or CSE.   It is, however, true that educational
      emphasis has changed, and many would say rightly
      so, towards greater development of such areas
      as creativity, imagination, analytical skills
      and inter-personal relationships, in short
      towards what is often cited as 'education of
      the whole person'.   Young people are, for
      example, better equipped than previous

generations to assess or interpret a television
programme or a political speech.   Concomitantly,
however, there has been less emphasis in schools
in recent years on what were previously or
perhaps still are in some quarters, seen as the
'basic skills', including correct spelling,
grammar and syntax, and facility with basic
arithmetic either mentally or in writing and
preferably both.   Thus a young person to be
employed in a situation relating to Value Added
Tax, for example, is likely to have to give an
immediate answer to 'what is 15 per cent of
£250?' and industrialists record their disappointment that frequently he or she cannot do
so.
     Such a debate tends to imply that
industry's requirements in this respect have
remained constant but this is certainly not the
case: *functional* literacy and numeracy needs,
i.e. those required for the purposes of the
work in question, e.g. to cope with the operating instructions on a machine, are now much
more advanced than previously and just how
complex they frequently now are has only been
obscured by repeated usage and familiarity.
It is worth considering, for example, how
previous generations of young people would have
coped with:

> *All the carburation systems are located in*
> *the lower body and the main progression*
> *systems operate in both barrels, whilst*
> *the idling and the power valve systems*
> *operate in the primary barrel only and the*
> *full load enrichment system in the*
> *secondary barrel.*[16]

With regard to numeracy skills the importance
of impressive mental agility is no longer clear
as a result of the almost universal use of
inexpensive pocket calculators, automatic
calculating tills in shops, which even tell
the shop assistant how much change to give, and
the introduction of computerised processes in
many businesses.   It does, perhaps, seem
paradoxical that industrialists continue to
complain that young people are not adequately
equipped with the 'skills' that industry
requires whereas many young people now leave
school with quite advanced proficiency in, for
example, the use of computers, or word

processing, or metalwork techniques, all of
which may, one hopes, be of direct and
immediate application in their future careers.

(3) *The drift away from science and technology*:
this is a charge about which it is easier to be
precise, at least as far as concerns the numbers
of young people involved.   Table 1.3 relates to
young people studying science and engineering,
at all levels of education from City and Guilds
up to university degrees and gives clear
evidence of the drift away from science and
technology.   At every level of education young
people have apparently felt more attracted
towards studying the arts, humanities and
social sciences.   In terms of percentages of
the total cohort to which the figures relate,
this trend shows up clearly in every line in
the table;   in terms of the numbers involved
there are often increases shown but it has to
be remembered that the years in question, 1971
onwards, were years during which the rapid
expansion of post-compulsory education in
Britain was still continuing.   The trends
shown are for the period since 1971 but these
are a direct continuation of the patterns for
at least the previous decade or more.   City and
Guilds examination students in engineering have
been declining both in numbers and, even more
strikingly, as a percentage of the steadily
increasing numbers taking these examinations
(down from 50 per cent to 28.2 per cent);   of
school leavers with two A-levels the percentage
with two A-levels in science subjects has
declined from 33.4 per cent to 30.1 per cent,
this fall being at a noticeably slower rate
than others in the table.   Of CNAA degrees
awarded, those in science and engineering comprised 69.8 per cent in 1970 but only 26.8 per
cent in 1982 - this is perhaps the most surpris
ing statistic in the table: the mushrooming of
numbers of students on CNAA degree courses in
those years, up from 2,910 to 29,323, largely
relates to the growth of the polytechnics which
are often seen as being in the forefront of
higher education in the fields of science and
technology, yet the figures in the table reveal
that in fact the development of polytechnic
courses and student numbers took place not so
much in those fields (graduates up from 2,000
to 7,800) as elsewhere.   In universities by

Table 1.3: Courses and Qualifications in Science and Engineering

	Year	Number (OOO)	%	Year	Number (OOO)	%
City and Guilds students in engineering	1971	170.0	50.8	1982	123.0	28.2
School leavers with two A-levels in science*	1971	27.0	33.4	1978	29.0	30.1
CNAA degrees in science and engineering	1970	2.0	69.8	1982	7.8	26.8
University degrees in science and engineering	1971	21.5	43.7	1982	26.8	37.3
Numbers starting EITB apprenticeship courses	1970/1	26.6	–	1982/3	10.5	–
University graduates entering 'industry'	1971	6.5	39.0	1982	8.4	29.0

*publication of statistics in this series was subsequently discontinued by the DES.

Source: R. Pearson, R. Hutt and D. Parsons, Education Training and Employment, Institute of Manpower Studies, Series No.4 (Gower, 1984).

23

contrast the trend, whilst in the same
direction, was at much slower a rate: nevertheless the decline from 43.7 per cent to 37.3
per cent is not unnoticeable.
    There are some caveats to all these
figures, as Pearson *et al.*[17] make clear, but
usually they are of a relatively minor nature
and do not affect the principal conclusions to
be drawn. In the case of the figures for
Engineering Industry Training Board apprenticeship courses, however, the massive fall from
26,600 to 10,500 obviously has to be related to
the general decline in apprenticeships particularly in the latter part of that period. The
final row in the table, which strictly does not
directly relate to the remainder, shows that
the percentage of university graduates entering
'industry' (widely defined) has fallen from 39
per cent to 29 per cent per year and has to be
related to the earlier comments regarding
general employment trends.
    In terms of all the available statistics
there can be little doubt as to the drift away
from science and technology. Nor are there
any signs of this drift abating: even in the
very recent period of retrenchment at university
level, over the years 1982 to 1985 the numbers
of graduates only suffered actual decline in
the subject areas *engineering/technology* and
agriculture and forestry.[18] This does, of
course, relate directly to the debate regarding
whether Britain does or does not have a shortage of scientists and/or technologists: that
is a question for which it is much more
difficult to produce hard evidence and is one
to which we shall revert in a later chapter.

    Points similar to those indicated above have
been raised in other countries and educational policy
has had to try to deal with such criticisms.[19] The
trends in question do, however, seem to be more
serious in Britain than elsewhere.

SUGGESTED REMEDIES

Most of the published works quoted thus far devote
much more space to recounting what is wrong than to
indicating how matters might be put right. The
National Economic Development Council report, however, does go into considerable detail regarding

possible remedies.   A main obstacle was seen to be
the examination system which dominates much of the
work of schools and has an *'almost exclusively
academic orientation'*;   in particular the proliferation of the 23 separate GCE and CSE examining
boards and their *'effective autonomy from influences
outside the education sector'* made it difficult to
introduce change.   Whether the new GCSE (General
Certificate of Secondary Education) examination now
being introduced (the new courses started in 1986/
87) to replace both GCE O-level and CSE, will substantially alter the situation in this regard is at
present not entirely clear but there are at least
grounds for thinking that it will.

If part of the problem lies with the teachers
themselves then a share of blame, in the NEDC view,
must also be attributed to the training they
receive: teacher training courses rarely include
more than the briefest of references to employment
and the world of work and the combined demands of
the training system make entry difficult for persons
with desirable industrial experience.   Both initial
and in-service training needed adaptation directly
to reflect the fact that *'the industrial world which
pupils face has been and is changing rapidly'*.   And
thirdly, according to NEDC, the system of financing
education needed reform so as to gear resources more
directly to the remedies needed: an obvious example
related to the shortage of well-qualified teachers
of mathematics, science and technical subjects where
additional resources or financial incentives could
be provided.   And finally it was up to industry
itself to articulate its demands much more clearly,
probably through the establishment of an appropriate
national body which could speak with one coherent
voice for the needs of industry.

These points are not, of course, new;   they
have all appeared elsewhere on previous occasions.
In the 1980s, however, it does seem that they are
being put forward with a new emphasis and urgency.
In the general field of links between education and
industry several new initiatives have taken place in
recent years, mainly on the lines of giving the
education curriculum a greater vocational orientation.   Both the educational system and industrial
organisations have tried to respond to the various
criticisms that have been expressed.   The most
significant of the new moves have been the Certificate of Pre-Vocational Education (CPVE) and
Technical and Vocational Education Initiative (TVEI)
courses, which will be referred to in a later chapter.

NOTES

1.   C.D. Cohen (ed.), *Agenda for Britain 2: Macro Policy Choices for the 80's* (Philip Allan, 1982).

2.   C. Freeman, 'The Economic Implications of Microelectronics', in C.D. Cohen (ed.), *Agenda for Britain 1: Micro Policy Choices for the 80's* (Philip Allan, 1982).

3.   E. Sciberras, quoted in Freeman, *ibid.*

4.   G. Routh, *Occupation and Pay in Great Britain 1906-79* (Macmillan, 1980).

5.   White Paper: *Better Schools*, Cmnd 9469 (DES/HMSO, 1985).

6.   Green Paper: *The Development of Higher Education into the 1990s*, Cmnd 9524 (DES/HMSO, 1985).

7.   Crowther Report: *15 to 18*, Report of the Central Advisory Council for Education (England) (HMSO, 1959).

8.   Newsom Report: *Half Our Future*, Report of the Central Advisory Council for Education (England) (HMSO, 1963).

9.   Robbins Report: *Higher Education*, Cmnd 2154 (HMSO, 1963).

10.   Dainton Report: *Enquiry into the Flow of Candidates in Science and Technology into Higher Education*, Cmnd 3541 (HMSO, 1968).

11.   Russell Report: *Adult Education: A Plan for Development* (HMSO, 1973).

12.   M. Carter, *Into Work* (Pelican, 1966).

13.   *The Times Education Supplement*, 22 October 1976.

14.   Green Paper: *Education in Schools*, Cmnd 6869 (HMSO, 1977).

15.   *Education and Industry, Memorandum by the Director General*, ref. NEDC (82)55 (National Economic Development Office, 1982).

16.   From description of carburettor, in J.H. Haynes, *Ford Cortina 1V Owners Workshop Manual* (Haynes Publishing Group, 1977).

17.   R. Pearson, R. Hutt and D. Parsons, *Education Training and Employment*, Institute of Manpower Studies, Series No.4 (Gower, 1984).

18.   Statistics from Central Services Unit for Careers and Appointments Services, quoted in, M. O'Connor, 'Just What the Country Doesn't Need', *The Guardian*, 22 January 1985.

19.   See various references in J.R. Hough (ed.), *Educational Policy, An International Survey* (Croom Helm, 1982).

Chapter Two

MANPOWER AND THE ECONOMY

The notion that a country should plan ahead for its
future manpower needs seems obvious. And it is
true that manpower planning or manpower forecasting,
as this approach is generally known, has been
adopted in some form or other in the great majority
of the world's countries. It is also true, however,
that the practical problems arising have come to
seem insurmountable and that the detailed forward
planning of manpower requirements has been accused
of doing more harm than good. It is therefore
somewhat of a paradox that the United Kingdom,
having shown little interest in manpower planning
during the years in which it was gaining ground in
other countries, has given the impression of becoming a zealous convert to it just when scepticism was
growing elsewhere.

PRACTICAL PROBLEMS IN MANPOWER PLANNING

It is easy to see how practical problems are likely
to arise with any serious attempt at manpower planning. Consider, for example, a proposal to
increase the supply of graduate industrial chemists,
in the light, presumably, of evidence that either
the quantity or the quality, or both, of such personnel seeking to enter industry, and especially the
chemical industry, has been seriously inadequate.
The government would take appropriate evidence from
interested parties and might then decide, for
example, to provide finance for a new degree course,
or for the significant expansion of one or more
existing courses, at a university or polytechnic.
This might entail commissioning a new building and/
or additional laboratories, the appointment of
additional members of the academic staff (who might

well be difficult to obtain in view of the revealed
shortage and of the typically depressed state of
academic staff salaries), and the recruitment of
other staff such as technical assistants.   All of
this could easily take five years, before the first
students could commence their studies.   Then the
course itself would take either three or four years
and after graduation it would be another year or two
before the new chemists were regarded as fully qualified and able to work largely on their own
initiative.

Thus the total time-lag is of the order of ten
years (probably nearer 15 years in the case of, say,
medical doctors or dentists).   Now it is only
necessary to consider how the needs of the economy
and of industry may have changed over such a long
period to realise that the previous manpower shortage
may no longer be a serious problem, it may have
largely disappeared, or there might even now be a
surplus.   It is also easy to see that the university
or polytechnic, having invested substantial time and
money in the development of the new degree course,
will be anxious to continue it regardless of any
evidence of changing national need.   This question of
a long time-lag is in fact one of the two major
problems related to any manpower planning exercise
and it is one to which no adequate solution has been
found: forecasts of labour market trends may be,
and increasingly are, refined year by year and are
kept as up-to-date as possible but significant
developments such as new degree courses, new buildings or new staff appointments, still tend to be
quite inflexible.

The second major problem relates to the match,
or lack of it, between the new graduates' qualifications and the jobs they eventually fit into: many
may not seek work as industrial chemists, or they may
not feel free to move to certain parts of the country
where the available jobs are located;   they may seek
to enter chemical retailing, or to teach, or to work
as, for example, a physicist (since their degree
course will probably have included some physics), or
they may end up in personnel work or in some form of
management.   In the UK labour market, in particular,
the relationship between educational qualification
and eventual employment is far from close and all
such eventualities are more than possible.   Job
substitution may also take place subsequently: after
just a few years working as industrial chemists, the
graduates in question may seek to diversify to other
opportunities, e.g. typically many move on to some

form of management.

Mismatch also takes place, for a variety of reasons, between level of qualification and level of employment within the one industry: the graduate may end up as a laboratory assistant whilst the chief scientist may, on paper at least, be rather poorly qualified. (One of the UK's most eminent university professors in recent years never graduated, at either first degree, master's, or doctorate level, from any university.)

All such problems are particularly true in the case of girls. It is a truism that labour markets, particularly for the successful products of higher education, have become much more open to girls in recent years, yet it is still very true that for the majority of girls most of the time the location of employment possibilities is heavily influenced by the husband's work, and the interruption of her career by childbearing and/or childrearing still militates against girls rising to the higher-level career positions. There have, to cite just one example, never been any women professors in my university during the period of 14 years or so that I have worked there.

Future Manpower Needs

> *The concept of forecasting manpower require-*
> *ments is today the leading method throughout*
> *the world for integrating educational and*
> *economic planning.*[1]

This was how one of the more eminent writers in the field of the economics of education summarised the place of manpower planning but he went on to emphasise the confusion between such terms as *forecast*, *projection*, *demand*, *requirement* and *need* which tend to be used imprecisely and almost inter-changeably. Consider, for example, an estimation of the number of dentists that will be required in, say, ten years time, on the basis of some particular assumption (which should always be stated), e.g. that the patient-dentist ratio should remain constant. There will undoubtedly be adequate, and probably more than adequate, *demand* for such dental services and the patients would feel that they *need* at least that number of dentists. Can one, however, pretend that it will be a national *requirement* in the sense that national economic or social prosperity, or some other desirable goal, would otherwise suffer? It is

29

clearly more difficult to be confident of this since
the links may seem quite tenuous: after all what,
it might be alleged, is the harm if patients
typically have to wait, say, six weeks to see their
dentist rather than three?

Blaug draws a sharp distinction between
forecasts, referring to predictions '*that depend on
the achievement of definite growth targets, that is,
a statement of what would happen if economic growth
were deliberately manipulated by government policy*'
and *projections* which '*predict the outcome of purely
spontaneous forces, that is, what will happen in the
normal course of events in an unplanned economy*'.
It is not difficult to see, however, that such a
distinction may in practice become rather blurred.
Currently, for example, the government's *projections*
show that the present total excess supply of secondary school teachers will continue for several more
years yet but with the size of the excess supply
depending in part on the numbers of pupils opting to
remain at school beyond the age of compulsory schooling, i.e. 16 years: as a consequence the government's
statisticians produce alternative 'High' and 'Low'
projections. Now we could also envisage government
policies to encourage more young people (how many
more?) to remain at school beyond age 16 and there
might be alternative *forecasts* of how successful
such policies might be: and such alternative forecasts would have to take into account the pre-
existing alternative projections. The resulting
figures would thus be some mix of the two.

Such manpower planning is often rendered particularly difficult in the UK in comparision to other
developed countries, where there are often strict
controls on the application of specialised qualifications. In France, for example, a qualified
teacher of mathematics will normally only teach the
subject of his specialisation whereas his UK counterpart may additionally teach one or more other classroom subjects and also e.g. help with games or other
activities. In the UK there are large numbers of
qualified school teachers who either do not teach or
who do not teach in state (LEA) schools but in
France the concept of an excess supply (or a shortage) of school teachers does not exist: when the
number of teaching posts to be filled each year
becomes known a public competition, including the
giving of a specimen lesson, is held, and those
judged the most able and most suitable are selected;
the remainder have either to seek other work or to
re-apply the following year. Normally, therefore,

there cannot be any question of there being
'unemployed teachers' as have been much in evidence
in the UK.

In an ideal and perfectly-functioning world, of
course, there ought to be no need for manpower planning: the relative earnings attributed to particular skills or occupations should rise or fall according to the situations of either excess supply or
demand and such salary differentials should then act
as signals either to attract more young people to
become, say, architects, or lawyers, or to influence
them to look elsewhere. Nor should the long lead
time referred to above necessarily prevent this
happening: the current economists' emphasis on
'rational expectations' has developed to take account
of the fact that we all do seek to anticipate the
future in various ways, including over time periods
at least as long (e.g. in connection with pension
arrangements or a mortgage). In practice, however,
such signals clearly do not work well, whether
because people do not have the requisite information,
or because of explicit or implicit government controls of labour markets - many highly qualified
personnel are employed either directly by the government or by organisations which derive much of their
income from government funding - or for some other
reason: shortages of particular types of qualified
manpower have been seen to persist for periods of
20 or 30 years or more.

Advocacy of the manpower planning approach is
therefore essentially an acceptance of the view that
the market signals so favoured by economists have
frequently proved inadequate in the past and seem
likely so to continue in the future, and must be
either supplemented or replaced by some more directly
anticipatory mechanism. Without such mechanism, a
country's economic performance will suffer and it
will be placed at a disadvantage *vis-à-vis* its
competitors:

> the fundamental axiom of the manpower require-
> ments approach is that highly qualified man-
> power constitutes a bottleneck to economic
> growth.[2]

One problem that will be developed more fully
later in this book but which must receive at least
passing mention here relates to the general practice
(labelled 'credentialism') by employers in all developed countries over the last 20 years or so to up-
grade the educational requirements applying to

particular jobs. Banks which used to be content to
recruit bank clerks at age 16 with GCE O-levels now
increasingly seek to recruit 18-year-olds with
A-levels or 21-year-olds with university degrees;
and the same is true of insurance companies,
libraries, health administration, and many other
occupations. *'Young person required by car dis-
tributor to valet cars on sale; must have 5
O-levels'* ran a recent newspaper advertisement: are
employers raising their entry standards because
better-qualified young people are readily available
or are schools seeking to increase production of
successful GCE and other external examination
results because they feel that this is what employers
want?

Presumably both influences are operating together and presumably too employers find it
convenient to use educational certificates as a
short cut to recruiting the kind of young person
they require: the possession of five O-levels is
quite irrelevant for car valeting but may indicate
some mix of intelligence, perseverance, and even
personality and presentability, all of which the
potential employer may seek. The *'Screening
Hypothesis'* sees educational qualifications as a
convenient device by which employers may *screen* or
filter out candidates for jobs in terms of their
suitability, even if the attributes required (e.g.
personality, appearance, punctuality) bear little
direct relationship to the subjects studied.

For our present purposes, all this further
complicates the manpower planning perspective,
especially with regard to general qualification
attainments, as distinct from specialised qualifications. If it has become common practice, as it
has, for many university graduates in arts and social
science subjects in recent years to occupy positions
in the various branches of the civil service formerly
held by persons with only GCE A-levels (previously
known as Executive-level posts), can we still confidently assert that the country urgently requires
more graduates or that the high cost of the latter
can be justified? This is a complex problem and a
full consideration of it would take us on to look at
how the specification of each of the jobs in question
had changed, e.g. hand-written entries in ledgers may
have been replaced by computer terminals and software, or pricing systems may have become much more
complicated (consider e.g. the role of the British
Rail booking clerk faced with a complex set of
alternative types of ticket, fare schedules, and

categories of passenger, to replace the previously
ubiquitous 'day return'.

This latter point causes us to realise that the
manpower planning approach may be applied in two
senses, firstly to the general level of educational
attainments in a country by, say, the whole of an
age cohort - e.g. the proportion of students obtaining five GCE O-levels, or three A-levels, or
university degrees in social science subjects - and,
secondly, to the specialised qualifications which are
intended as the entry routes to named occupations.
The former has received much attention in recent
years and is mentioned elsewhere in this book:
no-one would ever pretend that any more than a small
minority of graduates from, for example, a degree
course in History would go on to earn their living
by working as historians: their subject studies are
seen as developing the intellect and training the
mind in a general way and they may go on to a wide
variety of professions, many of which will require
further subsequent study, hopefully maintaining their
historical interest in their spare time. The
second connotation, however, that of the more
specialised expertise, is the one that has received
much the most attention in the manpower planning
literature and it is to this aspect that much of the
remainder of this chapter will be devoted.

MANPOWER PLANNING METHODOLOGY

Any approach to manpower planning must start from the
present situation, however irrational or higgledy-
piggledy it may seem: we may not like the fact that
25 per cent of qualified teachers of mathematics in
secondary schools do not teach any mathematics, but
we cannot just ignore it. It is therefore important to bear in mind at the outset that we cannot
necessarily assume that the current or any previous
position is necessarily correct or justifiable; if
we do not, any inherent mistakes in the present
situation will automatically be carried forward into
the future: for example, until just a few years ago
it would have seemed entirely reasonable for planners
to assume that one public bus must always have one
driver plus one conductor, whereas it is now obvious
that that approach would have led to a manpower
forecasting error of 100 per cent! Rather similarly,
driverless trains are now coming into use on some
rail systems, which would have been unthinkable until
very recently.

One would therefore have thought that any manpower forecasting exercise would commence with at
least some critical examination of the relevant pre-
existing manpower situation but in fact this aspect
has frequently been ignored completely: manpower
studies have almost always tended to assume that they
should seek to project forwards from the present
labour market position, without seriously taking into
consideration what imbalances may already pre-exist.
Subsequent correction of the latter by normal market
forces may largely invalidate the premises on which
the original calculations were based. Perhaps the
most obvious example of major structural change in
the UK labour market in recent years would relate to
the large-scale shake-out of labour, combined with
capital-labour substitution, from industrial and
commercial employers. To cite just one example from
many, British Airways announced in the summer of
1986 that it had been able to achieve around 20 per
cent *increase* in the number of passenger flights
whilst *decreasing* its staff by around 20 per cent.
The most obvious end-result has been the high unemployment statistics which are now all too familiar
but it is also true that any attempts at detailed
labour market analysis in those same years have been
rendered quite problematic.

If manpower forecasting has found such wide
favour in so many countries, one might think that it
would have become clear which was the most reliable
and appropriate forecasting method to use, but
regrettably this is not the case:

> *There is no single universally accepted method
> of forecasting requirements for specific
> occupations or occupational categories.*[3]

There are a number of alternative approaches, each
of which has both advantages and quite serious drawbacks; we must now consider each in turn.

Firstly, the views of employers: it would seem
blindingly obvious that the most direct and reliable
way of ascertaining employers' future needs for
particular kinds of manpower would be to ask them:
via some form of questionnaire survey or the equivalent, and making due allowance for such factors as
possible alternative growth paths for their organisations and the effects of technological change,
employers would surely be in a better position than
anyone else to indicate what their future requirements would be. Their responses would be appropriately collated and, within reasonable margins of

error, totals arrived at for specific industries or
for particular specialisms.   Regrettably, however,
it does not work out like that:

> *We discovered in our successive inquiries that*
> *one of the least reliable ways for finding out*
> *what industry wants is to go and ask industry*

was how Sir Solly Zuckerman summarised the outcome
in his evidence to the 1963 *Committee on Higher
Education*.[4]
     A major problem relates to the fact that many
employers will not have been in the habit of compil-
ing such statistics, they may have no particular
view of the future on which to base their forecasts
and frequently it may not be clear to them whether
they should, for example, assume an optimistic or a
pessimistic scenario for their industry.   Unless,
therefore, one or more assumptions regarding the
future are specifically stated - e.g. that national
economic growth will average a certain percentage
each year which will in turn mean that a particular
industry will need to have growth averaging four
per cent per year - then clearly different employers
will be providing answers based on quite different
premises.   And in the great majority of manpower
forecasting exercises based on seeking the view of
employers, no such assumptions have been stated or
even hinted at.
     Linked to this lack of precision of any overall
scenario is the fact that prospective employers, in
common with most respondents to most questionnaire
surveys most of the time do not like to give less-
than-optimistic answers: to indicate low or zero or
even negative growth, whether of output or of manpower needs, may be objective and realistic but it
goes against the grain of a basic trait of human
nature.   Experience from many countries shows that,
overwhelmingly, employers tend to be over-optimistic
in their replies.   Sometimes, indeed, their forecast
increases in labour requirements are so high that
there would be no way in which it would be possible
for these to be met within the constraints of time
and resources available.
     A famous example of the use of this approach in
the UK was embodied in the report of the Jackson
Committee, 1966:   it arranged for the Ministry of
Labour to ask both prospective employers and other
interested parties how many qualified scientists and
engineers would be required in three years' time,
apparently ignoring all the attendant problems such

as those indicated above, although the eventual
report did admit that,

> the quality of employers' estimates is likely
> to depend on the size of the firms and on the
> degree of sophistication in their manpower
> planning.

It can scarcely be doubted that the method of
manpower forecasting based on the views of employers
will continue to be widely used and will continue to
give rise to problems of interpretation; much could,
however, be done to improve the validity and reli-
ability of this approach if there were given as full
and careful as possible a specification of the
general background scenario envisaged. Often a
good way of bringing this latter point home would be
to request alternative answers depending on different
background assumptions, e.g. higher and lower rates
of economic growth.

It should also be increasingly possible in the
future to give more of a mix of the fairly subjective
views of employers with more objective indications of
longitudinal trends, via the use of increasingly
sophisticated computer software programmes for
advanced multiple regression analysis. An example
would be if an employer's demands for different
types of labour in each of, say, the last ten years
were extrapolated forwards to give an indication of
what the figures would be on the assumption that
previous trends were to continue; the employer
could then be invited to indicate what, in his
opinion, might be the estimated deviations to either
side of the underlying trends. This would, of
course, still leave extant the basic problems
referred to above, especially that of the mismatch
between educational qualifications and occupations
and how the relationship between the two is seen by
employers:

> Employers may not be interested in the
> educational qualification of, say, mechanical
> engineering: their concern may be the number
> of people carrying out a mechanical engineer-
> ing function, which is not at all the same
> thing. [5]

Much of the interest in this particular approach to
manpower forecasting in the UK in recent years has
related to the supposed national shortage of qualified scientists and engineers, to which we shall

revert in some detail in Chapter Four.

The second method relates to the use of international comparisons. This has found considerable
favour, often in a rather general and even unscien-
tific fashion, in recent years: critics of a
country's economic performance have found it a
relatively easy matter to note that, for example, a
smaller proportion of its graduates from higher
education were qualified in subject x or became
employed in occupation y than was the case in some
other country whose performance was more to be
admired. (By definition there will, of course,
always be *some* educational subject and *some* occupational category of which this is true.) By
extension, if the former country were in its forecasts of future manpower needs to seek to emulate or
at least approach more closely to the position of
the latter, then, supposedly, its economic prognosis
should improve. Of no country has this suggestion
been made more frequently in recent years than of
the UK with regard to its production of, or shortfall of, qualified scientists and engineers.

Earlier, basically the same approach but on a
rather more systematic or scientific basis was used
in France in the early 1960s as part of the longitudinal process of national economic planning:[6] the
distribution of the labour force over various
industrial and commercial sectors was related to
forecasts of required future educational output by
reference to norms derived from statistics relating
to other directly comparable countries. It may be
noted in passing, however, that one long-standing
criticism of French economic planning, which persisted throughout the 1960s and 1970s and was
perhaps only remedied in the 1980s, was that it paid
rather little attention to interactions between the
education system and the industrial and commercial
life of the country. A much-publicised example of
the same approach applied rather differently
occurred in Puerto Rico in the late 1950s, when the
country's planners made the heroic assumption that
a proxy for Puerto Rico's development in 25 years
time could be taken to be the contemporary USA: the
levels of educational qualification found in the
different categories of occupation in the USA in
1950 were assumed to be a reasonable model for the
Puerto Rico of the future. It must now seem so
obvious that such an approach would be fallacious
that its use in such a way is liable to give rise to
scepticism regarding manpower forecasting as a
whole: it may now seem difficult to believe that

37

anyone would seriously accept that the development path of any one country would be liable to follow so closely that of any other country or that any pattern of development would so closely resemble a previous experience of 25 years earlier. And it is certainly true that the forecasts in the Puerto Rico case showed wide errors from what eventually transpired. Nevertheless one must also acknowledge the position of the planning officials who had available no other reliable statistics on which to base their estimation of future labour developments and little or no qualified expertise on which to draw for the production of statistics or forecasts.

The widespread criticism that there has been of the method adopted perhaps fails to take account of the fact that the planners themselves must have been rather sceptical as to the outcome, particularly over as long a period as 25 years, but were well aware that, starting as they were from such a very low base in that Puerto Rico had a virtual dearth of highly qualified manpower of all kinds, the projected image did at least bring home to the government of the country how very great were the gaps between the levels of educational qualifications currently being produced and those that would be required in the future if a reasonable state of development were to be achieved. Perhaps also such experiences in a number of countries which have paid homage to what has become known as the international comparisons approach should add a note of caution to the recently-expressed concerns relating to the UK which were referred to above.

Thirdly, there is what might validly be termed the *Disaggregation of GNP* method but which has become widely known as the *Parnes-MRP* method because of its much-publicised use as part of the Mediterranean Regional Project in conjunction with Professor Parnes. This approach commenced with a projected target Gross National Product at some appropriate future date, perhaps some ten years hence or more; this GNP is then disaggregated by major industrial and commercial sectors, appropriate total labour requirements are deduced for each, these are then broken down into discrete occupations each of which then has applied to it precise requirements of levels of educational attainments.

It scarcely needs to be said that such a generalised approach retains within it all the problems, especially regarding the degree of substitutability both within and between occupations, that were referred to previously. The Mediterranean

Regional Project itself sought to apply this common
approach to countries in southern Europe - Greece,
Italy, Portugal, Spain, Turkey and Yugoslavia -
which are classified as developed countries but
which are among the poorer members of that elite
club.   At the outset the project team was forced
to realise that economic and educational development
in these six countries had reached different stages
and would continue to take quite different paths -
one has only to think, for example, of the contrast
between the industrialised north of Italy and the
country's agricultural and underdeveloped south, or
of the very considerable effect that the subsequent
emergence of a domestic automobile industry has had
on the course of economic development within Spain -
but the intention was to be able to plot a future
course for each country more systematically than had
been done previously and to some extent for each
country to be able to learn from the experience and
mistakes of the others.
     The practical problems were clearly recognised,
including by Professor Parnes himself:

> *even if forecasting were an exact science, to*
> *speak of ascertaining precisely the future*
> *occupational structure of the work force*
> *implies a degree of rigidity in occupational*
> *composition that is unrealistic ... there is*
> *no nation for which patterns of occupational*
> *mobility can be described with sufficient*
> *precision to permit making estimates of*
> *separations from and accessions to specific*
> *occupations ... there is frequently no unique*
> *and rigid relationship between educational*
> *background and occupational affiliation that*
> *would permit a knowledge of manpower require-*
> *ments to be translated unambiguously into*
> *'educational output' figures.*[7]

Such an approach has never been applied as such in
the UK, although one can postulate that it might
well have been: the UK's one serious attempt at
systematic indicative economic planning, the
Labour government's National Plan of 1965, proved
to be ill-fated and abortive since it was peremp-
torily abandoned when the county ran into yet
another economic and financial crisis the following
year.   There was, however, a degree of commonality
between the generalised approach adopted in The
National Plan and the Parnes-MRP method of manpower
forecasting and if, in different circumstances,

39

economic planning had continued and become established in the UK, this approach would seem likely to have appealed to the late Lord George Brown and his colleagues.

The other approaches to manpower forecasting may be dealt with more briefly here, partly in view of their rather technical nature and partly because their application has been relatively limited. They all relate to the calculation of *ratios* which are then extrapolated forwards into the future. Firstly, the *density ratios methods* which calculates, for each economic sector, the percentage of the labour force comprising qualified manpower and then applies this ratio to demographic forecasts of the future labour force after allowing for appropriate distribution across sectors. This approach has found favour in the USSR - which has also experimented with estimating stable ratios between different kinds of qualified manpower such as between scientists and engineers - and has also occasionally been used elsewhere. It obviously assumes either stability or a built-in and rather inflexible trend in the relationship between qualified and unqualified labour, which experience increasingly shows is no longer the case. Also the large-scale unemployment which has become common in many countries in recent years would inevitably make such calculations more problematic.

Secondly, the calculation of the relationship between additional industrial or commercial output and the relevant additional qualified manpower has become known under the rather complicated-sounding title of the *incremental labour-output ratio*. This is essentially the method used by the Zuckerman Committee in the UK in the mid-1950s. The crucial concept here is output per man and it is necessary to assume that this is either constant or on a reliable trend path over time. Much therefore depends on having adequate and reliable time-series statistics. This approach also rather begs an important question: once we have calculated output per man for, say, a graduate chemist (possibly a Ph.D), what does this tell us about the output per man for the technician (possibly with a relevant HNC or HND) who may work with him? Frequently, it may be impossible to extricate one effect from the other.

The methods considered in the previous paragraph sound more systematic, objective and scientific, but it is at least arguable that this impression is misleading, particularly in view of the rather gross

assumptions that have to be made.   The UK's Zuckerman Committee, for example, assumed a *fixed* ALOR
(average labour-output ratio) but only three years
later the ALOR proved to be *four times as high*:   the
ILOR must therefore have risen very steeply.[8]   From
a consideration of such drawbacks one can also see
the attractions of the employers' opinion method
considered earlier: if any or all of the ratio
relationships mentioned above are stable, then forecasting presents no problems and can all be done by
an appropriate computer programme which has built
into it the appropriate mathematical and statistical
techniques;   once, however, there are any instabil-
ities, then intuitively it seems advantageous to ask
employers (who else?) what any future trends are
likely to be.

EDUCATIONAL OBJECTIVES

All of the above, and indeed much of the present
book, is based on the assumption that it is a prime
function of any country's education system either to
prepare young people directly for their future working lives or at least to equip them with the skills
and aptitudes (and some would even say the attitudes)
that their future employers will require.   There is
no suggestion here that this should be the sole
function of education and we may for the moment
leave on one side the rather philosophical or even
semantic argument about whether the *principal* function of education should lie in this direction or
should be directed towards the development of the
whole person with all that this implies in terms of
cultural, literary, artistic and aesthetic awareness
quite apart from the development of personality.
     It may be argued that all such aspects have a
vocational connotation in that they may all be of use
in some form of employment or other and all tend
towards the production of a more rounded or complete
person.   There is therefore no clear dichotomy.
It may now seem ironic to us to read that the young
Don Bradman was torn between earning his living and
playing cricket, so accustomed have we become to
stories of the world's top sports players or pop
stars having astronomically-high earnings, reaching
up to millions of US dollars annually in some cases.
For most young people most of the time, however, it
is a question of probabilities: many young men and
women like to play tennis but only a very small percentage of them will ever make any money out of

playing tennis, a smaller proportion still will earn
enough from the game for this to be their main live-
lihood and the very high incomes that are quoted in
the media apply only to perhaps a handful of the
world's best players.

It remains true therefore that, provided the
above caveat is borne in mind, there is utility in
drawing the distinction between *'vocational'* and
'non-vocational' functions of schooling, if only to
enable us to try to focus more clearly on what
education is trying to achieve. The traditional
but allegedly increasing gulf between the education
system on the one hand and the industrial and
commercial world on the other, which has been
referred to previously, has been the subject of much
comment in the UK but has also been discussed in
other countries. But if educational attitudes were
to change and if teachers, at all levels, were to
come to accept that their prime function was to prepare their young charges for their future working
lives, would we be quite certain that this was the
right thing to do? In the words of a leading
writer in this field, Philip Coombs,[9]

> *It is well to note that there is potentially a
> serious philosophical conflict between this new
> 'manpower' interest in education and the
> traditional view of education's role in a free
> society. In the context of 'the manpower
> shortage', the educational system comes to be
> viewed as a 'brain power industry' whose social
> function is to develop human beings as instru-
> ments for building national economic and
> military strength. Under the older view, it
> was taken for granted that education contrib-
> uted indirectly to the economic and general
> welfare of the nation, but the overarching
> purpose of education in a free society was to
> enable individuals to realise their full human
> potentialities for their own sake.*

One can, of course, argue that no individual can
realise his or her full human potentiality unless he
or she has found appropriate and satisfying employment, to say nothing of those who are left unemployed, but this does not centrally affect the valid
point made by Coombs. It is, perhaps, a question
of finding the appropriate balance between the
vocational and the non-vocational aspects of
education and it would be a brave man indeed who
would claim that any particular educational system

had managed to get the balance just about right.
Professor Parnes argues that any educational planning, to be worthy of the name, must take full
account of what might be called the non-directly-
vocational, or cultural, aspects of education,
including the *'understanding necessary for wise
policy decisions in a democracy'*, *'the psychological
satisfaction which creative activity brings'* and
*'a capacity for satisfying and purposeful use of
leisure time'*: a cynic might say that if education
had to be assessed on those grounds, in the case of
the broad mass of ordinary working people it might
be adjudged to have failed lamentably. The point
remains, however, that the more strictly vocational
dimension of education cannot be, and one hopes
should never be, the whole story: in the words of
Professor Parnes,

> *no-one would maintain that the sole function
> of education is to contribute to ...
> economic growth.*[10]

CATEGORIES OF OCCUPATIONS

In a sophisticated economy there are many thousands
of different jobs. No manpower planning exercise
could ever take account of all of them separately,
so some form of grouping jobs together into categories or classifications is necessary. How may this
be done? Consider for example a broad generic
term in common use such as 'scientist' or even
'chemist': we may have a very hazy notion of the
kind of work that such people do and we may be able
to sub-divide each term further into e.g. biologist,
organic chemist, etc. But this would still leave
us with broad umbrella-type categories and the only
way sensibly to disaggregate in terms of the
functions or roles of the persons concerned would be
to refer to their levels of educational attainment:
a Ph.D in physics may be assumed to be doing, or
ought to be doing, a quite different kind of work as
compared with a person with an HNC or B.Tech qualification.

For any manpower planning exercise, however, to
classify occupations in terms of the educational
levels of the persons holding those positions may be
said to be the equivalent of throwing out the baby
with the bath-water: it would clearly, by definition,
remove any possibility of investigating mismatch
between educational qualifications and jobs held:

the young person with five GCE O-levels valeting
cars who was referred to earlier, the Ph.D engineer
who was cited in a recent newspaper as running a
grocer's shop, or the highly-successful chief general
manager of one of the country's largest building
societies who left school at 16 and progressively
worked his way up through successive management
layers, would all be obvious examples.   And similarly with regard to, for example, the significant
proportion of graduate engineers who do not work
directly as engineers at all.
     Most questions relating to substitutability
would therefore be removed by this method of
definition and could not then be investigated:

> *We conclude that occupations must be defined
> in terms of the nature of the job that is to
> be performed, without any reference to the
> characteristics of the people who take them
> up*[11]

was the conclusion that Professor Blaug came to, but
no ready objective way of doing so has found
universal approval and the subjective views of the
planners or researchers have often played a part.
It is also true that over the long period of a full
manpower planning exercise, which may be anywhere
between 10 and 20 years, the educational requirements of a variety of jobs will typically rise - as
with the case of the bank clerks noted earlier -
although it is probably true that the majority of
manpower planning exercises have not allowed for
such refinements.
     How much does all this matter?   In the words
of Professor Blaug again,

> *The point is that whenever we classify the
> work people actually do into more or less
> homogeneous job clusters, these clusters or
> skill levels turn out to be distributed among
> several educational levels.   We need, there-
> fore, to keep occupational classifications.
> separate and distinct from educational ones.*

It is therefore somewhat of a paradox that for the
purposes of manpower planning we require occupations
to be classified in terms of work done and *skills*
(as distinct from education) required just at a
time when, for very many jobs, the nature of the
work and the types of skill needed are changing more
rapidly than ever before.   We urgently need

statistics of occupational categories to be drawn up
on this quite different basis but the only point of
which we can be quite sure is that the categories
thus produced will be out-of-date almost immediately.
This reference to future changes in a sense
brings us back to the point at which this chapter
started, that the case for manpower planning being
needed at all rested on the inadequacy of normal
economic market signals, especially of relative
wage and price levels. In what has followed, price
and cost factors, including the costs of any
additional education or training, have not been
mentioned and implicitly relative wage levels have
been assumed to not change significantly. This may
be a reasonable and realistic assumption in the case
of some occupations, nurses and teachers for example,
but not with others such as computer programmers or
systems analysts.

Two marked features of executive-level earnings
in recent years have been firstly the proliferation
of non-monetary aspects of the remuneration package,
such as company car, private health schemes, and
even the payment of private school fees, and,
secondly, the stretching of salary differentials to
reach very large figures at the top end. The most
highly paid industrialist in Britain is now reported
to be earning just on one million pounds a year;
this begs the question of whether such a very high
figure can ever be justified although we may note
that it is still considerably below the earnings of
the top international tennis players or purveyors of
pop music.

The manpower planning approach requires us to
assume that such major changes in relative differentials will not act as efficient market signals to
attract labour of the right quality and quantity to
those occupations. Or rather, perhaps, that the
broad mass of the occupations in which highly-
educated people find themselves, including all of
those - the majority - in public sector institutions,
do not in fact evidence such significant movements.
Manpower planning also requires us to have faith in
our ability to predict over long periods, despite
all the evidence of how erroneous may be any figures
relating to events 10 or 20 years hence.

The issues raised in this chapter will recur
throughout much of this book and will have particular relevance to the next two chapters which will
both, in different ways, relate to manpower requirement problems.

NOTES

1. M. Blaug, *An Introduction to the Economics of Education* (Penguin, 1970).

2. *Ibid.*

3. H.S. Parnes, 'Planning Education for Economic and Social Development', in C. Baxter and others (eds), *Economics and Education Policy* (Longman, 1977).

4. Quoted in K. Gannicott and M. Blaug, 'Scientists and Engineers in Britain', in Baxter and others, *Economics and Education Policy*.

5. Gannicott and Blaug, 'Scientists and Engineers in Britain'.

6. For details of economic planning in France, see J.R. Hough, *The French Economy* (Croom Helm, 1982).

7. Parnes, 'Planning Education for Economic and Social Development'.

8. C. Moser and R. Layard, 'Estimating the Need for Highly Qualified Manpower in Britain', in M. Blaug (ed.), *Economics of Education*, Vol.1 (Penguin, 1968).

9. Quoted in Parnes, 'Planning Education for Economic and Social Development'.

10. Parnes, 'Planning Education for Economic and Social Development'.

11. Blaug, *An Introduction to the Economics of Education*.

Chapter Three

INVESTMENT IN EDUCATION

For an economist, *Investment* is a term with a
specialised meaning, rather different from that
understood by the layman.   To the latter the term
probably refers to the notion of putting some money
on one side, into an appropriate savings outlet, for
a rainy day or for some future large item of
personal expenditure;   thus paying cash into a bank
deposit account, or a building society savings
account, or the purchase of stocks or shares or
unit trusts might all in conventional parlance come
within the term investment, but an economist would
include none of these.   *Investment* in economics
refers to the acquisition or installation or construction of real, as opposed to monetary or paper,
assets which will enable future production and thus
subsequently *consumption*, i.e. the enjoyment of
goods and services, to take place.   Thus the
building or purchase of a ship, extending a factory,
installing new plant or machinery or even laying
down a road, will all be viewed as investment if
they aid future production process.   So too may a
local authority town hall, or civic centre, or
leisure amenity, although here the connotation is
not with the production of goods but with the future
flow of services or simply use.

HUMAN CAPITAL

The essence of the concept is that the real assets
will be long-lasting and entail provision for an
extended period of future years.   All such
investments together are collectively termed *capital*
and the distinction between capital and non-capital
(or more usually recurrent or simply current)
expenditure is one of the most fundamental in

economics and in theory is quite clear-cut.   In
practice, however, there may be considerable blur-
ring between the two, as will be obvious if we
consider the commercial traveller's car which is
used for family outings at weekends, or the telephone which may be used for a mix of business and
pleasure purposes.

The same concepts have also come to be used
more widely and to refer not solely to certain
things produced by people, but also to the *people*
who produce them.   Thus analogy came to be drawn
between expensive investment in a valuable piece of
machinery and perhaps equally expensive investment
in human beings, also to be considered valuable.
Expenditure on health care, for example, might pro-
long the working life of the country's leading
industrialists or scarce scientists or technologists,
or even musicians or artists, and would therefore
represent an excellent investment in the future
which would contribute significantly to the national
wellbeing in the years to come.   But it would
clearly do more than this: the individuals in
question would not be automated robots, they would,
hopefully, have lives outside work, with spare-time
interests.   If expenditure leading to an extension
of working life is investment, expenditure leading
to additional life outside work might be viewed as
falling under the umbrella term consumption.   In
that sense health-care is some mix of the two and
represents some combination of capital and non-
capital expenditure.

What about education?   Essentially the same
concepts and problems apply as have been outlined
above.   Education leads, or should lead, to a
more productive, more efficient, and more usefully
employable person and it is therefore clearly of an
investment nature.   But education also leads to
wider enjoyment of and pleasure in life outside
work, whether in cultural, aesthetic, sporting, or
other terms, and in addition the process of
education may itself be enjoyable (in contrast
presumably to health-care).   The great majority of
students attest that it is and indeed something
would be seriously wrong somewhere if this were not
the case.   In both these respects, therefore,
education must be considered as consumption, in
addition to also being viewed as investment.

Just what the mix will be in respect of any
particular course or level or part of education it
may be almost impossible to say.   An evening class
in, for example, flower-arranging or pottery, is

presumably almost entirely pleasurable; a day-
release course in machinery maintenance or industrial
safety may be almost entirely work-orientated. But
how to classify an A-level course in English Literature which hopefully should be enjoyable but which
also probably has as one of its prime aims the
furtherance of the student's future career? Or
the evening class in car mechanics where a main
objective is to save much of the cost of having the
car serviced? Presumably these twin elements will
always be present to some extent with any educational
course: there will always be some general effect on
the whole person and whatever the knowledge gained
it may always prove to be vocationally useful in
some way or other. All we can say is that there is
some indeterminate mix, which may vary from one
student to another, or even between different parts
of the same course. We must, however, recognise
that increasingly many, perhaps most, educational
policy decisions are taken in terms of national need
or future economic prosperity, i.e. with the investment aspect of education very much in mind.

Education and Economic Growth
In the terminology of economics, the objective of
all investment is to aid future economic growth,
which translates into additional goods and services
or into increases in people's real standards of
living. No-one actually wants to see electricity
pylons straddling the South Downs, cooling towers on
the horizon, or valuable and attractive farmland
giving way to six-lane motorways, all of these are
simply means to the end of improved living conditions
in the future. We have already seen that Britain's
economic performance, and especially her rate of
economic growth, have for many years compared
unfavourably with those of her principal competitor
countries: that that has been the case is undeniable.

It may, however, be necessary to remind ourselves that in most years at least some real
economic growth has taken place in this country as
in other developed countries. To verify that this
is so, it is only necessary to consider the numbers
and quality of consumer durables - refrigerators,
freezers, colour TV sets, videos, hi-fi, music
centres, micro-wave ovens, dishwashing machines,
cars, caravans - per head of the population today,
as compared with 20, 30 or 40 years ago. People
now live in homes that are more spacious, better

heated, and better equipped in every way than the standards that previous generations enjoyed. The same is true for all other developed countries, at varying rates and with varying degrees of success. It is, of course, a different story in the case of the developing countries since there the (usually) positive rate of economic growth is frequently less than the rate of growth of the population, so that the standard of living per head of population actually declines, on average, year by year.

Whence comes this economic growth? Can we be sure of its precise causes and in particular what can we say about the contribution which education makes to the growth process? The answers to these questions are extremely complex. There is perhaps no other aspect of economics where it is so difficult to pursue research or where the answers are so uncertain as with attempts to determine the causes of economic growth. The reasons for this are not hard to imagine: the circumstances of individual countries vary so widely both over time and when compared with other countries - in respect of natural resources, climate, obstacles to development, location, transport and communications, and social customs and attitudes (e.g. the place of women) - that it is not surprising that it might prove difficult to arrive at definitive answers.

In particular, for our present purposes, does education contribute to economic growth? On the one hand it seems intuitively obvious that it does and must do: if a country's educational system manages to bring more of its people to the level of functional literacy, these can subsequently be employed in a range of functions where there was previously a shortage of literate workers and where literacy is required - e.g. to read the printed instructions on a piece of machinery or on a packet of seeds - thus increasing the rate of production. At higher educational levels, an increased flow of, say, highly-qualified computer specialists or skilled technicians must surely increase industrial output, always assuming of course that their services are put to good use.

Various scholars have attempted to identify and even to quantify the precise contribution that education can make to economic growth but the results must be described as rather mixed and uncertain. In a path-breaking study over twenty years ago Bowman and Anderson[1] found relationships between level of basic education as measured by literacy rates and economic development as measured

by Gross National Product per head broadly to apply
across the whole range of the world's developing
countries.   There were, however, certain notable
exceptions and the case was no by means proved.
Their work suggested that such countries need to
attain a literacy rate of 40 per cent if they were
to achieve a minimally acceptable standard of living,
which was defined to be the then world mean GNP per
head.   Anderson[2] subsequently confirmed this level
of 40 per cent literacy from historical survey
material and an associated finding by Peaslee[3]
suggested that for at least 10 per cent of the total
population to have attended primary school was an
essential prerequisite.   Blaug[4] emphasises the
inadequacy of the data base underpinning such work,
especially where developing countries are concerned:

> *When it is realized that ... in India the*
> *census schedule defines a person as literate*
> *when he replies affirmatively to the question*
> *'Can you read and write?' ..., all confidence*
> *in even the limited results that have so far*
> *been established tends to vanish.*

This work relied heavily on statistical correlation
techniques, as also did a variety of subsequent
endeavours in the same direction, but such techniques tell us nothing about cause and effect
relationships.   An oft-quoted and much-criticised
piece of research by Harbison and Myers[5] discarded
primary enrolments completely and then weighted
higher education enrolments *five times as highly* as
secondary school enrolments, in their search for
matching relationships with economic growth, but
they gave no rational justification for either case.
    The practical applications of all such work
would always be limited but especially so in the
case of all developed countries where broadly speaking enrolment rates for both primary and secondary
education have been around 100 per cent for many
years.   In the place of such research there have
been some very technical studies of relationships
between workers' income per head and level of
educational attainment (Tinbergen) and between
occupational structure and output per worker (Layard
and Saigal) but unfortunately written in terms that
would be unintelligible to anyone without a strong
background in economics;   the best analytical
summary of this field is to be found in Blaug[6] but
non-economists are warned that they would probably
find the material quite indigestible.

51

Of more direct interest for our present purposes
are attempts to quantify the contribution that
education can make to the economic growth process.
Much the most celebrated of these, and the one that
is still always quoted in any references to this
topic, was the mammoth study by Denison[7] of the
growth of the economy of the USA for the period of
50 years to 1960. He derived aggregate production
functions (mathematical relationships between
economic inputs and output) and then examined the
remaining or 'unexplained' portion of economic
growth in relation to a number of factors, including
education. The ensuing calculations arrived at the
finding that over the period 1930-60 education contributed as much as 23 per cent of total economic
growth, which was more than any other source except
for the increase in the labour force in whom the
effects of the education were incorporated.

When the incidence of population growth was
discounted and the result expressed as a per capita
basis, the contribution to economic growth from the
education system increased to the quite remarkable
figure of 42 per cent. These findings do rest on
a complex technical base which in turn makes a
number of assumptions about the nature of technical
progress, for example there is an underlying incon-
sistency in the research regarding whether there are
or are not significant economies of scale over time.
But Denison's research remains much the most serious
large-scale attempt at quantification in this field,
and its findings have been widely quoted throughout
the world.

It is also possible, according to the *Screening
Hypothesis*, which is referred to elsewhere in this
book, that the education received merely makes it
easier for the employer to select candidates for
appointments, by acting as a filtering mechanism.
According to this view the knowledge gained is
irrelevant for the students' future economic performance, and therefore for economic growth, but the
level of education stands as a proxy for other attitudes which are far more important.

RATES OF RETURN

Once human beings had come to be seen as a form of
capital, akin to pieces of industrial machinery, it
was inevitable that economists would endeavour to
apply to them the same kinds of calculations of
investment criteria, profitability, and rates of

return, as had long been familiar in the worlds of industrial economics or accountancy. Only by so doing, it seemed, could we arrive at meaningful answers to such questions as, 'Should investment in education be increased (or decreased?', 'Would we do better to concentrate more resources at the primary school end of the process rather than on higher education?', or, 'How does the UK's perform- ance in this respect compare with those of other countries?' Calculations on these lines of the costs and benefits of education, and therefore known under the umbrella term of 'cost-benefit analysis', had been applied to education in some countries before the Second World War but only really developed as a serious field of study, both nationally and internationally from the 1960s.

It will immediately be obvious that whatever difficulties may arise in the computation of the 'costs' side of the equation - as they certainly do - these must pale into insignificance when compared with the attempted estimation of 'benefits': at a personal level, which of us could begin accurately to assess all the benefits of the education he or she had received? It has often been the case that researchers in this field have been able to produce apparently quite precise computations based on more or less reliable statistical data but have then had to make rather arbitrary adjustments to the figures to allow for various contingencies. This will become apparent when we consider some of the major findings.

Outside the world of education, cost-benefit analysis has been common in connection with major capital expenditure projects both in manufacturing industry and in relation to public (government) expenditure, throughout the post-war period but especially from the mid-1950s onwards. Originally developed mainly in the USA, the techniques in question soon spread to other countries including the UK: before a final decision was taken on any large item of investment (i.e. addition to capital) a cost-benefit analysis would attempt to quantify in financial terms all negative (cost) and positive (benefit) aspects of the scheme in question. Examples of major cost-benefit analyses of this kind in the UK have included those relating to the original M1 Motorway, the Third London Airport, or the Victoria Line underground railway in London.

Various of the technical and conceptual problems that arise are also applicable to cost- benefit analyses relating to education; three in

53

particular need to be considered here: each of
them tells us something about the limitations of
cost-benefit analysis as a practical policy
instrument.

Firstly, which costs and which benefits should
be included in the computation? The short answer
is that all costs and all benefits, whether
financial or non-financial, should be included but
the longer answer is that in practice it may not be
possible to adhere to this theoretical ideal. If
we think once again of our own education, which of
us could be quite sure that we can attribute directly
to our own schooling responsibility for, or some
share of responsibilities for, our interests in
music or reading or wine-making or physical activity
or whatever? In practice we have to be content to
include in any calculation as much as is both
feasible and quantifiable, whilst recognising any
shortfall as a clear limitation.

Secondly, how can such diverse effects, and
even some of the inputs, be measured in financial
terms, i.e. expressed in money? Most educational
costs, and a good many of the benefits, do in fact
originate in monetary values but the problems arise
in connection with those that do not. Consider
the input of *time* by the student which is increasingly being regarded as one of the most important of
all educational resources, and how this may be
assessed. Would it be reasonable to assess it by
reference to the hypothetical alternative use of the
time, i.e. to possible work that the individual
might otherwise have done, which in turn could be
valued at the wage rate that would have been payable?

It is a common technique of economists to do so
and it is not difficult to see why: often there is
no other course readily available. Yet this begs
two questions: firstly, if there is widespread
unemployment, as there has been in all countries for
at least the last decade, then it seems unrealistic
to think of our individual having the ready alternative of a job waiting for him, or if he or she were
to find such work, then presumably it is at the
expense of some other potential worker who is being
ousted. And, secondly, we have to revert to the
question of education being consumption or investment
or some mix of the two: if education is so pleasurable, as it is for most students most of the time,
then are we justified in regarding the time so spent
as a 'cost'? It is by no means clear that we are.

The third point relates to the timing of any
costs or benefits, especially the latter, and how

these are to be aggregated together into the eventual large sum. Consider someone being offered the
choice between the receipt of, say, £100 tomorrow,
or the same sum in one year's time; he would
clearly choose the former, if for no other reason
than that it could be 'invested' to produce, say,
£110 in a year's time (if the current rate of
interest were 10 per cent). Therefore, £110 in a
year's time may be said to equal around £100 now;
similarly, £100 in a year's time must equal around
£91 now. It is in fact a cardinal principle in
economics that any monetary amounts are meaningless
unless attached to a specific date or time period,
particularly in view of the need to allow for the
effects of inflation. Therefore a stream of future
monetary benefits which will accrue in years 1, 2,
3, 4, 5, needs to be re-expressed so as to be on a
comparable basis, say, all in year 1 values. Thus
if the stream originates as £100, £100, £100, £100,
£100, in current values, it will become in year 1
values, £100, £91, £83, £75, £68 (again assuming for
ease of calculation that the rate of interest is 10
per cent).

There are a number of technical problems
involved in making such calculations, such as the
choice of which interest rate to use, which can be
quite tricky and which have a considerable effect on
the eventual result, but for our purposes here we
may concentrate on the principle involved, namely,
that benefits in the immediate or near future figure
much more prominently in the final calculation than
benefits which may only be realised at some date
much further away. This effect may substantially
alter any evaluation of which may be the more profitable of two or more possible avenues for investment,
or, in educational terms, two or more different
levels or courses or types of education. Exactly
the same principle applies, incidentally, in the
case of costs but there it is much less likely to be
crucial to the outcome: with most investment
projects, educational or otherwise, most costs are
incurred at or near the inception of the investment
in question.

For a fuller discussion of these and other
problems of a technical nature relating to cost-
benefit calculations, the reader is referred to any
one of the several specialist volumes on this subject, such as Layard.[8] A shorter and convenient
summary of related questions may be found in
Henderson.[9]

Age-Earnings Profiles

We now need to consider how to attempt to measure the benefits from education. Our starting point is the rather obvious fact that the more highly paid in society are the ones who have received the more education and the more highly educated young people go, in turn, into those careers which offer the higher financial rewards. The unattractive and poorly-paid jobs tend to be filled by those who have had only minimal levels of education. There is a fairly close relationship between educational background and the pattern of lifetime earnings. This has been demonstrated to be true in many different countries.

It is not, of course, true for all individuals - we can all think of the Sir Billy Butlins who left school at 13 and rose to head large organisations and to draw very large salaries, and of the occasional Ph.D. who is content to have a humdrum, lowly-paid job, or who is even unemployed. We may also think of the pop music 'stars' or leading tennis players who have been referred to elsewhere in this book and who may have had very little in the way of formal education. The highest-paid sportsman, and one of the most highly-paid people, in the UK is a snooker player, for which formal education would scarcely seem to be a prerequisite. In such cases rather different considerations apply, notably a gross imbalance between high demand and very limited supply of exceptional talents.

To examine the available evidence, we would require statistics of the educational attainments and earnings of groups of people over their working lives, i.e. to be collected over a period of perhaps 40 years, known as *time-series data*. Such data generally does not exist, for obvious reasons. What does exist and can be used is snapshot evidence of cross-sections of society at one moment in time, or *cross-section data*. We should not now be looking at how, e.g. the *same* 16-year-old school leavers fare as they progress through their careers but at evidence relating to *different* people who all left school at 16 and who are now aged, say, 20, 30, 40, 50 and 60. As will become clear, there are serious drawbacks, but also some advantages, relating to the use of cross-section data in place of the time-series data; we will revert to this point later.

Statistics relating to earnings, educational qualifications and age, or *age-earnings profiles* as they have become widely known, have been collected in many countries. They are usually official or

semi-official in origin and are based on large
statistical samples of the working population.
They may usually be considered very reliable,
especially as broadly similar findings emerge from
such profiles in whichever countries they have been
carried out.   For the UK the most reliable of such
data remains the statistics derived from detailed
surveys carried out by the Department of Education
and Science for the financial year 1966-67, plus
unpublished data from the Department of Health and
Social Security, as used by Ziderman.[10]
Since the major findings from these surveys
tally closely with the evidence from all the other
countries where similar surveys have been carried
out, it seems probable that we may still have
confidence in them even though the base data are now
nearly 20 years old.   These findings are as
follows:

1.   From the commencement of working life
      earnings increase steadily to reach a
      peak before declining.
2.   Persons with higher education typically
      start their careers at higher salaries
      and achieve earnings throughout their
      working lives, and the earnings differ-
      entials between those with different
      levels of education typically increase
      steadily.
3.   For persons with higher levels of
      education earnings continue to rise for
      a longer period, so that the earnings
      peak is achieved later in life, and the
      eventual decline in earnings largely
      maintains the salary differential
      previously achieved.

Ziderman's graph of age-earnings profiles for males,
which is reproduced as Graph 3.1, shows these trends
clearly.   His graph for females was on similar
lines but gave less clear evidence for females with
higher levels of education on account of the
difficulty of being able to include in the survey
data for adequate numbers of women with higher levels
of education at successive ages.   (It is important
to remember here the point mentioned above regarding
the use of cross-section data in lieu of time-series
data.)   Results broadly similar to the above have
also been found for Canada, Denmark, Greece, Israel,
Japan, the Netherlands, New Zealand, Sweden, USA
and USSR, among countries conventionally defined as

57

Graph 3.1: Average Earnings for Levels of
Educational Qualifications in UK, 1966/67 (males)

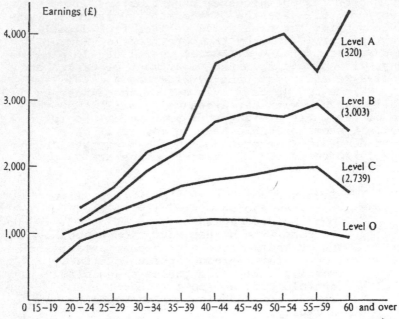

Key:
Level A — Higher university degrees or equivalent.
Level B — First degrees and all qualifications at this
            standard, including membership of certain
            professional institutions.
Level C — Qualifications below first degrees, such as HND,
            HNC, teaching certificates and nursing awards.
Level O — All males in working population.

Note: Sample numbers shown in brackets.

*Sources: Levels A, B and C: Survey of Earnings of
            Qualified Manpower in England and Wales,
            1966-67, Department of Education and
            Science, 1971, Table 6; Level O:
            Department of Health and Social Security
            (unpublished data).*[11]

developed, and for Chile, Colombia, India, Kenya, Mexico, Nigeria, the Philippines, Puerto Rico, Uganda, Venezuela and Zambia,[12] among the developing countries. In each case the more highly educated people do, of course, start earning salaries later - perhaps several years later - than people with less education, for the obvious reason that the latter are already at work whilst the former are continuing their full-time education beyond age 16 or 18, but even allowing for this the total earning power of the more highly educated is on average much higher.

It can hardly be doubted that this would also be found to be the case if we were able to have access to time-series data instead of cross-section data, which we theoretically or ideally require. The use of cross-section data may be said to have some advantages in that, since they give a snapshot view across people of different ages at one moment in time we do not have to worry about changing monetary values due to inflation or about the effects of successive periods of economic depression and reflation - the familiar 'Stop-Go'. This certainly makes the calculations much easier to do. Cross-section data do, however, suffer from a severe disadvantage in that they fail to capture the effect over time of economic growth, which translates into increases in real standards of living. The eventual earnings of the graduates of the year 1986, say when they reach age 50 in about the year 2015, should be very much higher in real terms than the earnings of the 50-year-old ex-graduates alive in 1986 which are used by the cross-section data. This is a real problem: the standard way to deal with it is to add to each age-earnings profile the annual expected increase in real income per head, based on past experience. This approach was inaugurated in the USA by Becker,[13] who may be said to be the founding father of the large literature that exists on age-earnings profiles, and was used in the UK by Ziderman[14] who decided to

> *conservatively assume that all earnings rise at the same rate of 2 per cent.*

The annual rate of economic growth in the UK has by no means always reached 2 per cent each year although it has done so on average. Perhaps a more significant factor relating to such an arbitrary adjustment, however, is that by applying the same percentage rate of increase to all earnings it

assumes that relative earnings differentials will
remain constant over the ensuing period of 40 years
or more, which past experience demonstrates is most
unlikely to be the case.   A further point worth
noting is that Becker demonstrated that one effect
of making such adjustments to the age-earnings profiles was to change the shape of the graph: the
decline at older ages disappears and the profiles
continue to rise throughout, to age 65, although at
slower rates in later years.   One can speculate
that this situation may subsequently have changed
again in recent years due to the increased incidence
of earlier retirements but as yet no definite
statistical evidence is available on this point.

Why is it that people with higher levels of
education on average receive higher incomes throughout their working lives than people with lower levels
of education?   A number of explanations are possible.
The most obvious one is that the 'graduates' from
each level of education really are more productive
and efficient than the persons emerging from the
educational level immediately below theirs: perhaps

> *the best educated are generally more flexible*
> *and more motivated, adapt themselves more*
> *easily to changing circumstances, benefit more*
> *from work experience and training, act with*
> *greater initiative in problem-solving*
> *situations, assume supervisory responsibility*
> *more quickly and, in short, are more productive*
> *than the less educated even when their education*
> *has taught them no specific skills.*[15]

On this basis, therefore, either an employee may be
rewarded more highly because of specific expertise
in, say, mathematics, or the effects of his or her
education, which may be in a not-directly-relevant
subject such as history, may be to produce a sought-
after ability to learn, react and adapt to ever-
changing situations.   All such attributes may
reasonably be included within the terms *'productive'*
and *'efficient'* and they may all have been imparted
in some way or other by the education received,
whether as the result of formal teaching and study,
speaking in debates in the Students Union, captaining
the cricket team, or simply mixing socially and
informally with other able young people.   This would
even be true if all that the young people learned in
the education system was perseverance and hard work.
All of these factors would represent the education
system *causing*, in some way or other, the future

enhanced efficiency.

But perhaps it does not. Perhaps the people in question were already, in some in-built or even genetic manner, the more able and the more efficient members of their age group before they entered the education system (after all, universities try to select out the most able 18-year-olds for entry) or would have become so during the years in question as the result of influences external to the education system or of general maturational processes. Or indeed that it is no more than social convention that graduates commence their careers with higher earnings than non-graduates and subsequently maintain and relatively improve them. Perhaps for employers the certificates or diplomas which are the end-products of all education systems throughout the world are simply a convenient and cheap way of choosing suitable personnel. Here we may think again of the advertisement which read '*Young person required to valet cars, 5 'O-levels' required*'. If we could prove that this were the case there would be an urgent need to re-examine the processes involved: what seems cheap to the future employer is in fact extremely expensive to society as a whole and perhaps some cheaper and quicker alternative should be sought, perhaps some modern 'high-tech' equivalent of the old-style aptitude tests.

In practice, however, it has proved impossible to disentangle these twin aspects, and it seems likely that some mix of the two may always be present. The position is also rendered much more complicated by the general tendency for a wide range of employers to require higher educational levels at entry. The commercial banks which used to recruit 16-year-olds with O-levels turned their attention to 18-year-olds with A-levels and then to 21-year-olds with degrees from universities or polytechnics; the engineering professions have turned from recruiting non-graduates and subsequently training them via part-time study to almost entirely all-graduate entry; teaching has become an all-graduate entry profession; nursing and surveying are increasingly seeking young people with higher entry qualifications, including graduates, and so are the armed forces and many other professions including virtually all types and levels of administration such as in hospitals or local government. These trends relate to an underlying 'chicken and egg' question: are more 16-year-olds (or 18-year-olds) choosing to remain in full-time education because of the wider career opportunities that are becoming available to those with extended education, or are employers turning their attention towards 18-year-olds with additional education because the bright 16-year-olds with O-levels whom they used to recruit no longer become available at that age?   It has proved impossible to disentangle this conundrum, for obvious reasons.

The same trends are to be found in all developed countries.   They make it doubly difficult to segregate out the 'educational' from the 'non-educational' factors in differentials in age-earnings profiles. We can be sure that the raw data which comprise age-earnings profiles overestimate the effect that education has on earnings, because of the incidence of all the 'non-education' factors, including innate I.Q. (although psychologists now seem uncertain whether this (i) can be measured or (ii) exists at all), natural personality, favourable home background, social class or simply family connections and the 'old boy network'.   To cite an example, the medical doctor is highly remunerated, in all countries, because of his long period of medical education and training but it is also true that the great majority of students in medical schools studying to become doctors - far more than in proportion - come from relatively priviledged family and social backgrounds.

But this still leaves the problem of how to quantify the proportion of income-stream differentials that derive respectively from education and from non-educational factors.   After a large-scale statistical study conducted in the USA, Denison[16] found the proportions to be respectively 66 per cent and 33 per cent and this finding has subsequently been quoted and utilised throughout the world, perhaps at least partly because no alternative finding has ever been shown to be more reliable.   Denison was writing in 1964 and the survey data results related to the period 1950 to 1955, so perhaps it is high time that the results of a more up-to-date study became available.   So widely-accepted has this correctional factor of two-thirds/one-third become that it has acquired a special name of its own, the *alpha coefficient*: since this term is applied to the figure of 0.66 it would in fact seem to be more accurate to call it the 'education coefficient' although for our purposes the terminology is scarcely the most important point.   Denison arrived at this conclusion by standardising income data for American high-school and college graduates for differences in father's occupation, rank in school class and I.Q. scores.   The data related to males only and said nothing at all about educational levels below high-

school; nevertheless the result was used by Denison
and has been used by many other researchers since to
apply to age-earnings differentials of both sexes
and at all educational levels.   At least some of the
adjustments Denison had to make to the original data
were based on little more than inspired guesses and,
as commented above, the results of I.Q. tests are now
widely derided.   Given all these caveats, the
universal use of the results of his research over the
last 20 years or more does present an interesting
example of the way in which a research finding which
is based on less-then-ideal foundations is taken up
and accepted.   It seems possible that Denison
deliberately overestimated the effects due to non-
educational factors so that he could confidently say
that education contributed *at least* 66 per cent of
any differential, i.e. any research findings based
on this coefficient are essentially *minimal* ones.

Blaug argues that for the UK an alpha coefficient of 0.66 may be too high for secondary-school
leavers since 'early leaving' is so highly correlated
with social class but may be too low for university
graduates since by then '*the divisive influence of
social-class membership ... has largely ceased to
exist*'.   If we were to attempt to apply such
reasoning it would seem that we would at least
require much lower alpha coefficients for those 50
per cent of young people - the females - for whom
the statistics, e.g. of progression from school to
university, are quite different than those for the
males.   Non-educational factors such as social
prejudice conspire to operate against them throughout
the educational system.   No such calculations have
ever been published and the figure of 0.66 has come
to be used universally, but it is important to be
aware of its inherent weaknesses.   However arbitrary
the effect, some adjustment of this kind is clearly
required to allow for the fact that although much of
a person's career success may be attributed to the
education he or she received, not all of it can and
allowance must also be made for other causal
factors.

Earnings Profiles - Gross or Net?

We have seen that clear and marked differentials
between the age-earnings profiles for people with
different educational backgrounds are an established
fact.   To quantify such differentials, if we simply
sum the differences in their earnings over their
careers - i.e. measure the area between any two

successive lines on a graph such as Graph 3.1 - and
suitably discount to allow for the effects of time,
will this suffice?   The answer must be No, it will
not, for two reasons, one of which is quite obvious
but the other rather more subtle: the graduate with
more education behind him (or her) may have incurred
higher direct costs, such as course fees as a result
of the education received and these must be allowed
for.   This point does not apply to all educational
courses everywhere but it does apply to some courses
in all countries and to all courses in some countries.
      The second point is related but much less
obvious.   Let us consider the full-time student and,
to avoid the charge of being sexist, make her femin-
ine: if she was not still in education she would,
the argument runs, be in a job and earning a salary;
to the extent that she is unable to do so, therefore,
she is forgoing income, and this *income foregone* must
be seen as a real cost to the student, and also
incidentally to the country or society which has lost
the benefit of her contribution to the country's
total production - assuming that her income gives a
meaningful measure of this contribution.   The latter
would be encompassed in the Gross National Product
(or Income, which is the same) albeit in such an
infinitesimal proportion that it would be quite
impossible to identify it;   after all, standard
National Accounting procedures lead to errors each
year amounting to several hundred million pounds, so
it is scarcely likely that it will ever be possible
to identify the contribution of any one individual.
The principle should, however, be clear.
      Incidentally, to digress just a little, the
measurement of such income forgone may look rather
different from the point of view of the society as a
whole than it does from the point of view of the
individual student, if the latter receives some form
of grant or bursary.   Say, for example, she could
have earned £6,000 per year and the grant she
receives is £1,500:   then she is only £4,500 out-of-
pocket (or even less since the £6,000 would be subject to income tax and national insurance but the
£1,500 would be tax free).   The 'cost' to society,
however, is the whole of the £6,000 (but not also
the payment of the £1,500 grant since this is merely
a cash transfer between different members of the same
society).   Such difference between the perspective
of the individual and of society will concern us
again, as we shall see shortly.   The final point to
make clear is that the concept of 'income forgone'
relates to young people of employable age whether 17-

year-olds in the UK or 7-year-olds in Indonesia; it
cannot apply to, say, 13-year-olds in the UK. There
would be no sense in which we could talk of 'income
forgone' for young people who were, for legal or
other reasons, unemployable. Thus, according to
calculations on the above lines, the raising of the
legal school-leaving age dramatically decreases the
total costs of certain educational courses.

Whether or not allowance should be made for
income forgone in any cost-benefit calculations has
been the subject of a long-standing dispute between
academic economists of different persuasions. The
late Professor Vaizey[17] argued that since the concept was not allowed for in a wide variety of other
economic calculations relating in some way or other
to national income, such as the time of housewives,
mothers, or all kinds of voluntary work, it would be
misleading to include it in the case of education.
Professor Blaug[18] strongly opposed this view, for the
reasons already given. Much would seem to depend on
the purpose for which any cost-benefit calculation is
made and this would normally be for the purpose of
drawing comparisons; there would be little point in
doing such a complicated sum in isolation. If that
comparison is to be drawn outside the boundaries of
the educational system, e.g. with investment in
manufacturing industry, or with health-care, then
Vaizey's argument would seem to have much validity.
But if, as has more often been the case, comparisons
are being drawn between one element of education and
another, then Blaug's argument is the stronger and
it is certainly the one that has become more widely
accepted.

The above sets out the standard argument relating to 'income forgone'; the importance of allowing
for it in any calculations may, incidentally, be seen
when it is realised that it frequently exceeds the
whole of the direct costs of the education in
question. The trouble with this argument, however,
is, as was indicated previously, that it assumes that
the student would be able to find a job if she wished
to do so and in a world where mass unemployment is a
long-term problem in every country in the world we
have to ask whether this is a valid assumption. Or,
if she is fortunate enough to find a job, is she
depriving someone else who would otherwise have
filled that post and who is made unemployed because
of the decision to appoint her, so that there is *no*
net increase in production? If we must accept that
this is the most likely situation, as it seems we
must, then we are refuting one aspect of

'*conventional wisdom*' à la Galbraith[19] and many
accepted cost-benefit calculations stand in need of
revision.

THE CALCULATION OF RATES OF RETURN

All of the above has been necessary to pave the way
for an examination of the application of cost-benefit
analysis to education.   That application may be made
from the perspective of society as a whole, giving
the *social rate of return*, or from the point of view
of the individual, giving the *private rate of return*.
This is a crucial distinction and one that we have
already met.   A further distinction is between the
calculation of rates of return relating to the
average over the whole of the education received,
e.g. from approximately ages 5 to 24 in the case of
a Ph.D, called *average rate of return*, and that
relating to only one incremental or marginal part,
course or year, of that education, the *marginal rate
of return*.   In all, therefore, we have the various
possibilities set out in Table 3.1, although it
should be recognised that the apparently clear-cut
distinctions shown are sometimes blurred in
practice.

Table 3.1:   Cost-Benefit Analysis: Rates of Return

	From perspective of the individual	From perspective of society as a whole
Average over all education received	Average private rate of return	Average social rate of return
Incremental part of education	Marginal private rate of return	Marginal social rate of return

The choice of which of the above to use will
obviously depend on the purpose of doing the calculation, which may relate to such questions as
whether it is worthwhile for our individual student
to invest more in his or her education, or what
return society as a whole gains from such additional

investment.   Therefore, no one of the above four
categories is 'best', they each serve different
purposes, and a considerable body of literature
exists, world-wide, in respect of each.   The principles involved in the calculation of each are
identical, only certain of the practical details
differ.

Private Rates of Return
Individual students looking at the costs they would
incur or the benefits they would in all probability
receive from investment in education would have to
begin by adding up all the costs incurred.   For most
students on most courses it is not necessary to start
worrying about such financial details as teaching
staff costs, the costs of buildings, recurrent
resources such as fuel and materials or loan charges:
the students will pay, or will have paid on their
behalf, annual course fees which should represent
both recurrent costs and the annual equivalent of
capital costs.   The students will also incur other
costs such as purchases of books and supplies of
paper, together with their normal living expenses;
for many higher education courses in the UK - but
much less commonly in other countries - the students
will receive grants and the amount of the full grant,
currently £1,800 per annum for most undergraduate
students, may be taken to represent all these other
costs, since these are what it is intended to cover.
     A problem here is that only the minority of
students who come from families with relatively low
parental incomes receive the full grant, the others,
the majority, supposedly receiving *parental contributions*' from their families to make up the difference;
it is well known that many students do not receive
the full amount but there are no accurate statistics
as to the extent of the shortfall.   We therefore
have no option but to assume that students receive,
from one source or another, the amount of the full
grant.
     There then arises the problematic question of
income forgone, as was discussed previously.   In the
present climate of high unemployment, would the
alternative scenario - the *'opportunity cost'* in the
language of economics - be that the student would get
a job?   Keeping to the perspective from the point of
view of the individual, the balance of probability is
that he or she would, but that, assuming that the
total level of employment stays constant, some other
unfortunate and unidentifiable person would be

deprived of work as a consequence. For our
individual student, therefore, we must include a
cost allowance for income forgone, possibly with a
probability factor to allow for the inherent uncertainty: e.g. if there is a 90 per cent probability
that the student could obtain a job which paid
£5,000 per year, then the income forgone would be
entered at 90 per cent of £5,000 = £4,500.

Now the benefits from the education - measured,
as we have already seen, by the differential in age-
earnings profiles after allowing for the alpha
coefficient (0.66) and for a long-term growth factor
(commonly 2 per cent), and leaving on one side the
'consumption' aspect of the education - need to be
related to the costs. All figures, but especially
the benefits, will need to be suitably discounted to
allow for the effects of time, i.e. to re-express all
the sums as at a common date, commonly the year of
graduation. After all the future benefits have been
so discounted, this gives their *Present Value*. If
we knew for certain the correct percentage rate to
use in this discounting exercise, we would arrive at
a single total (present) figure for benefits which
could be compared with the single total figure for
costs; if the former exceeds the latter, the
education may be regarded as a profitable investment.

This *Present Value* method is technically
different from the alternative *Internal Rate of
Return* method even though the sums superficially look
the same. With the latter, and more commonly used,
method, various alternative discount rates are used
in turn to re-express the future values in current
figures until one is arrived at which equates, as
closely as may be possible, the total benefits with
the total costs, thus avoiding the problem of having
to select the most appropriate discount rate. This
Internal Rate of Return, so called because it is
deduced internally from the calculations, may then be
compared with (i) alternative investment possibilities and (ii) the current cost of borrowing money.
The final decision may seem obvious if we have either
of two contrasting examples:

(a) Internal Rate of Return = 20 per cent
     Return on next best alternative
        investment = 10 per cent
     Cost of borrowing money = 12 per cent
     Decision: Enrol for the course.

(b)   Internal Rate of Return = 10 per cent
       Return on next best alternative
          investment = 20 per cent
       Cost of borrowing money = 12 per cent
       Decision: Do not enrol for the course.

In practice, of course, it is likely that there may
be some intermediate position and that the decision
may not be so clear-cut.
      Private rates of return have been calculated
for many different types and levels of education in
many different countries.   For the UK, the most
widely-publicised results have been those produced
by Ziderman[20] and based on the age-earnings profiles
given above in Graph 3.1.   Tables 3.2 and 3.3
summarise the results for average and marginal
private rates of return respectively: in each case
the first column gives the results where the whole
of the income differentials have been related to the
education received, and the second column gives the
results where an alpha coefficient of 0.66 has been
used.   Not all students successfully complete their
courses and the third column in Table 3.3 gives the
results when a further adjustment has been made for
the probability of dropping-out.   The two columns
are given in Table 3.2 and the three columns in
Table 3.3 so that the effects on the results of
making such adjustments may readily be seen.
      A number of comments are required in connection
with these tables.   Firstly, the wording indicates
that the intention was to calculate average rates of
return over the whole of the education received, as
shown in Table 3.2, and returns for additional increments or slices of education beyond GCE A-level,
which is normally taken at about age 18, as shown in
Table 3.3.   Census survey statistics were available
for income streams for holders of each of First
(Bachelor's) degrees, Master's degrees, and
Doctorates, save only that there were too few females
available with higher degrees to enable valid calculations to be made, which is why these are not shown
in Table 3.2.   For the A-level base income stream,
however, no such statistics existed and the researchers had to take as a proxy the salaries attaching to
Executive class employed in the Civil Service, for
which GCE A-level standard was the normal entry
requirement.   (We should note in passing that
similar jobs now increasingly recruit graduates.)
At the time, this seemed a not unreasonable thing to
do for males although it probably included some *over-
estimation* of typical salaries and therefore some

Table 3.2: Average Private Rates of Return on
Degree Education from Age 15, 1966-67 (per cent)*

	No 'ability' adjustment	'Ability' adjusted†
Males		
First degree	15.0	12.5
Master's degree	15.5	12.5
Doctorate	16.0	13.0
Females		
First degree	20.5	18.0

*All rates of return are rounded to nearest 0.5 per cent.
†Rates of return sensitivity tested for ability and other
 factors, by reducing earnings differentials by one-third.

Source: A. Ziderman, *Does it pay to take a degree?
           The profitability of private investment in
           university education in Britain.*

Table 3.3: Marginal Private Rates of Return on Male
Education, 1966-67 (per cent)*

	I No 'ability' adjustment	II 'Ability' adjusted†	III Adjusted for drop-out
GCE A-level			
(from no qualification)	10.0	8.5	Negative
First degree	22.5	20.0	16.5
(from GCE A-level)	(23.5)	(21.5)	(18.5)
Master's degree	20.0	16.5	Negative
(from first degree)	(19.0)	(16.0)	(Negative)
Doctorate	19.5	16.0	2.5
(from first degree)	(14.5)	(11.0)	(Negative)

*All rates of return rounded to nearest 0.5 per cent.
†Rates of return sensitivity tested for ability and other
 factors, by reducing earnings differentials by one-third.
Note: Figures in brackets are sensitivity estimates of the
rates of return with school teachers *excluded.*

Source: See Table 3.2.

underestimation of marginal rates of return.   For
females, given the unsatisfactory state of female
labour markets such errors would be so great as to
invalidate the findings and therefore the marginal
figures in Table 3.3 relate to males only.   This
problem obviously does not apply to the average rates
shown in Table 3.2.
     Overall, the results shown in the tables may be
summarised as follows:

(i)   The rates of return shown in the tables
        are high, certainly high enough to indicate
        that the additional educational investment
        is well worth while.
(ii)   The differences between the figures shown
        in the first and second columns are not
        excessive and generally would not affect
        the final decision, suggesting that the
        question of the alpha coefficient need not
        after all be such a worry as had been
        feared.
(iii)   The average rates of return for females
        are exceptionally high, even though it is
        well known that on average females earn
        considerably less than males; the reason,
        of course, relates to the 'lower-level'
        alternative for females, for which the pay
        is usually very much worse.
(iv)   The final column in Table 3.3 suggests
        that if prospective students were to take
        seriously the possibility that they might
        not complete the course, many would never
        enter at all (assuming that a not-completed
        course has no effect at all on future
        earnings).
(v)   If schoolteachers (who arguably have
        relatively low rates of pay compensated by
        advantageous non-monetary considerations)
        are excluded - as shown by the figures in
        brackets, returns to first degrees rise
        marginally but others fall.

Social Rates of Return
Most of the principles set out above regarding
private rates of return also apply to social rates
of return, with certain notable differences in the
practicalities of the calculations.   Chief among
these are that account should be taken of incomes
before deduction of income tax instead of after,
and that all the costs of the education should be

included, comprising all those that are met by the
government or education authority and not by the
student.   This latter point, incidentally, explains
why social rates of return are almost always lower
than private rates of return.   The vexed question
of income forgone has already been discussed: the
conclusion must be that, in the case of social rates
of return, in a world of high unemployment it should
be omitted.

Much the most problematic remaining point refers
to the concept of *'spill-over benefits'*:   each
educated graduate, so the argument runs, enters a
career where he will be working with other people.
On account of the graduate's greater efficiency or
productivity, output, turnover or profits will be
raised, a by-product or spill-over benefit of this
process being that his or her colleagues have some
share in this enhanced production and they in turn
become more productive and efficient.   Logically
this should in turn lead to increases in their levels
of real wages.   In addition what have been termed
'second round spill-overs' may follow in the form
of, for example, increased incentives to suppliers
of services, such as research.   Although no way has
ever been found of quantifying all the possible
spill-over effects, a rough-and-ready calculation
by Becker[21] suggested that the combined effect of
these may be so great as to *double* published rates
of return, which conventionally have never and do not
now include any allowance for spill-over effects.
This is a good example of the kind of generalised
approximation that was referred to previously: after
meticulous and detailed calculations, economists have
no qualms in suggesting that the ensuing results
should be doubled.   One can see why they do so and
why on balance the result is more likely to be more
accurate if some such correction factor is included.
Nevertheless to do so makes clear the degree of
approximation to which we are working: this is a
point of which it may be necessary to remind oneself
whenever one finds rates of returns reported as being
correct to two decimal places.

Perhaps the most widely-quoted study of social
rates of return in the UK was that by Morris,[22] based
on the same incomes survey data for qualified manpower as was used by Ziderman.   These were then
applied to cost statistics disaggregated by level of
education and, unusually, by subject area, to give
marginal and average social rates of return, as
shown in Tables 3.4 and 3.5.   The footnotes to the
tables indicate some of the adjustments that were

Table 3.4: Marginal Social Rates of Return in Different Educational Qualifications and Subjects (%)

Educational qualification	Subject discipline				
	All subjects	Arts	Social science	Science	Engineering
Full-time education					
Men					
A-level/unqualified					
Ability: unadjusted	7.5	–	–	–	–
adjusted	7.0				
First degree/A-levels					
Ability: unadjusted	11.0	12.5	12.0	9.5	10.0
	(12.0)	(13.5)	(13.0)	(11.0)	(11.5)
adjusted	9.0	9.5	9.5	8.0	8.0
	(10.5)	(10.5)	(10.0)	(8.5)	(8.5)
Master/first degree					
Ability: unadjusted	1.0	–	–	3.0	
	(2.0)			(4.0)	
adjusted	<0.0	–	–	2.0	
	(0.0)			(2.5)	
Doctorate/first degree					
Ability: unadjusted	1.5	<0.0		1.0	
	(2.5)	(1.0)		(2.0)	
adjusted	<0.0	<0.0		0.5	
	(1.0)	(0.0)		(1.0)	
Women					
First degree/A-levels					
Ability: unadjusted	5.5	6.0	9.0	<0.0	–
	(6.5)	(7.0)	(10.5)	(0.0)	
adjusted	4.0	3.0	6.0	<0.0	–
	(5.0)	(4.0)	(6.5)	(0.0)	
Vocational education					
Men					
ONC/unqualified					
Ability: unadjusted	7.5	–	–	–	–
adjusted	6.5				
HNC/ONC					
Ability: unadjusted	>20.0	–	–	16.0	>20.0
	(20.0)			(16.5)	(20.0)
adjusted	>20.0	–	–	13.0	19.5
	(20.0)			(13.5)	(20.0)
HNC.PQ/HNC					
Ability: unadjusted	20.0	–	–	–	>20.0
	(20.0)				(20.0)
adjusted	16.0	–	–	–	>20.0
	(16.0)				(20.0)

Notes: (1) The ability factor has been adjusted by one-third.
       (2) The figures in parentheses show the social rates of returns excluding research costs.
       (3) Returns exclude the earnings of school teachers.

Source: *V. Morris, Investment in Higher Education in England and Wales.*

Table 3.5: Average Social Rates of Return from
Compulsory School-leaving Age in Different
Educational Qualifications and Subjects (%)

Educational qualification	Subject discipline				
	All subjects	Arts	Social science	Science	Engin-eering
Full-time education					
Men					
A-levels					
Ability: unadjusted	7.5	–	–	–	–
adjusted	7.0	–	–	–	–
First degree					
Ability: unadjusted	9.5	10.0	10.0	9.0	9.0
adjusted	8.0	8.0	8.0	7.0	7.0
Master's dgree					
Ability: unadjusted	7.5	–	–	7.0	
adjusted	6.0	–	–	5.0	
Doctorate degree					
Ability: unadjusted	6.5	–	–	6.0	
adjusted	5.5	–	–	4.0	
Women					
First degree					
Ability: unadjusted	7.5	6.5	8.0	4.5	–
adjusted	6.0	4.5	5.5	2.0	–
Vocational education					
Men					
ONC					
Ability: unadjusted	7.5	–	–	–	–
adjusted	6.5	–	–	–	–
HNC					
Ability: unadjusted	14.5	–	–	10.5	13.0
adjusted	12.0	–	–	8.5	10.0
HNC.PQ					
Ability: unadjusted	15.5	–	–	–	15.0
adjusted	13.0	–	–	–	11.5

Notes: (1) Returns are based on costs including research.
(2) Returns exclude the earnings of school teachers.

Source: V. Morris, *Investment in Higher Education
in England and Wales.*

made to the data, including the alpha coefficient of
two-thirds and the problematic question of whether
to include as a cost universities' expenditure on
research. The rates of return shown are, as
expected, lower than the private rates of return met
previously. First degrees are evidently 'worth
while' but postgraduate degrees are not: the marginal returns to Master's degrees or doctorates are so
low as to represent very poor investments. The
lower level Higher National Certificate courses on
the other hand have very much higher rates of return
than the higher level courses which are conventionally
regarded as more prestigious. Rates of return are
rather higher for first degrees in arts and social
science subjects than for science and engineering:
this reflects the higher costs associated with the
latter and is contrary to the current 'conventional'
wisdom' that Britain needs more scientists and
engineers. If the results of this study were to be
translated into practical educational policy, there
would be a significant expansion of part-time
advanced further education courses, previously denot-
ed as Higher National Certificate but now coming
under the umbrella of the Business and Technical
Education Council.

There have been many other examples of calculations of rates of return, both private and social,
to investment in education. Good reviews of such
results world-wide were given by Psacharopoulos in
1973[23] and 1981.[24] For the UK reference may be made
to just one other study, that by Birch and Calvert[25]
which examined the rates of return to becoming a
teacher and the main findings of which are summarised
in Table 3.6. The most striking finding relates to
the very high rates of return for women becoming
teachers, even though on average women teachers
receive lower salaries than men teachers: the cause
lies with the alternative forms of employment and
typically low rates of pay open to such women. if
they had not decided to train as teachers. As the
authors comment,

> *the high rates of return enjoyed by women*
> *teachers are more a commentary on the poor*
> *state of the female labour market than they*
> *are evidence of high salaries for women*
> *teachers.*

For male teachers in order to obtain better rates of
return it was important to qualify as a graduate.
Table 3.6 indicates two notable adjustments that were

Table 3.6: Alternative Estimates of Private Rates
of Return on the Investment in a Teaching Career from
Age 15 Adjusted for Holiday 'Perks' (1970)

	Percentages economically active	Percentages in employment
Males		
All graduates	14.1	14.4
graduates: secondary	14.3	14.6
graduates: primary	11.2	11.4
All non-graduates	9.6	9.8
non-graduates: secondary	9.7	9.9
non-graduates: primary	9.4	9.6
Females		
All graduates	29.3	31.0
graduates: secondary	29.8	31.5
graduates: primary	28.3	29.9
All non-graduates	29.0	31.0
non-graduates: secondary	29.8	31.5
non-graduates: primary	28.8	30.5

Source: D.W. Birch and J.R. Calvert,
How Profitable is Teaching,

required, for the probability of being unemployed
and to take into account the 'perks' of having long
holidays.   The comments made previously regarding
all such arbitrary adjustments should be borne in
mind here.

Views of the usefulness of applying cost-
benefit analysis techniques to education vary widely.
Writers such as Blaug and Psacharopoulos are clearly
in favour;   the most serious critic was Vaizey:

> *the range of inaccuracy may be so large as to*
> *render the estimates literally meaningless ...*
> *large differences in the returns to different*
> *levels or types of education would have to be*
> *apparent before the results have any great*
> *significance for educational policy making ...*
> *the usefulness of such studies is very*
> *limited.* [26]

The very large number of cost-benefit studies related
to education that have been carried out attests that

such a degree of pessimism has not commanded majority support.

The rates of return resulting from cost-benefit studies achieved greater prominence when they were publicised in the 1985 Green Paper *The Development of Higher Education into the 1990s*, where the impression was given that the government was in favour of such calculations. Nevertheless it is probably as well to conclude this chapter on a note of caution particularly regarding the question of accuracy in results. As we have seen, there are several major grounds for suggesting inaccuracy, perhaps the most important ones relating to non-pecuniary aspects of jobs, in the case of private rates of return, and to the question of spill-over benefits, in the case of social rates of return. A reminder may also be necessary regarding 'consumption benefits': people do not, and presumably never will, take decisions relating to the acquisition of additional education on financial grounds alone. Therefore any fit between the results of cost-benefit studies and subsequent educational decisions can at best only be approximate.

NOTES

1. M.J. Bowman and C.A. Anderson, 'Concerning the Role of Education in Development', in C. Geertz (ed.), *Old Societies and New States* (Free Press, 1963).
2. C.A. Anderson, 'Literacy and Schooling on the Development Threshold: Some Historical Cases', in C.A. Anderson and M.J. Bowman (eds), *Education and Economic Development* (Aldine, 1965).
3. A.L. Peaslee, 'Primary School Enrolments and Economic Growth', *Comparative Education Review* (February 1967).
4. M. Blaug, *An Introduction to the Economics of Education* (Penguin, 1970).
5. F. Harbison and C. Myers, *Education, Manpower and Economic Growth* (McGraw-Hill, 1964).
6. Blaug, *An Introduction to the Economics of Education*.
7. E.F. Denison, *The Sources of Economic Growth in the United States* (Committee for Economic Development, New York, 1962).
8. R. Layard (ed.), *Cost-Benefit Analysis* (Penguin, 1972).
9. P.D. Henderson, 'Investment Criteria for

Public Enterprises', in R. Turvey (ed.), *Public Enterprise* (Penguin, 1968).

10. A. Ziderman, 'Does It Pay to Take a Degree? The Profitability of Private Investment in University Education in Britain', *Oxford Economic Papers* (July, 1973) and reprinted in C. Baxter *et al.* (eds), *Economics and Education Policy* (Longman, 1977).

11. *Ibid.*

12. Blaug, *An Introduction to the Economics of Education.*

13. G.S. Becker, *Human Capital, A Theoretical and Empirical Analysis, With Special Reference to Education* (Princeton University Press, 1974).

14. Ziderman, 'Does It Pay to Take a Degree?'.

15. Blaug, *An Introduction to the Economics of Education.*

16. E.F. Denison, 'Proportion of Income Differentials Among Education Groups Due to Additional Education', in J. Vaizey (ed.), *The Residual Factor and Economic Growth* (OECD, 1964).

17. J. Vaizey, *The Economics of Education* (Faber, 1962).

18. Blaug, *An Introduction to the Economics of Education.*

19. J.K. Galbraith, *The Affluent Society* (Pelican, 1958).

20. Ziderman, 'Does It Pay to Take a Degree?'.

21. Becker, *Human Capital.*

22. V. Morris, 'Investment in Higher Education in England and Wales', in G. Fowler *et al.* (eds), *Decision-Making in British Education* (Heinemann, 1973) and reprinted in Baxter *et al.*, *Economics and Education Policy.*

23. G. Psacharopoulos, *Returns to Education* (Elsevier, 1973).

24. G. Psacharopoulos, 'Returns to Education: An Updated International Comparison', *Comparative Education*, Vol.17, No.3 (1981).

25. D.W. Birch and J.R. Calvert, 'How Profitable is Teaching?', *Higher Education Review* (1974). For more recent findings on similar lines, see R.A. Wilson, 'The Declining Return to Becoming a Teacher', *Higher Education Review*, Vol.15 (Summer 1983), and R.A. Wilson, 'The Social Returns to Producing Teachers', *Higher Education Review*, Vol.17 (Summer 1985).

26. J. Vaizey and others, *The Political Economy of Education* (Duckworth, 1972).

Chapter Four

EDUCATION SUPPLY AND DEMAND - TWO CASE STUDIES

We may now consider, as case studies, examples of
two areas which highlight the intricate problems
involved in trying to reconcile the demand for
specialised highly qualified manpower with the
supply of potential entrants that may be available.
This chapter will deal firstly with the supposed
shortage of qualified scientists and engineers in
Britain and secondly with the problems involved in
planning the numbers of teachers required to teach
in schools.

SCIENTISTS AND ENGINEERS IN BRITAIN

Does Britain have a shortage of scientists and engineers?   This is perhaps the most problematic question
considered in this book.   Reports of a persistent
and on-going shortage of scientists and engineers,
particularly at the graduate level, have appeared at
regular intervals for at least the last thirty years,
yet this contention has been supported by remarkably
little hard evidence and has frequently been denied
to have any substance.   We may conveniently begin
our discussion of this question with the latest
relevant official inquiry, the Finniston Report,[1]
which confined itself to engineers rather than
scientists although many of the points at issue are
common to both.

The Finniston Report
Finniston set out to examine the existing stock of
engineers and their usage, but found this difficult
to do in view of the lack of adequate information:
*There are no comprehensive and up-to-date data on
the numbers and distribution of engineers in this*

country'.   If one of the most sophisticated
economies in the world has no such statistics, small
wonder that the poorer countries of the Third World
have such massive problems of identification.
Finniston went on to use the data from the 1971
National Census, which were nearly 10 years out-of-
date and incomplete in a number of respects: these
showed that Britain had in 1971 some 239,000 graduate
engineers, of whom less than 39 per cent were employed in manufacturing industry;   36 per cent were
employed in the 'white-collar' categories, professional and scientific services (including education)
and public administration and defence, and insurance,
banking and finance.   A further 197,000 engineers
were qualified to HNC/HND level and of these 51 per
cent worked in manufacturing industry and 21 per
cent in the same 'white-collar' categories.   There
were far fewer scientists: 148,000 with degrees (30
per cent in manufacturing industry, 53 per cent in
professional and scientific services including
education) and 20,000 with HNC/HND (54 per cent and
28 per cent respectively).   As to how accurate or
reliable these figures might be by 1980, there was
no way of knowing and the Report's comment,

> *We consider the lack of adequate information*
> *about the numbers and distribution of*
> *engineers employed in the UK economy a*
> *serious deficiency*

seems rather an understatement.   It is also noteworthy that such statistics, even if they were fully
up-to-date, would still have inherent in them all the
disadvantages of being related to level of educational qualification rather than job actually done which
were noted in the previous chapter.
     This latter point is particularly important in
this instance since surveys commissioned by
Finniston showed:

> *a high degree of individual mobility in those*
> *aged under 30 between employers, between*
> *functions and between engineering and non-*
> *engineering occupations ... there is a clear*
> *trend for engineers, as they get older, to move*
> *away from the design and specification work in*
> *which many begin their careers into more general*
> *management or other 'outside' work.   It emerged*
> *from replies to our survey that many young*
> *engineers currently employed in primarily*
> *technical functions foresaw themselves*

> *progressing in their careers in posts in which they would not directly be applying their engineering knowledge.*

This mobility of engineers away from working as engineers as such became one of the chief concerns expressed in the Finniston Report and led on to the view that there would be little point in seeking to increase the flow of new graduate engineers if the stock of those already available was apparently not being used efficiently. Of crucial importance here were the experiences of the young engineers and the influences that led them to diversify their career patterns. Those who had moved on:

> *tended to earn rather more than graduates of similar age still employed in engineering practice*

whilst they typically commented adversely on their previous experiences:

> *Many of the respondents were critical of their earlier experiences in engineering practice in terms of job satisfaction, status and pay: a number said that they had left engineering jobs because they positively disliked engineering. The survey of 'lapsed' engineers served primarily to confirm something we found already well acknowledged in other countries, that an engineering background provides an excellent basis for a wide variety of rewarding career opportunities in the modern economy.*

All this was in line with the 1971 Census data which showed that,

> *people initially qualified as engineers are to be found working in almost every sector of the economy, both as engineers and in many other roles.*

It thus emerges that working as an engineer is in some respects unattractive perhaps especially in terms of status, that an engineer's training makes him an attractive recruit for other (non-engineering) employers, and that this problem is also found in other developed countries (but is perhaps more acute in the UK). Similar comments could obviously be made in respect of qualified scientists.

With regard to the supply of new engineers,

Finniston noted that a major and significant change
in the chief route of entry had occurred since the
mid-1960s: previously the majority of engineers had
finished their full-time education at age 16 or 18
and subsequently obtained their professional qualifications via part-time study whilst in full-time
employment, with only a small minority achieving
degrees. By 1980 most engineers (over 80 per cent)
were coming through full-time degree courses at
universities or polytechnics *'as has long been the
case in other industrial countries'*: at long last,
therefore, Britain was in this respect catching up
with her competitors. From 1965 to 1980 the numbers
of young people completing degree courses in engineering increased by around 50 per cent, but decreased
significantly as a proportion of all degrees
completed, as the attractiveness of other degree
courses grew even more rapidly. Finniston found
that young people still at school were often not
attracted to study mathematics and physics to A-level
(normal pre-conditions for entry to engineering
degree courses), had little knowledge of or interest
in engineering as a career, and were largely unaware
of alternative routes of entry, and whereas

> *in other industrial countries the demand from
> young people for an engineering education is
> consistently high and the competition for
> places fierce ... an engineering formation is
> well recognised in these other countries as an
> assured route to a variety of attractive and
> rewarding careers'*

the same could not be said of the UK.
    Quite apart from the numbers involved, there was
also here an implicit reference to quality: if, as
had usually been the case, the A-level grades
required for entry to degree courses in engineering
were lower than those required for many other degree
courses, then perhaps many of the country's brightest
young people, as assessed at age 18, were not being
attracted to engineering and some remedial policies
were needed to correct this. (This point should
not, however, be overstated: the 1985 Green Paper
The Development of Higher Education into the 1990s
showed that A-level scores for entrants to degree
courses in Engineering and Technology were only
marginally below the average for all subjects.)
    In trying to assess total demand for engineering
recruits on the part of employers, Finniston again
found a dearth of substantive evidence available but

was able to cite various examples and references all
pointing in the direction of a shortage:

> *Evidence to us from some employers and trade*
> *associations suggested that there are*
> *insufficient engineers in Britain for current*
> *demands and that manufacturing industry faces*
> *a chronic and growing shortage of engineers at*
> *all levels and for the whole range of engineer-*
> *ing disciplines ...   Further evidence of*
> *unsatisfied demands is shown by the negligible*
> *unemployment among engineers, despite recent*
> *high aggregate unemployment and minimal levels*
> *of industrial and economic growth ...   There*
> *are evident problems of shortages of engineers*
> *to meet specific current demands in parts of*
> *British industry.*

The Report was in parts quite critical of some of
the present practices of companies employing
engineers: frequently the engineers they employed
were either not fully utilised or were utilised in
ways in which their professional expertise was
scarcely required, there was often little representation of engineering expertise at the highest levels
in the management of the company, the engineers
employed typically felt undervalued and misunder-
stood, and many companies had not appropriately
adjusted their salary levels to a situation in which
the greater part of all new entrants were now highly-
qualified graduates who expected to be paid accordingly.   On average young graduate engineers continued to be paid at about the same salaries as non-
graduate recruits.

Finniston saw the existing scenario continuing
well into the future even though the committee did
not feel that such future shortfall could be quantified.   In a paragraph which has perhaps been the
subject of more criticism than any other aspect of
the Report, it commented:

> *We have not attempted to quantify national*
> *requirements for engineers of different types*
> *and levels in the future.   Since it is not*
> *realistic to anticipate with any confidence*
> *any specific future industrial scenario, it is*
> *equally unrealistic to attempt to quantify*
> *future engineering manpower requirements except*
> *in the most general and indicative terms.   Our*
> *scepticism of such forecasting is strengthened*
> *by the lack of any adequate data base for*

83

> *assessing current demands and requirements.*
> *We nonetheless firmly believe that the demand*
> *will exist to provide employment for as many*
> *engineers as can feasibly be produced for many*
> *years to come and we see no danger of creating*
> *an over-supply of engineers.*

One must, of course, sympathise with the position
in which the committee found itself, particularly
with regard to the lack of an adequate data base but
even so it does seem rather confusing on the one hand
to say that future requirements cannot be quantified
and on the other hand to express firm belief in a
continuing shortage well into the future.   The
problems to which the Report referred were and are
real but they are no worse than those applying to
other manpower forecasting situations, in fact generally less so once we bear in mind that perhaps the
majority of manpower planning exercises have had to
take place in the far more difficult conditions prevailing in Third World countries.   The committee was
therefore, by implication, rejecting the whole concept of manpower forecasting, which seems unfortunate
in view of the subject matter of their Report.
Perhaps the committee should more usefully have
commissioned the major (but necessarily expensive)
manpower forecasting exercise that would have thrown
more detailed light on future needs, and then devoted
part of their report to discussing the likelihood and
size of any possible error terms in the figures thus
produced.   When Finniston went on to argue:

> *There is no danger of producing too many*
> *engineers, since an engineering formation can*
> *lead to a wide range of careers in and outside*
> *engineering.   The national objective should*
> *be to produce as many engineers as possible*

did it overstep its brief?   There would seem to be
rather little point in deliberately aiming at
increasing the supply of graduate engineers in the
full knowledge that significant proportions of the
new graduates will not in fact ever work at engineering, which point should be combined with the fact
that the production of graduate engineers is extremely expensive (in view of both the length of course
and the amount of costly technological equipment and
laboratory space required) and requires careful
justification.
     The Finniston Report therefore echoed the theme
of the UK's supposed shortage of qualified engineers

(and scientists) which has been enunciated by leading industrialists, which has been oft repeated in the national press, and which has recently been encapsulated as part of the government's policy of aiming to achieve a shift in education and training towards scientific and technological subjects.   Finniston's conclusions are in this respect in line with the views expressed in earlier official reports as were cited previously.   The theme of a national shortage of engineers and scientists has been with us since at least the Second World War and probably earlier, and it has continued unabated in the years since the Finniston Report was published.   The Institution of Electrical Engineers,[2] in evidence to the House of Lords Select Committee on Science and Technology, demonstrated the need to expand the annual output of graduate electrical engineers by between 80 per cent and 100 per cent.   The Institute of Production Engineers[3] has called attention to the worrying continuing shortage of qualified engineers in UK industry, which *must be seen as a contributory factor to the erosion of Britain's manufacturing base*.   The recently-formed Engineering Council has repeatedly drawn attention to the same question. Thus, from institutions which might collectively be termed 'the professionals' on this issue there seems to be unanimity.

The Views of Academic Economists
It would be surprising if academic economists of the highest repute had not also studied this same theme. Indeed they have, and they too are virtually unanimous in their conclusions, but in the opposite direction: they can find no hard evidence that such a shortage exists.   To say that the contrast between their findings and those of the professional engineering bodies quoted above is surprising would be an understatement.

Scepticism about methods used to forecast demand and supply figures for particular types of manpower and doubts about any firm conclusions regarding either surpluses or shortages have existed for many years but in the early 1970s they came into renewed prominence with the publication and subsequent re-publication of a study by Gannicott and Blaug.[4]   In strongly-worded language these writers castigated recent official reports and especially the Jackson Report,[5] for using forecasts of demand based on inadequately-structured questionnaire surveys of employers, for making the unstated assumption of a

very low degree of substitutability both within and
between occupations, for basing notions of shortages
on the acceptance of forecasts likely to have been
erroneous, for taking estimates to be minima which
could be exceeded with impunity and, above all, for
ignoring completely any price, wage or any other
monetary effects. Via movements of relative earnings, the latter should signal the existence of
additional economic demand and constitute the only
mechanism which could ever bring together movements
of supply and demand. After pointing to what they
saw as further inconsistencies, Gannicott and Blaug
commented,

> All this adds up to the conclusion that the
> Committee has failed to make its case for a
> long-term shortage.

Broadly similar views have appeared from almost all
the economists who have taken an interest in this
question. Writing at about the same time, Wilkinson
and Mace[6] paid particular attention to the published
statistical data available for the 1960s: noting
that vacancies in engineerings jobs had decreased,
that the activity rate for people with engineering
qualifications had declined slightly, that the rate
of production of new engineers had declined, and
that the level of engineering salaries had shown
fluctuating relative increases and decreases, they
concluded,

> It is hard to make any case for a general
> shortage of engineers ... (official) forecasts,
> which have a doubtful theoretical basis, are
> now found to be misleading in practice.

Mace[7] later repeated such views even more strongly,
referring to proponents of the 'shortage' view as
using *'pseudo-scientific terms'*, *'questionable
evidence'* and *'an almost religious crusading zeal'*.
Bosworth[8] also found against the 'shortage' view,
although in somewhat qualified terms:

> The rate of return evidence does not suggest
> any significant shortage of engineers relative
> to scientists ... there is no case for arguing
> that there are widespread unsatisifed demands
> for this type of labour.

Bosworth drew attention to the weak relationship
between persons becoming qualified in science,

engineering or technology to degree or equivalent level and the same persons subsequently being employed as professional scientists, engineers and technologists - less than 42 per cent according to the 1971 Census. This would suggest that any worries about possible shortages of scientists and engineers have to be seen in the context of possible failure to make efficient or adequate use of the scarce skills of those who are already qualified. A further puzzle, which was highlighted by Bosworth and Wilson,[9] was that even though it was widely agreed that considerable substitution between scientists and engineers was possible, crude calculations of the gaps between the numbers of qualified personnel available and the numbers of specialist jobs as scientists and engineers suggested a possible shortage in the case of engineers but a large surplus in the case of scientists. This would seem to be logically impossible save for the point already made above regarding the traditional mismatch between qualifications and area of work specialisation, and for definitional problems: it is far from easy to specify precisely what is a 'scientist' or an 'engineer'.

Nor can it be right to ignore the more complex situations that must arise once we disaggregate each of these terms: can a biologist realistically seek work as a nuclear physicist? Or a chemical engineer as a civil engineer? A good friend of the writer switched jobs in mid-career from electrical to mechanical engineering and then back again: how typical is such ready substitutability? Rather little evidence is available regarding this question.

Bosworth and Wilson, writing in 1979, projected forwards to 1985 largely on the basis of demographic calculations and came to the qualified view that, far from a shortage, there was likely to be an excess supply of graduate scientists and engineers of around 50,000 nationally, even allowing for the proportion of such people always likely to be economically non-active (e.g. females) at any one time. They conclude:

> *Our crude comparisons of supply and demand*
> *projections for 1985 point, if anything, to*
> *a slowly growing excess supply of this type*
> *of labour. On this evidence we find it*
> *difficult to support the demand for increasing*
> *the new supply of qualified scientists and*
> *engineers above the present levels.*

Further light can be thrown on this debate by considering other aspects of careers as professional scientists and engineers. Traditionally, as noted above, the route towards becoming a professional engineer lay via GCE O-levels or A-levels followed by part-time or evening course study, combined with practical training and possibly an apprenticeship with an employer, leading to qualification as a member of an appropriate professional body. Only over the last 20 years has this pattern largely given way to entry via a relevant degree, usually obtained by full-time study at a university or polytechnic. Over 96 per cent of Chartered Engineers under the age of 35 and 79 per cent of the total are now graduates.[10] However, whether due to the traditional entry route, to the 'dirty' image of the profession, to the allegedly relatively low salary levels (for which Finniston found it difficult to assemble conclusive evidence), or to some other cause, engineering as a profession has long had lower status and prestige in the UK than in other countries such as France or West Germany. Engineers in senior and middle-management positions still tend to be qualified to no more than HNC/HND level[11] and these may exert an extra-proportional influence on the public image.

For whatever cause, there is clear evidence that many young people are not attracted towards engineering as a profession; surveys have shown that fewer students from middle-class backgrounds apply, and such courses draw more on applicants from working-class backgrounds. If all such comments are true in the case of boys, they are even more so in the case of girls: in spite of recent increases, the numbers of girls on engineering courses rarely reach 5 per cent of the total. It also seems to be true that similar comments are valid, perhaps to only a slightly lesser extent, in the case of scientists: apparently many of our brightest school pupils do not seek to study science, well-qualified scientists frequently have no wish to teach in schools and generally we do not in the UK associate either scientists or engineers with the most senior positions in government, the civil service, commercial life, or even industry. Mrs Thatcher is reported to be the first scientist ever to attain the highest level of government.

Over their careers, many scientists and technologists express disappointment with their position, status and pay, and many seek to move away from working as scientists or engineers as such. A recent special survey by *The Times* concluded,

> *The engineer in Britain, unlike many of his*
> *or her counterparts abroad, remains the poor*
> *relation of the professional classes, although*
> *at long last there are some signs that*
> *attitudes are changing.*[12]

All this is partly a failure of communication:

> *engineering and the art of making things are*
> *disowned in Britain or at best go unrecognised*

because there is little or no understanding that

> *engineering is never dull and often very*
> *exciting.*[13]

Recruitment of high-quality entrants to science and engineering is undoubtedly an important issue and one in respect of which the current position relating to the teaching of mathematics and science is crucial. By contrast, worrying about a supposed overall shortage seems much less important since it seems clear that the country is making only very imperfect use of its existing stock of qualified scientists and engineers.

At the time of writing it had become more difficult than ever before to recruit well-qualified teachers of science and mathematics into secondary schools. Fewer and fewer science and mathematics graduates are applying for places on teacher training courses, as they presumably feel that more attractive careers are available to them elsewhere. The future health of these subjects in schools now seems very problematic and there is every probability that we shall be unable to maintain the existing flow of students on to degree courses in science and engineering, let alone increase it.

In summary, therefore, the debate outlined above must now relate essentially to two questions:

(i) Can the UK maintain the existing supply of graduate engineers and scientists? The answer seems problematic and this may become a severe national problem in future years.

(ii) Does the country wish, as a matter of national policy, occupations not directly relevant to engineering to be staffed (in part) by qualified engineers - e.g. general

management, personnel or the Civil
Service? Finniston argued that they
should and this has in fact been happening
implicity for many years (although not to
such an extent as in other countries in
Europe). If this is to be so, then the
nature and content of engineering education
may have to change from its current focus
which is arguably of a relatively narrow
technological nature to include wider considerations relating to people and society.
This would affect and perhaps lower
(because of the reduction in expensive
laboratory/workshop time) the current high
cost of engineering education. There
would need to be strong educational or
other advantages to justify processing
through such high-cost education students
many of whom were not destined subsequently
to work as engineers.

TEACHERS: DEMAND AND SUPPLY

We may now consider, as a second case study of manpower planning, the labour market for school teachers
in the UK in maintained schools. That this market
is 'planned' there can be little doubt, indeed it is
perhaps more 'planned' than almost any other labour
market in the country: the government oversees the
supply of new teachers via its authorisation of
courses of initial teacher training and control of
intake numbers on to such courses and directly
influences the demand for new teachers via its control of the expenditure of the employers, the local
education authorities. Nevertheless for many years
the labour market for teachers has evidenced considerable imbalances between demand and supply, both in
total and at the level of individual subject specialisms: the persistent shortage of qualified teachers
for perhaps the first 70 years of the twentieth
century turned, remarkably quickly, into an excess
supply in total but with severe shortages continuing
in such subject areas as mathematics, the physical
sciences, creative design and modern languages, all
at secondary school level, and with a forecast
future shortage for primary school teachers.
    The main constituent of the total demand for
teachers is obviously the national birth-rate, which
gives the numbers of children who will be entering
primary schools some five years later. This

has proved remarkably difficult to estimate in
recent years: the annual total of live births in
Britain fell steadily, against all expectations, from
some 876,000 in 1964 to some 569,000 in 1977, i.e. by
over 35 per cent in 13 years, before rising again and
then relatively stabilising at around 600,000 to
650,000 in the early 1980s. Similar falls took
place at about the same time, for reasons that are
still not entirely clear, in all other developed
countries. Yet the numbers of entrants to initial
teacher training courses in the UK continued to grow
inexorably throughout the later 1960s and into the
early years of the 1970s. The Robbins Report had
envisaged that entrants to Colleges of Education
might increase to reach some 26,400 by 1967, whereas
the actual entry for that year was some 35,000. By
1971 there were in all some 113,000 students in the
public sector institutions which provided most of the
places for initial teacher training: by 1981 this
figure had fallen dramatically to 27,000[14] and many
colleges had to close or to amalgamate with other
institutions. The implications for and effects on
the colleges are considered in Chapter Ten; here we
confine ourselves to questions of teacher supply.

Robbins had considered that the numbers of
students in Colleges of Education in Great Britain
should mushroom at a more rapid rate of increase than
was suggested for any other sector of higher education. This confidence, combined with the fact
that the Robbins targets for Colleges of Education
for earlier years were in fact exceeded by wide
margins, perhaps helps to explain why the planners
were so slow to react and why headlong expansion of
the numbers of new teachers in training continued for
long after it should have been apparent to all concerned that there would be a considerable excess
supply of teachers. The Head of the Teacher Training Branch at the DES later wrote that years of shortage had conditioned everyone to the idea of growth
and that *'work on teacher supply projections had
fallen into abeyance'*.[15] Not, of course, that work
could not have been found for all these additional
teachers in an ideal world: there are, after all,
practically no limits to the extent to which ideal-
istic planners free from budgetary constraints might
seek to reduce class sizes in schools and to extend
curricular options. In practical terms, however,
given the poor long-term performance of the British
economy, retrenchment was inevitable whichever government was in power and the numbers of teachers
employed, whose salaries comprise much the major

element in recurrent educational expenditure, had to
be brought under stricter and stricter control.

The effects of the switchback pattern of births
were, when combined with other demographic factors,
felt very differently in different LEAs: a survey[16]
of the 15-year-old population conducted by the major
local authority associations showed that the fall in
the numbers would be only some 15 per cent or less
in Cornwall or Somerset, but around 50 per cent in
Manchester and Knowsley; in Tameside and Wolverhampton, they would continue to fall for 15 years, in
Shropshire and Clwyd for only 6; some LEAs had their
peaks of such numbers as far back as 1977, others
would not have theirs until 1986, whilst the trough
years will extend from 1985 until 1994. Small
wonder, perhaps, that future planning of educational
requirements is so difficult at LEA level.

Teacher supply is not, however, planned at the
disaggregated local level but nationally. The only
serious previous attempt at local control at employment level, the Quota system in force from 1957 to
1975, had a very curious history: the numbers of
teachers it specified for each locality were orgin-
ally set as *maxima* but in the course of time they
came to be regarded as *minima*. It is now assumed
that new teachers will move to where the jobs are
available and broadly speaking this is what happens
even though there have always been more teachers
available, and better qualified teachers, in the
affluent south-east, and relatively more teaching
jobs available in the northern regions.

Nationally, the number of live births for the
appropriate dates has to be combined with estimates
(sometimes termed 'guesstimates') of the numbers of
under-fives to be accommodated in schools, of those
staying on after the age of compulsory schooling,
and of pupil-teacher ratios and curriculum needs.
Governments have had separate policies for each of
these but usually more short-term than medium-term
or long-term in nature, thus making reliable future
predictions more problematic. Little has been
heard recently, for example, of any possible expansion of provision for the under-fives. The overall
pupil-teacher ratio has been declining slowly but
steadily (from over 22.1 in 1967 to 18.2 by 1984,
but with variations of at least 50 per cent at LEA
level) but is now predicted to stabilise; as
schools typically decline in size over the next few
years they would need more generous staffing allowances if similar curricular provision were to be
maintained; the post-compulsory staying-on rate

after rising for many years had started to decline
before the massive rise in youth unemployment in the
early 1980s nudged it back up again. The decline
in the birth-rate has related almost entirely to
social classes III and below and not to social classes
I and II whose children have predominantly stayed on
at school after age 16: should we therefore expect
a considerable further increase in the staying-on
rate in another few years' time? Annual wastage of
teachers due to death, retirements and resignations
is normally stable and predictable but rose markedly
in the early 1980s as many teachers opted to take
early retirement. None of these variables is
liable to evidence sudden or dramatic movements but
even, for example, a fall of only 0.1 per cent in
the overall pupil-teacher ratio would, when applied
to a national total of some 8.5 million pupils, mean
that nearly 2,000 extra teachers were required.

It is not a sexist remark to say that many of
the calculations relating to teacher supply have been
upset by women. On average, women entering the
teaching profession in the early 1960s remained for
only three years: on marriage and/or childbirth they
departed and mostly did not seek to return. Now
women teachers initially remain for some six years
and on marriage and/or childbirth either take
maternity leave and return to the classroom after
just a few months or take a few years' absence to
rear a young family and then very many seek to
return to teaching. The Pool of Inactive Teachers
(colloquially the PIT), comprised largely of married
women liable to return to teaching, by the 1980s
looked set to overturn many of the calculations
emanating from the Department of Education and
Science regarding teacher supply. The National
Advisory Council on the Training and Supply of
Teachers could, in the early 1960s, refer to married
women as '*a promising new source of recruitment*' but
by 1981 the successor Advisory Committee on the
Supply and Education of Teachers could urge against
this trend on the grounds that, *inter alia*, '*employers
will prefer newly trained teachers partly because they
will on average be better trained than those seeking
to return*'. ACSET went on, in 1982, to advocate
that returners should not exceed 40 per cent of
primary school appointments and 20 per cent of
secondary; by 1984, however, the former figure had
been exceeded since over 50 per cent of primary
school posts filled that year went to returners to
the profession, almost all of them married women.

This single aspect of teacher supply may, in

fact, be taken as symptomatic of the problems to
which the whole of this subject gives rise: despite
(or perhaps even because of?) the conflicting exhort-
ations quoted above, the DES has no clear policy
regarding married women returners: nor is it clear
how it could have, since the actual appointments
decisions are taken not even at the level of the
100-plus LEAs, but (largely) at the level of the
individual schools.   The size and importance of
this problem is clearly shown by the figures: by
the early 1980s the DES was predicting, rather
belatedly, that the number of returners annually
securing teaching appointments would rise steadily
from 11,000 to 18,000 over a decade: these figures
are to be compared with the total output of new
teachers from all teacher training courses of only
some 15,000 by the mid-1980s.

By late 1984 a DES Discussion Paper[17] could
forecast that total pupil numbers in England would
continue to decline from the peak of 8.5 million in
1977 to just on 6.6 million in 1991 before recovering
to some 6.9 million by 1996.   The numbers of teachers
required would fall from some 400,000-plus to anywhere between 370,000 and 396,000, depending primarily on changes in pupil-teacher ratios, by 1991.
In a section on 'redeployment' there appeared the
ominous comment: *'redeployment measures ... would
release up to 6,000 primary teachers and 9,000
secondary teachers for redeployment'*.   When in
early 1985 the annual White Paper on *The Government's
Expenditure Plans*[18] was published, it was, despite
all the talk of further cuts, actually less pessimistic in this respect than its immediate predecessors: it envisaged the employment of 400,000
teachers for 1985-86 whereas the equivalent 1984 and
1983 White Papers[19] had forecast for the same year a
range of 390,000-395,000 and a range of 380,000-
395,000 respectively.

In the summer of 1982 perhaps 7,000 newly-
trained teachers were unable to secure posts in
teaching;   the DES forecast that the *excess supply*
would continue but decline, reaching perhaps 3,000
or less by 1986.   But by that year it was forecast
that the upturn in the numbers of young children
entering primary schools would have created an *excess
demand* for primary teachers, rising to perhaps 3,000
annually by 1989, that could not be filled from the
number of qualified teachers available.   Such are
the rigidities in the teacher training system that it
will be well into the 1990s before these imbalances
are rectified.   The problems arising from such

rigidities have in fact led to a fairly dramatic
change of balance in the number of new teachers
emerging from the one-year PGCE or the longer con-
current courses respectively as shown in Table 4.1.
Educational arguments have increasingly favoured
longer courses but such arguments have now taken
second place to the practicalities of planning: the
one-year course is flexible and easy to manipulate
and has thus increasingly found favour and retrenchment has been concentrated entirely on the longer
courses.   The PGCE course produced only some 15 per
cent of new teachers in 1963, by 1981 some 52 per
cent.

Table 4.1: Students Admitted to Courses of Initial
Teacher Training in England and Wales

Year	PGCE	Three- and four-year courses	Other courses	Total
1963	3,840	19,640	2,781	26,261
1972	10,365	37,381	2,886	50,632
1981	10,118	7,483	1,969	19,560

Sources: *Statistics of Education;   Department of*
         Education and Science (Statistics Branch).

     By 1985 the DES felt that the situation had
stabilised to such an extent that it could confidently indicate target intakes, separately for primary
and secondary, for B.Ed and PGCE, and for universities and public sector institutions through to
1989, as shown in Table 4.2.   These figures start
from the total for 1985 of 17,652, some 10 per cent
less than the total for 1981 shown in Table 4.1, and
then provide for increases totalling some 18 per cent
by 1989.   Most of the increase will relate to
courses preparing for teaching in primary schools,
where the numbers of pupils will be rising.   Overall,
approximate parity will be achieved between university and public sector institutions and between B.Ed
or long courses on the one hand and PGCE on the other.
In those senses the nature of the political compromise contained in these figures is quite apparent.

Table 4.2: Proposed Intakes to Teacher Training Courses in England and Wales, 1985-89

	1985 (already allocated)	1986	1987	1988	1989	Numerical increase (average)	% Increase overall 1985-89
PRIMARY							
Primary B.Ed							
Universities	340	425	525	600	700		
Public Sector	6,110	6,375	6,625	6,850	7,050	325 p.a.	20
Primary PGCE							
Universities	670	750	825	900	975	260 p.a.	47
Public Sector	1,500	1,700	1,875	2,050	2,225		
Total	8,620	9,250	9,850	10,400	10,950	586 p.a.	27
SECONDARY							
Secondary B.Ed (and other undergraduate training courses)							
Universities	354	425	475	525	575		38
Public Sector	1,660	1,750	1,900	2,050	2,200		–
Secondary PGCE							
Universities	4,488	4,500	4,500	4,500	4,500		–
Public Sector	2,530	2,575	2,575	2,575	2,575		–
Total	9,032	9,250	9,450	9,650	9,850		9
OVERALL TOTALS	17,652	18,500	19,300	20,050	20,800		18

Source: Letter from Secretary of State to Chairman of University Grants Committee, 25 March 1985.

The UGC and NAB respectively went on to allocate target student numbers by course and subject of study to each institution involved in teacher training, with wide differences in the varying treatments they received. During the 1985-86 academic year, however, it became apparent that the adverse publicity resulting from the teachers' strikes and declining living standards had led to sharp falls in the numbers of students applying for teacher training places in certain subject areas, particularly the physical sciences, and that the intake targets set for those subjects would not be met. Of those young people who did still want to teach, increasing numbers sought refuge in the comparatively safe havens offered by the independent schools. When put together, such considerations showed all too clearly the problems involved in advance planning in this difficult area.

By now it will be apparent that when all the factors considered above are brought together there will always be great difficulty in ensuring an approximate balance between teacher supply and demand, barring radical changes in the system of teacher employment which seem unlikely. We cannot do better than conclude with the words of a recent perceptive critique[20] of the system of teacher supply and demand in England and Wales:

> *Perhaps the most glaring weakness of the present system is that it is only half a system. By this we mean that there is no strong link between the assessment of teacher requirement and its subsequent supply on the one hand, and the employment of the teachers on the other. Even if requirement and supply of teachers is assessed with 100 per cent accuracy the planning cycle is broken since local authorities may not employ them, due to other priorities or lack of funds.*

CONCLUDING COMMENT

The two case studies given in this chapter are intended merely to serve as examples of the practical problems involved in anticipating future manpower needs. There are many other specialised labour markets, e.g. that for medical doctors, where similar problems arise. The imponderables seem as difficult as ever yet it seems that the country really has no option but to continue to make the best

forecasts it can, in the full realisation that these
will never be entirely accurate.

NOTES

1. Finniston Report: *Engineering Our Future*,
Cmnd 7794 (HMSO, 1980).
2. Institution of Electrical Engineers,
*Evidence to House of Lords Select Committee on
Science and Technology* (IEE, 1984).
3. Institution of Production Engineers,
Press Release No.6852 (I.Prod.E, 1984).
4. K. Gannicott and M. Blaug, 'Scientists
and Engineers in Britain', in B. Ahamad and M. Blaug
(eds), *The Practice of Manpower Forecasting*
(Elsevier, 1973), and reprinted in C. Baxter,
P. O'Leary and A. Westoby (eds), *Economics and
Education Policy: A Reader* (Longman/OU, 1977).
5. Jackson Report: Committee on Manpower
Resources for Science and Technology: *A Review of
the Scope and Problems of Scientific and Techno-
logical Manpower Policy*, Cmnd 2800 (HMSO, 1965).
6. G. Wilkinson and J. Mace, 'Shortage or
Surplus of Engineers: A Review of Recent UK
Evidence', *British Journal of Industrial Relations*,
Vol.11 (1973).
7. J. Mace, 'The "Shortage" of Engineers',
Higher Education Review, Vol.10, No.1 (1977).
8. D. Bosworth, 'Technological Manpower', in
R. Lindley (ed.), *Higher Education and the Labour
Market* (SRHE/Leverhulme, 1981).
9. D. Bosworth and R. Wilson, 'The Labour
Market for Scientists and Technologists', in
R.M. Lindley (ed.), *Economic Change and Employment
Policy* (Macmillan, 1980).
10. Engineering Digest, *Education*, Vol.164,
Part 16 (1984).
11. R. Smith, *Access and Recruitment to
Engineering* (Kingston Polytechnic, mimeo., 1984).
12. *The Times*, 5 October 1984.
13. Sir Kenneth Corfield (Chairman of Standard
Telephones and Cables plc), *The Times Higher
Education Supplement*, 19 October 1984.
14. L.M. Cantor and I.F. Roberts, *Further
Education Today* (Routledge & Kegan Paul, 1983).
15. H. Harding, 'The Hencke Report', *Education*
(December 1978).
16. Quoted in Macfarlane Report: *Education for
16-19 Year Olds* (DES, 1980).
17. *Schoolteacher Numbers and Deployment in*

the Longer Term - A Discussion Paper (DES, 1984).

18.   *The Government's Expenditure Plans 1985-86 to 1987-88*, Cmnd 9428-II (HMSO, 1985).

19.   *The Government's Expenditure Plans 1984-85 to 1986-87*, Cmnd 9143 (HMSO, 1984) and *The Government's Expenditure Plans 1983-84 to 1985-86*, Cmnd 8789-I (HMSO, 1983).

20.   T. Blackstone and A. Crispin, *How Many Teachers?*, Bedford Way Papers No.10, University of London Institute of Education (Heinemann, 1982).

Chapter Five

INDUSTRIAL AND VOCATIONAL TRAINING

It is first necessary to consider what is the meaning
of *training* and what, if anything, distinguishes
training from education: in common parlance the two
terms are used almost interchangeably, or at least
with a great deal of overlap (*teacher training*, for
example, has for long been taken to be synonymous
with *teacher education*). Training is often envisaged to be more oriented towards the acquisition or
advancement of more specific skills, to have a more
restricted focus, and/or to be provided in
industrially-based settings, but none of these gives
us a complete distinction.

TRAINING AND EDUCATION

Over twenty years ago Professor Edgar Dale described
the essence of the distinction between education and
training in the following terms: education emphasises
creative interaction and is symbolised by a man thinking critically: it asks 'how' *and* 'why'. Training,
on the other hand, emphasises imitation or memoris-
ation and is oriented towards things as they are; it
asks only 'how'. Education emphasises long-range,
broad goals with flexible ceilings and unlimited
horizons whereas training emphasises short-range,
limited, inflexible goals with fixed ceilings. The
educated person is at home in an atmosphere of
uncertainty and challenge whereas the trained person
is only at home in familiar situations with habits
and values unexamined.[1]
     Clearly, then, the typical university graduate
in history who will never use his historical knowledge
throughout his or her subsequent career has been
educated but not trained whereas the novice car
mechanic taught the correct sequence in which to

tighten a series of nuts and bolts has been trained
to carry out that particular task but has, presumably, derived no wider or consequential benefit.
But what of the school pupil who is taught that
correct spelling requires 'i before e except after
c'?   Or the law student told the distinction
between registered and unregistered property?   Both
of these would conventionally come within 'education'
but it is difficult to think that there is any
creativity or critical thinking involved in either,
so should they more correctly be regarded as training?   And what of the car mechanic who has to understand *why* the timing of an engine needs to be
advanced or retarded or the apprentice hairdresser
who needs to understand the interactions between
different chemicals?   Both of these would conventionally be classified as training but in terms of
their spillover effects and wider implications,
perhaps they are more akin to education.
     The distinction between the two terms is, then,
complicated and often difficult to draw: *'much that
passes for education is in fact training'*[2] and
presumably vice versa.   And this may be no bad
thing, indeed it may be positively desirable that,
regardless of whether it is formally designated as
education or as *training*, any learning sequence
should include a wide variety of different
experiences.   In fact,

> The dichotomy 'education or training' does not
> serve us well.   It is when we consider
> education *and* training that we gain an insight
> into the role of each in the process we call
> learning.[3]

There are, however, two inter-related reasons
for including in this book a separate chapter
entitled *Industrial and Vocational Training*.
Firstly the practicalities are that the provision of
much of what is conventionally termed 'training'
whilst obviously important in a book on *Education and
the National Economy*, has followed a different path
and been subject to different influences as compared
with the mainstream education system, and secondly
that training has often been regarded as the
inferior counterpart or poor relation of the two.
Taking the second point first, Dale stresses the
superiority of the educated over the trained person
in that *'Education emphasises changing ends and
changing means'* whereas training tends to mean
continued dependence on an instructor, is frequently

boring, and '*often becomes a drab, unevocative routine*'. This is the approach that has often been adopted, historically, but must now be increasingly open to question in an era when productive processes have become so complex and frequently computer-orientated and when there is a close inter-relationship between education and training, as noted above. Thus a more typical view now is that of Ely:

> *Training and education are both important and, if training is done in the context of education, the whole is probably greater than the sum of its parts.*

The first of the two points cited relates to the differing and often complex systems for the provision of industrial and vocational training which have usually developed under the aegis not of the Department of Education and Science or its predecessor the Ministry of Education but either of other government departments or of industrially- or commercially-based training organisations. Most of the complex rules and regulations relating to the provision of education - e.g. that teachers must be suitably qualified and certificated - have therefore not applied and it has to be said that the development of such training has until very recently passed almost unnoticed by observers of the educational scene.

Perspective on Training
The term 'training' may embrace a variety of different activities but Machlup suggests that they may be grouped into three:

(i)   *on the job learning through experience* which happens to all workers to varying degrees, which may involve no instruction as such, and which may simply be a matter of recognising that 'trial-and-error' type learning takes place in most situations throughout life: perhaps such activities scarcely constitute *training* as such at all, even though at the end of the process the person should emerge better able to do the job in hand,

(ii)   *on the job training* involving supervision and/or instruction, *in situ*, and

(iii) *off the job training* involving the provision of formal training programmes in the factory or workplace.[4]

It is, of course, easy to see that in practice there may be some combination of all of these. A distinction that has had a pervasive effect on thinking about training over the last 20 years or more has been that drawn by Becker[5] between *specific training* and *general training*, on the following lines:

> *specific training* imparts knowledge or skills usable within the firm providing the training but not, or only to a negligible extent, elsewhere; specific training thus increases the trainee's future productivity but only within that firm.
> By contrast,
> *general training* imparts knowledge or skills usable universally or at least on behalf of a number of different employers, thus it raises the trainee's future productivity wherever he may be working in the future.

Now logically, if we may assume that workers are freely able to move to other employers, there is a clear difference in the incentive to a firm to provide and finance training: in the case of *specific training* this will clearly be worth their while since they will receive the benefits but in the case of *general training* they are liable not to receive the benefits and so the reverse is true: each firm will try to recruit new entrants who have received general training provided and financed by other firms. Firms would only be willing to provide general training if they could pass on the costs to the employees in the form of lower wages (which employees may be willing to accept in return for the training), whereas specific training (such as an in-house orientation programme) is always worthwhile for the firm since the costs will be offset by the workers' future increased productivity. Therefore, workers will typically have the choice of general training accompanied by lower pay now but with the expectation of higher pay in the future, or specific training with the converse of these.

Clearly general training is always likely to be the more important of the two and if we think of full-time education as the ultimate form of general training, the individual bears the heavy costs of income forgone in exchange for higher expected earnings in the future. In many instances the

distinction between the two forms of training does
not relate to whether or not the knowledge or skills
gained are transferable but to how easy it is for
the workers to move to other jobs.   Thus such
devices as the cheap mortgages granted by the major
banks to their employees to retain their services
will tend to turn general training into specific
training.   So too, in present-day terms, will the
labour-market effects of the mass unemployment that
has now become all too common throughout the Western
world.

An obvious objection to Becker's approach is
that no simple distinction between general training
and specific training can be drawn either because in
the real world knowledge and skills tend to be *partly*
transferable but partly not (consider for example
the car mechanic trained in particular Volvo or BMW
procedures), or because the degree of mobility of
workers may (a) be at some intermediate position,
(b) be unknown in advance, or (c) vary at some
future date.   In an age of rather frenetic company
mergers and take-overs it is worth mentioning that
any one of these could, in Becker's terminology,
meaninglessly convert general training into specific
training.

The practical attitudes of firms are also
important:

> *A much more telling criticism of Becker is*
> *that firms are likely to treat labour training*
> *as a fringe benefit;   although it may be*
> *initially introduced to deal with the costs of*
> *a high rate of labour turnover, training soon*
> *comes to be regarded as a welfare service to*
> *which the cost-benefit calculus is not applied.*
> *It can be no accident that few firms keep*
> *accounts of the direct costs of training pro-*
> *grammes and that even fewer firms make attempts*
> *to measure the benefits of training.*[6]

Despite such caveats, Becker's work has had a profound effect on thinking about such questions as who
should bear the costs of training, why apprentices
are invariably paid less than skilled workers even
while performing identical tasks, and why workers'
real earnings tend to rise during their careers.

There has been much criticism of traditional
attitudes to industrial training in the United
Kingdom, most notably in a recent report commissioned
by the Manpower Services Commission and prepared by
Messrs Coopers and Lybrand.   In this report

employers were castigated for attaching little
importance to training, for seeing little connection
between training and competitiveness and profitability, for delegating training decisions to line
managers with short-term horizons, and for seeing
training as an overhead to be cut back at times of
low profitability.   The report came to the rather
pessimistic conclusion that there was little real
pressure for employers to change their attitudes.[7]

THE DEVELOPMENT OF INDUSTRIAL TRAINING POLICY

In contrast with some of its major competitor
countries, the United Kingdom has never managed to
achieve a coherent national policy relating to
industrial training, much in the same way as there
have never been coherent national policies relating
to other aspects of labour markets.   There has, in
particular, been a failure to consider medium- to
long-term trends in labour markets and the consequent effects for training needs, in lieu of an
often undue concentration on the immediate, short-run
situation.[8]   Such government policy as there has
been in this area has usually related primarily to
the latter.   In so far as there has been a general
consensus, it has been to the effect that the place
for industrial training is in industry and that there
has been a general need to encourage firms to undertake more training, either directly themselves or
through an agency acting on their behalf.   This was
the rationale behind the Industrial Training Act 1964
which led to the creation of Industrial Training
Boards; this Act was in turn largely repealed by the
Employment and Training Act 1973 which sought to
place greater responsibility for industrial training
matters on the firms themselves.

The Apprenticeship System
Historically, the main form of industrial training
offered in the United Kingdom was through the apprenticeship system under which boys, and much smaller
numbers of girls, were indentured for a period of
five years to follow what was supposed to be a
systematic course of skill acquisition related closely to working alongside a skilled craftsman in the
particular trade.   In its heyday the apprenticeship
system recruited large numbers of boys, over one-third
of all those leaving secondary modern schools (but
only 6 per cent of girls) and at its best provided an

excellent preparation for the skilled job which, in
those days of virtually full employment, was assured;
in such industries as iron and steel, shipbuilding,
electrical goods or coal-mining, for example,
employers took their duties seriously and often set
up training schemes (typically including part-time
day or block release) and appointed full-time training officers to oversee the progress of their
apprentices.   Elsewhere, however, the system was
patchy, firms began to find the costs prohibitively
high (one estimate was that around 1980 the net cost
to the firm of an apprenticeship in engineering was
around £12,000),[9] often there was little more than a
pretence at any training worthy of the name and boys
became embittered at being *'so-called apprentices'*
on much lower wages than their contemporaries, i.e.
at being what they often saw as no more than a source
of cheap labour.[10]
     From an egalitarian point of view, a major
criticism of the apprenticeship system was the
minimal provision for girls, who would not be considered for apprenticeships in many industries.   All
these factors have contributed to the rapid decline
in apprenticeships in recent years but the dominant
cause has undoubtedly been the worsening economic
situation, the ready availability of cheap alternative labour, and firms' needs to reduce costs
wherever possible.   The total number of apprenticeships in manufacturing industry peaked at 236,000 in
1968 since when it has fallen steadily to well under
90,000 by the 1980s.   It is significant that more
recent training schemes, as considered below, were
all for much shorter periods, all applied more
equally to both boys and girls, and all had as a
stated aim the achievement of better quality in
training.

Industrial Training Boards and the Manpower Services
Commission
In the years following the 1964 Act, Industrial
Training Boards came into existence to cover the
major industrial groups, some 23 in all, with the
twin objectives of increasing both the quantity and
quality of training.   The volume of training certainly increased considerably under the ITBs but
doubts arose over the suitability and costs of some
of the training schemes promulgated and firms
naturally objected to the levies which they had to
pay.   The new Conservative government was not
persuaded that the bureaucracy involved was justified

and in November 1981 the government decided to close
16 of the ITBs, the major ones remaining being those
for Construction and Engineering.

From 1974 onwards the ITBs had operated under
the aegis of the Manpower Services Commission which
had come into existence as a result of the 1973 Act.
Initially, the MSC's primary role was to stimulate
training in this way but its work subsequently
increased in scope, diversity and importance, and
it has now become much the major national body
involved in training and related matters. The MSC
brings together representatives of employers, trade
unions, local government and the education service
and, by deliberate government decision, operates
under the tutelage of the Department of the Environment and not of the Department of Education and
Science with which it has rather little contact. A
glance at the long entry under the MSC in any local
telephone directory will show that it has now taken
over a wide variety of activities including, for
example, running the local Job Centres. The MSC
has pioneered a number of highly significant initiatives relating to training and we may now consider
the major ones in turn:

The Training Opportunities Scheme (TOPS) was taken
over by the MSC although the scheme had previously
been in existence since 1972. In its original form
it was limited to young (or even not-so-young) people
aged 19 or over and to those who had been away from
full-time education for at least three years -
conditions which clearly indicated the intentions of
the scheme - although these requirements were later
relaxed somewhat. The courses are essentially
retraining and cover a wide range of skills and
occupations, from clerical/secretarial to automobile
repairs and maintenance. Courses may last up to a
year although a more typical duration is three
months, and are full-time. Government Skill Centres
and firms training centres participate in the scheme,
but most courses are operated in colleges of further
education, thus bringing to attention once again the
question of whether a meaningful distinction can
really be drawn between education and training.
TOPS courses reached a peak early in 1978 with a
total of around 100,000 students[11] and with favourable employment prospects for the persons so trained,
but subsequently the numbers have gradually declined
as, under the critical influence of the severe unemployment problem confronting young people, the
trainees increasingly found themselves unable to

obtain jobs where they could use their newly-acquired skills.

The Youth Opportunities Programme (YOP).   Influenced by the success of TOPS - the similarity between the acronyms is significant - the MSC in 1978 introduced YOP, aimed at jobless school-leavers and with the ambitious target of offering a training place to every young person unemployed for 12 months or more and wanting such a place.   The majority of the programme places have been designated as *'Work Experience'* and typically consist of a mix of formal tuition and practical experience spread over a period of around three months, especially in such areas as engineering, construction and clerical/secretarial. YOP experienced phenomenal growth, with an estimated 630,000 young people on such courses by 1982-3; about one-half of these were school-leavers, this proportion having risen steadily since the inception of the scheme; some two-thirds of the entrants had not achieve any passes at either GCE O-level or CSE Grade 1.
       The years of rapid growth of YOP were also the years of the rise of unemployment to reach massive proportions, especially among the young, and increasingly young people emerging from YOP courses found themselves unable to get jobs.   There also arose, especially from some trade unions, a repetition of the criticism for long applied to apprenticeships, namely that YOP was little more than a source of cheap labour.   At the same time it became increasingly difficult to find satisfactory work experience placements for such large numbers of young people and programmes had to shift into colleges, often bearing a marked resemblance to other college courses already in existence.   For all these reasons YOP, despite its undoubted successes, became the focus of considerable criticism and by 1982 the MSC felt that the time had come for a major new initiative.

The Youth Training Scheme (YTS).   Introduced in 1982, after having been outlined by the MSC in a major paper entitled *A New Training Initiative* published in May 1981, and endorsed by the government in a White Paper with a similar title in December of that year, at a time when national unemployment was hovering around 3.25 million and when perhaps 50 per cent of school-leavers were unable to find a job. Apart from specifying agreed standards of skills to be attained, perhaps the principal objective of YTS

was to provide a way for all young people under the
age of 18, and also some adults, to continue to
receive some form of education/training/planned work
experience; the intention was that all those leaving
school at age 16 without jobs, perhaps 300,000 young
people, would receive a full year's training.

Since the scheme included the teaching of basic
skills such as numeracy and communication previously
considered to be the prerogative of the schools,
since it had an estimated annual budget of £1,000m.
at a time when the education service seemed starved
of money, and since the scheme would reduce the
unemployment statistics 'at a stroke' without any
real creation of additional job opportunities, it is
not surprising that the scheme had its critics. YTS
trainees were initially to receive £25 per week, i.e.
the same as YOP trainees, after the government had in
the face of strong opposition withdrawn its original
proposal to allow only £15 per week and no Supplementary Benefit.

Early estimates were that the scheme might
recruit some 500,000 youngsters and represent a large
increase in work for local colleges contributing to
the scheme; in the event, there was a considerable
shortfall with 'only' 316,000 recruited in England
and Wales in 1983-4, and with perhaps one-third of
these failing to complete the programme. Some two-
thirds of entrants opted to follow schemes provided
by employers and industrial organisations. Reports
of trainees' reactions included references to
criticisms and disillusion; a common reaction was
to see YTS as an inadequate substitute for a paid
job and to seek to withdraw if a job, apparently
almost any job, became available. In the circumstances just how much true training is being
achieved must be a matter for conjecture. To put
these criticisms into context, to get such a massive
scheme off the ground at all in such a short space of
time was a quite remarkable achievement - in round
terms the numbers completing the scheme approximated
to the total number of university students in the
country - and there were bound to be teething
troubles.

YTS has now been extended to two years, which
may give room for more coherent and credible training
programmes, but the government's proposals that much
of the additional cost should fall on employers have
inevitably met with considerable opposition. The
launching of the two-year YTS has been accompanied
by full-page advertisements in national newspapers
which have emphasised that a youngster embarking on

the scheme,

> *Will begin his course by trying out several*
> *different skills before he chooses the one*
> *he'll train for through to the end of the*
> *second year*

and alleged that this has been the approach adopted
by our competitor countries, including in the Far
East (one of the first lessons this writer had to
learn, incidentally, when he visited South-East Asia
was *not* to call it the Far East). That this was
the case was hotly denied in a critical article[12]
which showed how the emphasis in other countries,
especially Japan, had veered away from specific
skill-acquisition at that age towards more general
educational preparation.

UNIVERSAL YOUTH TRAINING

From 1981 and the *New Training Initiative*, national
policy has been aiming at *universal* youth training,
based on the twin justifications of economic performance and individual opportunity. The latter
requires little comment: if the tragedy of massive
youth unemployment can be alleviated by having young
people better prepared for work, this would surely
command wide support (although the argument, which
is always valid for any one boy or girl, is unlikely
to be so for their age cohort as a whole unless
additional jobs are forthcoming). But from the
standpoint of economic performance the justification
may be less convincing, partly, again, because there
may be no jobs for many of the young people to go on
to, and partly because of the changing nature of
work itself:

> *For all the excitement about new technology,*
> *many jobs will in future still demand little*
> *more than attention and discipline from their*
> *incumbents. To place persons with foundation*
> *training in such jobs is not only to leave*
> *much of the learning unused but also to frus-*
> *trate the expectations raised by the training*
> *itself.*[13]

The outcome may therefore be seen in terms of stark
alternatives: the training '*may be treated with*
cynicism in view of the lack of jobs' or, particularly if an adequate educational component is

included, '*may be valued by young people quite apart from subsequent employment prospects*'.[14]

YOP was severely criticised for providing little training and much direct labour to its participants and on the introduction of YTS the MSC took a series of steps to try to ensure that the training given and received was of genuine quality: at least three months out of the 12 were to be spent in education and training off the job and training in planning and diagnostic, personal and life skills, guidance and counselling, monitoring of achievements and a record of attainments on leaving, were all to be included. Training was intended to go beyond the needs of particular jobs and to include 'core skills', transferable within a 'family' of related occupations (echoes here of Becker's 'general' training), but employers preferred a pattern closer to Becker's specific training and there was in practice some retreat from this stated principle.

Criticisms of YTS

Whether YTS would really provide high quality training would depend heavily on the goodwill of employers and by 1984 serious doubts were being expressed about the eventual outcome. Statements such as:

> *a lack of enthusiasm amongst young workers for YTS is indicated by the government's insistence that careers officers report YTS refusals to the DHSS for reduction of Supplementary Benefit*[15]

sounded particularly ominous in terms of the motivation of the participants.

Various other criticisms were soon being voiced of the principles embodied in YTS, one of the most crucial relating to the balance between the imparting of general, transferable, skills intended to serve the young people well in a variety of future situations and to improve their employability and quite specific skills relating to immediate, hard-to-fill, vacancies. YTS included a considerable element of the former but there were critics who saw its approach as too academic and too concerned with such questions as completion of the 12-month course and certification. Also seen as suspect were the motivations of some of the participating firms and organisations keen to make use of redundant training facilities and instructional staff.[16]

There was strongly-expressed criticism of the kinds of firms in which trainees were placed, often in '*small, non-unionised, low-paying workplaces*' such as shops and other small businesses, of the way employers had complete control over hiring and firing trainees, and of the way the trainees are excluded from the cover of the Employment Protection Acts, of most of the Race and Sex Discrimination Acts, and of adequate Health and Safety provision. [17] At about the same time a detailed investigation of the practicalities of MSC-controlled training in one London borough, Southwark, found that whereas,

> *I was told that the trainees were actually mastering 'transferable skills': ... yet ... the trainees seemed to spend a lot of their time sweeping floors, cleaning up, running errands, etc.*

The same writer also commented:

> *Trainees on these same schemes could also be found learning social deportment, good interview manners and dress sense, a whole variety of techniques of impression management which seemed to belong more to a finishing school for the children of some rising middle-class.* [18]

ADULT RETRAINING

At least, however, for young people training places were being made available for those ready, willing and able to take advantage of them; in the case of adults, however, it is a sad commentary on the lack of an overall national training policy that in the 1980s an unemployed adult had little chance of being able to retrain and provision for adult training was even on the decline. The reason for this lamentable state of affairs lay in the government's insistence on applying commercial criteria to adult training, in sharp distinction to the youth training approach: in the period following the Rayner enquiry, several Skillcentres judged to be cost-ineffective were closed, a separate Skillcentre Training Agency was set up with the requirement that it achieve breakeven funding by the following year, and there was little incentive for either individual adults or firms to incur the increased training costs if future job prospects were at best uncertain and at worst, e.g. in some of the country's more depressed regions,

quite bleak.   More than one commentator has observed
that national policy relating to the training of
adults lags sadly behind that relating to the training of young people.[19]

THE FINANCING OF TRAINING

Reverting to youth training, it is not easy to dis-
cern how significant are the effects of the various
financial arrangements that have come and gone, save
where these have directly affected the pockets of
the young people themselves as compared with the
alternatives available elsewhere.   The general
approach adopted in this country may be described as
pragmatic, with successive governments coming, perhaps rather reluctantly, to commit to training
steadily increasing sums from central funding, whilst
at the same time expecting that significant costs
should fall on and be borne by the co-operating
firms.   For the young people, in the days of full
employment the heaviest cost falling on them related
to income forgone whilst training: this was the case
with the overwhelming majority of apprentices.   In a
world of large-scale youth unemployment, however,
that argument loses much of its validity and the
government's approach has been to accept, again
rather reluctantly, that the young people should be
neither better nor worse off whilst on a training
scheme, the obvious alternative in this case being,
normally, the level of Supplementary Benefit.
    Nor are the lessons to be learned from our
competitor countries immediately obvious since these
vary from West Germany's example of largely financing
vocational training publicly through taxation to
those of Japan or France where industry is expected
to bear the cost.   In the United Kingdom an increasingly sharp distinction has arisen between the
mechanisms for financing youth training and adult
retraining respectively, as indicated above, but it
is not easy to see the logic of this and it is far
from clear where the dividing line between the two
should be drawn - at some particular age, for
example, or should it relate to previous job
experience?
    Labour market economists[20] have recently drawn
attention to the fact that one of the most significant but least-noticed aspects of the employment of
young people has been that, for those fortunate
enough to be in work, average wages relative to those
of adults rose quite sharply over time, from only 45

per cent of the latter in 1953 to some 63 per cent
by 1976 (and this was over a period when adult wages
were also rising steadily in real terms).   The
reasons for this trend are rather obscure but it is
possible to suggest a number of possible consequences
that may arise, the foremost being that if over time
the trend is reversed and the wages of young people
start to revert towards their previous relative
levels, then logically more young people should be
employed and youth unemployment should start to
fall, leading to consequent effects on training
requirements and attitudes.

A secondary possible effect is that a government attracted to the principles of free market
economics might well take the view that since those
people who have a job are clearly better off in real
terms than their predecessors they ought logically
to be prepared to bear a greater proportion of the
cost of their own training (the obvious analogy
being that of student loans).   Whether such effects
will come to pass must at present remain to be seen.
The latter point would be the reverse of an alternative suggestion that, since unemployment is here to
stay and therefore labour surpluses will continue in
the majority of occupations for the foreseeable
future, the government should establish the scale of
training activity on the basis of social objectives,
in much the same way as higher education was allowed
to expand fairly freely in the post-war period;[21]
perhaps the main problem involved in so doing would
be the heavy strain on public expenditure, quite
apart from the economic waste involved in providing
training that might not subsequently be put to good
use.

Demographic Effect
All such arguments will be greatly affected by the
changing size of the 15-19 year age group cohort as
it falls from 4.6 million in 1980 to about 3.4
million in 1996, with the fall being least in the
case of young people from middle-class families,
large numbers of whom have typically gone on to
full-time higher education and good job prospects,
and greatest in the case of young people from
working-class families many of whom have ended up
on the various training schemes outlined above and/
or found themselves unemployed.

The numbers of young people requiring training
will therefore fall very substantially over the next
decade or so, before recovering somewhat thereafter.

Since the same demographic effect should also lead, hopefully, to a substantial fall in youth unemployment, much of what has been written above and elsewhere relating to young people at the start of their working lives will be liable to require amendment at that time.

THE TRAINING CURRICULUM

Critical to the success of YTS and similar schemes is the content or curriculum of the training. In contrast to traditional school curricula, this is almost entirely labour market orientated, closely related to industry's perception of its needs, has little to do with education *per se*, and therefore embodies quite different norms and values. Even so, its content must be inherently problematic. Manpower analysis is unable to predict what skills will be required in the economy in the years to come and the MSC itself expects demand for labour to change substantially during the 1980s; therefore, training in specific job skills is bound to lead to much waste and inefficiency, hence the attractiveness of training in more general, transferable, skills.[22] The demand for traditional craft skills has been steadily declining for many years but it is not at all clear what will replace them. Against this background YTS seeks to cater for '*low attainment, unskilled and inexperienced minimum age school leavers ... with probable negative antecedent attitudes and likely teacher debilitation*'.[23]

What will eventually be very important but is not yet clear will be the credibility to be attached to the certification on completion of the course. It can be argued that the most successful trainees will in fact be those who manage to get a job during the course and that those acquiring the certificates will be the less successful; leaving aside this rather jaundiced '*job-recruitment model*', it can scarcely be doubted that the level and wording of the certification issued will be crucial to the trainees' prospects not just of getting a job at some future date but also of going on to further education or training courses.

The new labour-market orientated curriculum could therefore be seen by one observer to have the following three characteristics:

> *(i)   the dramatic extension of 'labelling' to all school leavers for the first time*

115

> *(ii)*   *the effective raising of the minimum*
>   *school leaving age*
>   *and*
> *(iii)* *the determination to direct young people*
>   *toward a limited range of putative jobs*[24]

although none of these could be described as unarguable.

    There can be little doubt that for the great majority of the young people on such courses 'success' would be seen in terms of getting a job even though these would usually be jobs with low status, poor prospects and considerable insecurity, therefore one critique argued that:

> *educational success in terms of these courses*
> *would still be defined as 'failure'.*[25]

INTERNATIONAL COMPARISONS

In recent years a considerable number of studies have shown the extent to which Britain's record in the field of vocational training compares sadly with those of its competitor countries elsewhere. Perhaps the most thorough and authoritative of these, entitled *Competence and Competition* and published in 1984, was carried out by the Institute of Manpower Studies on behalf of the National Economic Development Council and the Manpower Services Commission, and compared the provision of vocational education and training in Britain with that in Japan, West Germany and the USA. The most critical of all the report's findings was that Britain was the only one of the four countries in which most 16-year-olds leave school in search of a job without being offered any further vocational education. All the other three countries had comprehensive training provision available - in West Germany, for example, over 65 per cent of young school-leavers enter some form of training. Costs are shared between employers, the state (at either federal or local level) and the young people and their families, in varying degrees.

    The report concluded with a long list of recommendations which commenced with the need for at least 85 per cent of school-leavers to achieve 'acceptable standards' in a core curriculum including the 3 Rs, and to seek to withdraw 16- and 17-year-olds from the labour market so as to be able to concentrate on obtaining a work-related qualification and then to enter employment at age 18. YTS needed to be occupation-orientated, with employers ensuring that work experience schemes are relevant, trade unions playing a fuller role in devising schemes, and individual trainees taking more responsibility and initiative for their own training once they were better informed regarding how to derive most benefit from learning opportunities.   In practically every one of the various education and training statistical tables given in the report, the UK ranked last of the four countries.[26]

A series of commentaries on vocational training systems in various countries have appeared in recent years, all of them finding that the training available in Britain suffered in comparison with those on offer elsewhere and with those referring to West Germany drawing the sharpest comparisons.   The 'foolish realism' of politicians and employers in the UK in concentrating on immediately required skills instead of taking a longer term view of 'formation' was particularly criticised.[27]   One Member of Parliament found that the differences largely boiled down to attitudes, especially the attitudes of UK employers whose niggardliness with regard to training contrasted sharply with the '*combination of far-sightedness and a tradition of social and moral responsibility*' manifested by their German counterparts.[28]

In France, too, far higher proportions of young people receive significant training provided or facilitated by their employers even after allowing for the fact that nearly double (71 per cent against 38 per cent) the proportion of the 16-18 age-group remain in full-time education.[29]   The stated national objective, that no young man or women should enter upon active life without having obtained a vocational training validated by a state diploma, has now virtually been achieved.[30]   A detailed examination of the content of such training found this to be both ambitious and demanding: trainees for the building industry, for example, were found in mathematics studying axiomatically-developed geometrical theorems and in French having readings from Baudelaire and Victor Hugo, and with a total of some 30 hours of practical tests ahead of them at the end of the course.   It was naturally tempting to draw a link with the productivity per employee in the French building industry, which was around one-third higher than in that in the UK.[31]   In Japan no fewer than 93 per cent of each age-cohort choose to remain at school until age 18, after which some 40 per cent enter full-time higher education;   for the remainder

117

a network of vocational training is provided by industry itself, a provision to which it is strongly committed.[32]

About all that can be said in mitigation of some of the above criticisms is that a number of them pre-date the development and expansion of the Youth Training Scheme; if the YTS is able to fulfil the hopes that have been placed on it, Britain's training record should at last start to appear less disadvantageous when compared with those of other countries.

In-School Provision

It may seem a contradiction in terms to refer to the provision of vocational training in schools, i.e. within the mainstream educational system. In a sense this is true, but it is undeniable that the various attempts to impart a vocationally-relevant bias to parts of the secondary school system spring from the same causes as the attempts to develop and expand vocational and industrial training outlined above. The two most notable developments in schools in the 1980s were the Technical and Vocational Training Initiative (TVEI) and the Certificate of Pre-Vocational Education (CPVE). Both are aimed at nudging education in the direction of curricula that are of directly vocational relevance, whilst at the same time retaining considerable general education. A common strategy for TVEI, for example, has been to retain a core curriculum to the extent of 70 per cent of the pupils' time, whilst introducing the TVEI material in the remaining 30 per cent, whilst other pupils are following a variety of other options. Both are probably best seen as experimental, pilot schemes which are likely to be the precursors of other such initiatives, both inside and outside school boundaries. Indeed the importance of this distinction may come to be seen as less and less relevant in the future.

RECENT TRENDS

By the mid-1980s there were grounds for believing that industrial and vocational training needs were occupying a more central place in the government's thinking than previously as a series of new initiatives emerged. In January 1984, only just over two years after the *New Training Initiative* of December 1981 referred to above, the White Paper *Training for Jobs*, in a move that was seen partly as

a commendation of the work of the MSC and partly as
a criticism of the education system, proposed the
transfer of one-quarter of the funding of work-
related non-advanced further education courses away
from the local authority rate support grant (and
therefore from the DES) to the Manpower Services
Commission.   This White Paper also announced that
the MSC was to have enhanced authority as the
'national training authority'.   Then in the Spring
of 1985 came the White Paper *Education and Training
for Young People* which recommended the extension of
the YTS to two years, as already indicated, and
which also announced that additional funds would be
made available for teacher training relating to
TVEI.
    Vocational training in the United Kingdom may
now be seen as being at a crucial stage.   The former
apprenticeship system, which probably generally worked well for those fortunate enough to be included
within it, has largely gone, probably for ever.   In
its place, and for much larger numbers of young
people, have arisen shorter courses seeking to combine skill training with some measure of more general
instruction;   the Youth Training Scheme is by far the
most ambitious of such attempts and by the time its
two-year version has come fully into effect will
represent a real attempt to bring vocational training
in the UK up towards the levels enjoyed in other
countries.   What will be the credence and standing
of the completed YTS qualification, particularly in
the eyes of employers, it is as yet too early to say
with certainty but early signs are that the scheme
is winning wider support than its predecessors were
able to do.
    YTS clearly has not overcome various related
problems such as those concerning sexism and racism.
Still far more boys than girls receive any form of
training and those girls who do receive training tend
to be heavily concentrated in certain occupations
such as clerical/secretarial, food-related and other
service occupations.   It is difficult to deny that
many doors effectively remain closed to girls, as
they also do to young people from ethnic minority
communities.   The latter continue to face disadvantages in this as in other spheres.   Doubtless they
have to face some discrimination, including on the
part of employers, even though the MSC does its best
to ensure that its courses are open to all.
    The training needs of adults have been a matter
of some concern but are now being developed via proposals for an *'Open Tech'* programme, which aims to

improve access to education and training for people at technician or supervisory level. The programme would open up opportunities for those who are prevented by, for instance, location or timing or unnecessarily restrictive entry criteria, from undertaking conventional courses.[33] This is but one more example of how attitudes to training needs have changed and become more realistic. Overall it is now possible to be more optimistic regarding national provision for training than at any time for many years past.

NOTES

1. E. Dale, 'Education or Training?', *The Newsletter* (October 1965), and reprinted in *Programmed Learning and Educational Technology*, Vol.22, No.1.

2. A. Howe, 'Education or Training: Is There Any Difference?', *Programmed Learning and Educational Technology*, Vol.22, No.1.

3. D. Ely, 'Education and Training: Two Paths or One?', *Programmed Learning and Educational Technology*, Vol.22, No.1.

4. F. Machlup, *The Production and Distribution of Knowledge in the United States* (Princeton University Press, 1962).

5. G. Becker, *Human Capital, A Theoretical and Empirical Analysis, With Special Reference to Education* (Princeton University Press, 1964).

6. M. Blaug, *An Introduction to the Economics of Education* (Penguin, 1970).

7. M. Jackson, 'Employers Ignorant of Need for Training', *The Times Educational Supplement*, 20 December 1985.

8. R. Lindley, 'Education, Training, and the Labour Market in Britain', *European Journal of Education*, Vol.16, No.1 (1981).

9. J. Atkinson, *Evaluation of Apprentice Support Awards* (Institute of Manpower Studies, 1982).

10. M. Carter, *Into Work* (Pelican, 1966).

11. This and subsequent statistics taken from L.M. Cantor and I.F. Roberts, *Further Education Today, A Critical Review* (Routledge and Kegan Paul, 2nd edn, 1983). I am also grateful to the authors for allowing me to consult the manuscript of the third edition of this invaluable book.

12. J. Wallington, 'Sunset Training', *The Times Educational Supplement*, 23 May 1986.

13. P. Ryan, 'The New Training Initiative After Two Years', *Lloyds Bank Review* (April 1984).

14. *Ibid.*
15. *Ibid.*
16. M. Belbin, 'The YTS - A Programme of Early Opportunity and Long-Term Uncertainty', *BACIE Journal*, Vol.38, No.44 (July/August 1983).
17. D. Finn, 'The Manpower Services Commission and the Youth Training Scheme: A Permanent Bridge to Work?, *Compare*, Vol.14, No.2 (1984).
18. P. Cohen, 'Against the New Vocationalism', in I. Bates *et al.* (eds), *Schooling for the Dole* (Macmillan, 1984).
19. K. Graham, 'Adult Training, Who Pays and Who Delivers', *Manpower Policy and Practice* (Winter 1985).
20. J. Baxter and B. McCormick, 'Seventy Per Cent of Our Future: The Education, Training and Employment of Young People', *National Westminster Bank Quarterly Review* (August 1984).
21. Lindley, 'Education, Training, and the Labour Market in Britain'.
22. T. Edwards, *The Youth Training Scheme. A New Curriculum, Episode One* (The Falmer Press, 1984).
23. *Ibid.*
24. *Ibid.*
25. M. Young, *Knowledge and Control, New Directions for the Sociology of Education* (Collier Macmillan, 1971). The quotation originally referred to vocationally-orientated school courses but has subsequently been taken to have wider reference, including to vocational training.
26. Institute of Manpower Studies, *Competence and Competition, Training and Education in the Federal Republic of Germany, the United States and Japan* (National Economic Development Office/Manpower Services Commission, 1984), and M. Durham, 'Why Ailing Britain Needs a Good VET', *The Times Educational Supplement*, 31 August 1984. See also R. Russell and D. Parkes, 'Keeping Up with the Schmidts', *The Times Educational Supplement*, 4 January 1985.
27. S. Maclure, 'An Industrial Education Lesson for UK?', *The Times Educational Supplement*, 1 February 1985.
28. G. Lawler, MP, 'Land of Youth Opportunity', *The Times Higher Education Supplement*, 4 January 1985.
29. H. Steedman, 'Running to Stay in the Same Place: Quantitative Comparison of Provision for Technical Education and the Training of Young People in France, England and Wales', *Compare*, Vol.14, No.2 (1984).
30. D. Kallen and S. Rivero, 'Early Entry Into

Working Life in France', *Compare*, Vol.14, No.2 (1984).

31.   S.J. Prais and H. Steedman, 'Vocational Training in France and Britain', *NIESR Journal* (February 1985), and R. Eglin, 'France Works Wonders in Bricks and Mortar', *The Sunday Times*, February 1985.

32.   L.M. Cantor, 'Vocational Education and Training: the Japanese Approach', *Comparative Education*, Vol.21, No.1 (1985).

33.   A.M. Lewis, *Descriptions of the Vocational Training Systems - United Kingdom* (European Centre for the Development of Vocational Training, Berlin, 1983).

Chapter Six

WOMEN IN THE ECONOMY

It may seem paradoxical to include in this book a
chapter on *'Women'*.   On the one hand generalised
terms such as *students*, *graduates* or *workers*, as
used throughout this book, should normally be taken
to include women who do, after all, comprise around
50 per cent of the population; no separate chapter
on women should therefore be necessary.   On the
other hand it is undeniable that many of the references quoted in this book are orientated primarily
towards the experiences of men either because these
have seemed to the various authors to be numerically
more important or somehow of greater interest, as
with most references to *engineers*,[1] or because the
available statistical data relates to men, as with
Denison's original calculation of the alpha
coefficient,[2] or because, possibly more by omission
than by deliberate intent, the position of women is
simply overlooked.   There are still major related
texts that do not seem to include a single reference
to women.[3]   Were the respective paths of men and
women through education, careers and lifestyles
identical, this would perhaps not matter very much.
But they clearly are not.   Women clearly undergo
quite different experiences throughout the whole of
the long process which we are here considering.
      This widespread tendency to either undervalue or
ignore the roles of women in published works in this
area has recently been attacked[4] in strong terms:

> sociologists concerned with industry and class
> show little interest in women's work.   This is
> unpardonable ... Giddens' conclusions that
> women are 'peripheral' to the class system and
> their location is mainly determined by ascrip-
> tive and non-economic criteria are fairly
> widely accepted ... To ignore working women is

to understand only part of the industrial and
class system.

GIRLS AND EDUCATION

Typically, boys and girls are treated differently by
their parents and by society generally from the
moment of their birth.   This process continues
throughout their school lives, with quite different
attitudes and norms about the two sexes being
communicated to the pupils.   Teachers, probably
unconsciously, reinforce the stereotyped ideas picked
up before and outside school:

> *Girls, even at pre-school and primary levels,
> are encouraged to develop verbal rather than
> mechanical or spatial skills and later are
> nudged into more 'feminine' subjects.   Girls
> are expected to be more polite and acquiescent,
> whereas boys are expected and allowed to be
> more disruptive, individualistic and aggress-
> ive.* [5]

Girls gravitate towards subjects which are seen as
more acceptable for them or which they have, through
complex processes, come to see as more suitable or
interesting, and they also gravitate towards those
courses seen as the softer options: many tests have
shown that girls are at least as able as boys and
they are frequently more hard-working and better
motivated at school.

In the years immediately after the Second World
War, more boys than girls took external examinations
at all levels, more stayed on at school after the
age of compulsory schooling, and more went on to
higher education.   Table 6.1 shows how the position
has changed, the statistics given covering the period
from 1974-5 to 1983-4, the latest year for which
figures are available.   Prior to 1974-5 the figures
were published on a rather different basis and the
same trends cannot easily be followed back to earlier
years.

Apart from indicating the generally more
successful outcomes achieved by both boys and girls
in 1983-4 as compared with nine years earlier,
Table 6.1 shows that girls had become more successful
than boys in external examinations at every level
except the highest.   Still relatively more boys than
girls, i.e. a higher percentage of the respective age
group, achieve two or more A-level passes - in 1983-4

Table 6.1: Educational Qualifications and Higher Education, Boys and Girls, 1974-5 to 1983-4

	1974-5				1983-4			
	Boys		Girls		Boys		Girls	
	Numbera	% of age group	Numbera	% of age group	Numbera	% of age group	Numbera	% of age group
School-leavers with:								
2 or more A-level passes[b]	44.8	13.1	35.0	10.8	55.9	14.1	40.0	13.2
1 A-level pass[b]	9.3	2.7	11.3	3.5	11.5	2.9	12.5	3.3
5 or more higher grade[c,d] O-level or CSE results	12.4	3.5	17.5	5.2	20.4	5.3	25.1	6.9
1-4 higher grades[c] O-level or CSE	63.4	17.9	69.6	20.7	71.3	18.5	81.0	22.2
No higher grades but[c] 1 or more other grades	103.4	29.1	93.3	27.8	130.9	34.0	113.5	31.1
No GCE or CSE qualifications[c]	63.5	17.9	54.4	16.2	40.2	10.4	27.1	7.4
All school-leavers	242.8	68.4	234.8	69.9	262.8	68.3	246.7	67.6
School-leavers entering:								
Universities	24.72	–	14.20	–	24.25	–	16.81	–
Polytechnics	4.13	–	1.95	–	7.80	–	5.11	–
Other further education[e]	0.29	–	0.26	–	0.78	–	1.27	–
Totale	29.14	–	16.41	–	32.83	–	23.19	–

Notes: (a) Numbers in thousands.
(b) Of 17-year-olds on 31 August preceding academic year.
(c) Of 15-year-olds on 31 August preceding academic year.
(d) Higher Grades = GCE Grades A to C (equivalent to former pass level), plus CSE Grade 1.
(e) Basis of compilation changed over the period, so direct comparison may not be valid.

Source: *Statistics of Education – School Leavers CSE and GCE (DES, annually).*

125

14.1 per cent against 13.2 per cent.   But in the
succeeding lines in the table girls fare better than
boys, with the differential becoming gradually more
marked as one reads down the respective columns.
This seems to support sociologists' findings that
girls are socialised into not aiming for success at
the highest level but are content to achieve at a
somewhat lower level.

It was certainly still true in 1983-4 that far
fewer girls than boys sought or achieved entry to
universities (16.8 per cent against 24.2 per cent) or
polytechnics (5.1 per cent against 7.8 per cent).
This again must relate strongly to a combination of
societal and individual expectations.   The figures
for All School-Leavers (i.e. approximately those who
left school at the end of their fifth year), by
contrast, show that whereas in 1974-5 a higher proportion of girls than boys opted to leave school at
that stage (69.9 per cent against 68.4 per cent) by
1983-4 the reverse was true (67.6 per cent girls
against 68.3 per cent boys).   This gives some
indication of the way such trends are slowly changing.

Gender differentiation by school subject is
still strong: boys predominate in such subjects as
physics (where *ten times as many* boys take the CSE
examination and three times as many take O-level as
girls), mathematics (twice as many as girls at A-
level), chemistry and technical drawing.   More
girls than boys take biology, French, English
Literature and art.   *Over thirty times as many*
girls take home economics as boys.   Just how
blatantly sexist the education system could be may
be seen by the wording of past CSE examination papers
in Housecraft:[6]

> *Launder a selection of your own and your
> husband's clothes ...*
>
> *Iron his shirt, that you have previously washed,
> and press a pair of trousers ready for him to
> change into ...*

Supposedly, inequalities in schools arising
from sexual differentiation were ended by the Sex
Discrimination Act 1975 and shortly afterwards, in
the 1977 Green Paper *Education in Schools*, the
Department of Education and Science acknowledged,
virtually for the first time, that sexual differentiation in schools was a problem that needed to be
drawn to the attention of teachers and education

authorities.   The Act said that schools should not
divide pupils for subjects by sex but,

> *There is still little positive action in*
> *schools to encourage pupils to make informed*
> *choices.*[7]

No-one could pretend, therefore, that the Act has
succeeded in ending sexual differentiation in
schools.   Overt discrimination relating to such
matters as subject choices has probably largely
ended but the more insidious implicit pressures
either remain much as before or are only changing
quite slowly.   The position statement by the
National Council for Civil Liberties still seems
relevant:

> *Schools are, at least partly, responsible for*
> *the beliefs common amongst girls that training*
> *is unimportant, their jobs are inessential and*
> *their husbands are financially responsible for*
> *them ...   The education system is, we believe,*
> *creating discriminatory attitudes and low*
> *expectations in new generations of children.*[8]

It seems clear that as a result of the process
of schooling the majority of girls develop lower
career and lifestyle aspirations than boys, accept
that they will go into largely menial and subservient
jobs and see rather little point in extended education or training.   There is evidence that working-
class girls in particular typically see school as
boring and irrelevant and look forward to leaving as
soon as possible.[9]
Recent research[10] has shown that by 1985
attitudes towards girls in schools, especially by
the boys, seemed to have changed little if at all:
boys are shown to dominate classrooms physically as
well as verbally, and to monopolise the teacher's
vision and talk.   In the playgrounds, too, the boys
occupy the centre spaces while the girls sit or walk
around the edges, often simply watching the boys'
activities.   Throughout schools,

> *An enormous amount of time and energy is*
> *expended by boys on what amounts to the*
> *social control of girls.*

The girls, on the other hand, *'service'* the boys in
that,

> *they help them with homework, fetch sweets and*
> *crisps and, during lessons, provide 'an endless*
> *supply of pens, pencils, rubbers and other*
> *equipment.*

It was precisely because the eighty-plus per cent of
schools which are co-educational embody 'normal'
relations between the sexes that the researcher saw
them as inhibiting girls' educational development.
Separate evidence indicates that modern developments
such as computers and 'hi-tech' innovations in
schools are monopolised by boys.   One scathing
critique concluded:

> *according to such criteria as economic power,*
> *technological skills and personal independence*
> *(the education system) is failing women very*
> *badly ... there is no evidence of any serious*
> *intention to change matters.*[11]

The inequalities persist on to education after
school.   Females comprise only around one-third of
all university undergraduates and predictably they
have tended to be concentrated in such subject areas
as language and literature, arts and (especially
before the cuts) education.   By the mid-1970s even
after initiatives to encourage girls in that direction,
still only around 5 per cent of students in engineering and technology were female, other categories in
which females were seriously under-represented being
science (30 per cent), medicine and dentistry (36 per
cent), architecture (24 per cent) and agriculture (29
per cent).[12]   It has long been a statistical
curiosity that in total more girls than boys go on
to some form of full-time post-school education but
they typically go on to lower level courses, often to
some kind of diploma or certificate course at their
local technical college.   Once again subject
selectivity is paramount:

> *Women are to be found preparing for caring,*
> *supportive and service roles in employment*
> *(pre-nursing, secretarial, hairdressing) and*
> *rarely for those preparing them for a more*
> *directly instrumental relationship with the*
> *world (construction, engineering, physical*
> *sciences).*[13]

It is perhaps particularly striking that whereas as
noted above until quite recently some two-thirds of
university students studying medicine were male (the

proportions changing to around 50:50 only in the
1980s), on the related but lower-level 'medical,
health and welfare' group of courses in colleges of
further education nearly 90 per cent of the students
have always been female.

EMPLOYMENT

From the above evidence it might seem that by the
time they leave the education system the future
careers of young women have been broadly predetermined. There is a measure of truth in this
statement in that for very many girls by then their
horizons have been confined and their range of
potential future choices limited; it would however
obviously be wrong to place all the blame for this
state of affairs on the education service which
largely reflects the norms and values of society as
a whole. These in turn affect the development of
attitudes and expectations by young people, so that
girls often expect to, and even more so boys often
expect them to, have working careers which are
restricted in terms of opportunities, working
conditions and financial rewards.

Historically, this has always been the case.
Women have always occupied positions in society
subservient to those of men and where women have gone
to work similar relationships were continued into the
workplace. Of course, in past centuries very many
women did not go to work at all in the sense of going
out of the home to an employer's separate premises
but were content to, or were confined to, work within
the home - either work such as spinning or knitting,
the product of which would be remunerated in cash by
an employer who would call at the house, or housework,
childcare and related chores. During the twentieth
century the numbers of women going out to work
steadily increased until by the time of the 1951
Census women constituted 31 per cent of the working
population of the UK. By the 1980s this had reached
around 40 per cent. Within the female labour force,
married women comprised only 38 per cent in 1951, a
figure that has now risen to some 75 per cent.
Married women were only some 22 per cent of the total
labour force in 1951 but this percentage had doubled
by the 1980s.[14]

The factors leading to the increase in the
numbers of married women at work have been categor-
ised by Parker *et al.*[15] under the three headings of
opportunity, capacity and *motivation. Opportunity*

increased because of the post-war shortage of labour,
changes in the occupational structure including
expansion of employment in fields employing large
numbers of women such as the retail trade and welfare
and administrative functions, social disapproval and
traditions about a woman's place being in the home
weakened, discrimination gradually lessened including
by legal measures, and industries adapted their
requirements in terms of hours and type of work in
order to get the women workers they required.
Capacity extended with better health, food, the
benefits of the welfare state and the spread of
labour-saving devices in the home. *Motivation*
stemmed from a mix of financial incentives and the
wish to escape from boredom and loneliness at home.

The rise in the percentage of married women
seeking to work, or to return to work, since 1945 has
been described as so *'dramatic'* as to amount to a
'revolution'.[16]   The participation of women in the
labour force will always be subject to some limitations arising from their parallel roles as wives and
mothers.   Even with the small *'nuclear'* size
families that have now become the norm, child-rearing
takes time - a great deal of time - and gives rise to
various contingencies such as one parent having to
stay at home whenever a child is ill.   In the past
this burden has fallen almost solely on mothers
rather than fathers, due to a complex mix of
attendant circumstances including societal expectations: male bank clerks, for example, would have
found it very difficult to take time off work for
such purposes.

Perhaps the majority of women, and certainly
the majority of men, would not have wanted it otherwise and it was only very slowly that demand
increased for those women who so wished to be liber-
ated from such constraints, especially those that
made it difficult for women to have reasonable and
meaningful career aspirations.   It is also worth
recalling that the widespread *'social stigma
associated with working married women'*[17] did not
change significantly until well after 1945,
especially among the middle classes;   by the 1980s
it can, of course, be argued that an exactly reverse
social stigma has now developed.

As with men, the proportion of women workers
who are in jobs classified as *'manual'* has steadily
declined from the figure of around two-thirds for
1951, although the *numbers* of women employed as
manual workers actually continued to increase over
the post-war period, at least until the present

phenomenon of mass unemployment arose anew in the
late 1970s. The number of *unskilled* female workers
approximately doubled in the years after 1951 whilst
the numbers of those classified as *semi-skilled* rose
very slowly and the numbers of *skilled* fell
substantially. This structural change within the
manual category has to be borne in mind against the
much-publicised parallel trend, namely the steady
increase in the numbers of female workers employed
in *clerical* work, usually in cleaner and more
attractive working conditions. By the time of the
1981 Census women in employment were distributed as
shown in Table 6.2.

By occupational category, women workers tend to
be concentrated in *professional and scientific
services*, the *distributive trades* and *chemicals*,
metal manufacturing and *engineering*, with very few
in such categories as *construction*, *agriculture*,
mining or *gas*, *electricity* and *water*. In *clothing
and footwear* some three-quarters of all workers are
female, this being the highest concentration in any
occupational category. Apart from the nurses and
teachers who dominate the *professional and scientific services* category, elsewhere women tend to be
concentrated in those categories where the work has
relatively lower-status, lower-pay and worse
prospects.

Within the *professional* category women are to be
found largely at the lower end, with only low levels
of representation as lawyers, surveyors, architects,
accountants, technologists, scientists, dentists,
clergy or draughtsmen ('draughtspersons'?).
Successive censuses have shown high concentrations
of women in such occupations as typists, secretaries,
maids, nurses, canteen workers and sewing machinists
(all over 90 per cent), and charwomen (no need to
worry about 'charmen'?) and office cleaners, hairdressers, laundry workers, waitresses and kitchen
hands (75-90 per cent female). All these categories
have undesirable connotations in terms of type of
work or working conditions or rates of pay, or more
usually all three, and may clearly be seen in sharp
contrast to the high-status, higher professional
occupations referred to above which are clearly more
desirable from various points of view.

Although there clearly have been some changes
over time which space does not permit us to explore
here, such as the decline in the numbers of domestic
servants or the increase in the numbers of hairdressers (both categories dominated by women),

Table 6.2: Distribution of Women by Occupational
Class, 1981

		Number	Percentage
1.	Professional		
	Higher	103,230	1.0
	Lower	1,548,880	15.7
2.	Managerial		
	Proprietors	229,130	2.3
	Managers	509,300	5.2
3.	Clerical	2,873,760	29.1
4.	Forewomen, Inspectors	261,730	2.7
	Manual Workers		
5.	Skilled	517,580	5.2
6.	Semi-skilled	2,751,480	27.9
7.	Unskilled	1,083,790	11.0
Total		9,878,880	100.0

Source: National Census, 1981.

This table shows that by 1981 'only' just over 41
per cent of women were employed in manual occupations
and that the figure for clerical occupations had
risen to just over 29 per cent.   Significantly more
women were classified as lower professional (mainly
teachers and nurses) but the percentages who were
higher professional (e.g. doctors, dentists) or
proprietors remained quite small.

> ... *little evidence has emerged of any signifi-
> cant erosion in the traditional division of
> labour by sex.   Within each occupational group,
> there is a tendency for women to be concentrated
> in a narrow spectrum of jobs.*[18]

It also has to be remembered that all of the above
understates the disadvantageous positions in which
women find themselves: some two-thirds of school
teachers are women but men predominate at the higher
levels of the profession, nursing is predominantly
a female occupation but the senior posts tend to be
dominated by men, women tend to be junior clerks

rather than senior clerks, most hairdressers may be
women but the men may be in charge, waiters tend to
be in charge of waitresses rather than vice versa,
and so on throughout practically every occupation.
That serious and persisting differentiation, discrimination and inequality by sex exist in respect of
work in Britain, as in every other comparable country,
cannot be denied.

Occupational segregation of men and women has
been steadily declining throughout the twentieth
century, not only in terms of the numbers employed in
each category but also in terms of such attendant
factors as terms of employment - e.g. the virtual
ending of the practice, widespread before and after
the Second World War, that on marriage a woman
rendered herself liable to dismissal - or pay - e.g.
the long and hard-fought battle for *nominally* equal
pay in the teaching profession.   In terms of
numbers, however, the trend seems to have been
reversed and occupational segregation seems to have
worsened since around the mid-1970s, paradoxically
the years when the Sex Discrimination Act of 1975
should have been taking effect.

The severe recession and growing unemployment,
a marked tendency towards less work on the part of
the older age groups, some slight fall in activity
rates for women with young children, and an increasing shift towards part-time work by mothers after
childbirth at a time when the birth-rate was rising,
are probably all contributory factors.[19]   Employers,
it is alleged, have become increasingly unwilling to
offer a job to a woman as the recession has deepened
and unemployment risen.   In that sense attitudes
against women in at least some kinds of jobs have
almost certainly hardened.   (It may, incidentally,
be noted in passing that the almost universal
assumption would be that the *employer* - i.e. whoever
is in the position of taking such decisions about
staff - would be male.)

The relationship between the inferior educational experiences of girls, as discussed previously,
and the typically disadvantageous work situations in
which they, as women, subsequently find themselves
may on the one hand seem obvious:

> *It is sometimes argued that the lowly position
> of women workers in the occupational hierarchy
> is in part due to their inferior education and
> training.   Such an inferiority results in their
> concentration into a narrow range of occupations,
> and thereby reduces their ability to enter*

> *higher status and better paid jobs and compete*
> *more effectively with their male counterparts.*[20]

But on the other hand we must be aware of the
'chicken and egg' question raised here: do women
fare less well at work than men because of their (on
average) worse education, or do they typically
receive an inferior education because they are seen
as being predestined to occupy more lowly employment
positions than men? Both are, at the same time,
cause and effect, and both are obviously heavily
dependent on general attitudes about women in
society.

Training

What about the subsequent vocationally-relevant
training that women may expect to receive? Joseph
reports an interesting calculation relating to
female workers in 27 major industrial categories in
terms of the numbers who were given day release for
part-time study at further education institutions
during working hours, compared to the *'expected'*
numbers of female workers who *should have been*
released (i.e. the proportion of all workers
released) by reference to the sex composition of the
work force in each industry.

The calculation was repeated for the years 1971
and 1978, in order to see whether there were any
clear trends over this period. In practically every
one of the 27 industrial categories the numbers of
females actually released were much less than the
numbers that, in proportional statistical terms,
should have been released, the most glaring example
being in electrical engineering, where the numbers
actually released were less than one-sixth of the
'expected' figure in 1971 and a little over one-fifth
in 1978. Almost all industrial categories showed,
to a greater or lesser extent, a similar record of
unequal treatment in the matter of granting work-time
release for study, the only exception being public
administration. There was some lessening of the
unequal imbalance over the period studied but by 1978
serious inequality between the sexes in this respect
persisted throughout almost every other category
(except for coal and petroleum products). This is,
of course, just one example of the many continuing
inequalities relating to the working lives of women.

THE ECONOMIC CASE FOR EDUCATING WOMEN

In view of the forgoing catalogue of differentiation, discrimination and disadvantage applying to their working lives, to what extent is it worth while, on economic grounds, investing in the education of women in the first place?

> *At first sight it would appear obvious that the returns to women's education will be lower than the returns for men, since the average earnings of women are about half the male average*

was how Maureen Woodhall began a study[21] of this question but she ended by concluding that,

> *Even when the benefits of education are measured solely in terms of earnings, the social and private rate of return is not very markedly below the rates calculated for men in several countries, and in a few cases, the female rate of return is actually above the rate observed for men.*

There were a number of main reasons for this finding. At each level of education, educated women were far more likely to remain in the labour force either full-time or part-time than women with less education; they were still likely to interrupt their working careers while having young children but it was more probable that they would later return to work. Therefore the additional education results in both the women themselves benefiting, in the form of higher lifetime earnings, and society benefiting from their higher productivity in the labour market. (This was written before the return of mass unemployment.) Secondly, although the absolute lifetime earnings of women will on average always be lower than those of men, in relative terms educated women may enjoy a greater advantage than men (i.e. because the alternative career opportunities available would typically be relatively worse) and they would also typically face less market discrimination than women with less education. Here one would now have to add that the current economic recession has hit less well educated women particularly harsly - more harshly than men with equivalent levels of education and more harsly than more highly educated women.
Although there is no known way of quantifying it, women's non-market work, especially child-

rearing, also needs to be taken into account,
especially in view of the fact that sociological
research has shown that the mother's own educational
achievement has a strong influence on the future
educational performance of her children.   Loss of
earnings due to time spent thus should be regarded
as *'family investment in the human capital of their
children'*.[22]   In a full assessment of all factors,
Woodhall argues that account should also be taken of
psychic income - there is a greater probability that
more educated women will do work in which they can
more fully express themselves and which they enjoy.
A series of surveys of women's attitudes has shown
such factors, combined with pleasant working
conditions, to be rated very highly and a major
OECD report by Seear concluded that such non-monetary
considerations may induce women to accept and remain
in jobs with low financial returns.[23]

It is also true that since educated women tend
to be concentrated in jobs, such as teaching or
public sector administration, where their earnings
may not fully reflect the economic worth of the work
they do (or, in economists' jargon, their *marginal
product*), any calculation of rates of return for
investment in the education of women would be particularly difficult.   And it would be rendered even
more problematic by the non-monetary considerations
outlined above.   Nevertheless the principles set
out by Woodhall are clear and can hardly be disputed.
They lead to the conclusion that, in the UK as in
other countries, there is serious under-investment in
the education of women.

Much the most important statistical enquiry to
have taken place into the position of women at work
in the UK was organised by the Office of Population
Censuses and Surveys and the Department of Employment
in 1980, its results being published in 1984.[24]
This study produced over 260 statistical tables and
it would be impossible to do full justice here to all
the mass of information assembled there but a number
of significant points emerge clearly.   Marital
status *per se* was shown not to affect whether or not
women work but rather the family roles played within
marriage, particularly relating to the care of the
youngest child.   The proportion of women working
had risen with successive birth cohorts of women.
Almost all women who had a child had a break from
employment but now a higher percentage of women
return to work (over 90 per cent eventually) and more
do so more quickly.   The report states, on page 187,

> *half the women who had a first baby between*
> *1975 and 1979 had returned to work within*
> *4 years*

but such a finding is not borne out by the statistical data (nor could it be in a 1980 survey), which do
however give such a result in respect of first
babies born between 1970 and 1974 (Table 9.15 in the
report).   The report continues:

> *Overall, women are spending an increasing pro-*
> *portion of their lives in employment, though*
> *very few adopt the typical male pattern of*
> *continuous lifetime employment as a full-time*
> *worker.   Most interruptions to employment are*
> *caused for domestic reasons.*

There are general assumptions which, still, affect
girls' decisions whilst at school and subsequently:

> *Girls tend to make educational, training and*
> *job choices predicated on the assumption that*
> *they will be wives and mothers.   They will*
> *have a working life interrupted for childbirth*
> *and childbearing, usually characterised by*
> *partial employment ...   Boys, by contrast,*
> *expect that they will be the primary wage*
> *earner and that employment is or should be the*
> *main lifetime occupation ...*

The labour market was shown to have a marked degree
of segregation between men and women, with women in
a restricted range of occupations, typically at
lower levels than men, and on average at lower levels
still if part-time.

Frances Cairncross has recently emphasised[25]
that whereas most men are obliged to work throughout
their lives until they reach retirement age, most
women have the choice of whether or not to do so and
can certainly choose intermittent periods of going
out to work and not doing so, if they wish.   The
OPCS/DoE survey confirms this but with reservations
regarding those women, probably an increasing number,
for whom there is effectively no such choice.   The
generalised notion of women having the freedom to
choose was also refuted, in stronger terms, by
Sanders and Reed.[26]

THE PRODUCTIVITY OF WOMEN WORKERS

Any assessment of the position of women in the
economy must centre on the perception that female
labour is lower in quality and has a lower market
value than male labour.[27]   There are two distinct
possibilities: firstly, due to discrimination it
may be that women are typically paid less than men
because their work is assessed as being less productive than that of men even though in reality it
is not (i.e. in economists' jargon they receive less
than the marginal revenue product of their labour)
and, secondly, female labour *is* of lower quality,
due to a number of attendant circumstances.
Prominent amongst these would be the position of
women in the household and their responsibilities
for childbearing, childcare and domestic duties.
Therefore those employers who seek long-term commitment, uninterrupted employment, full-time work,
possibly flexibility regarding hours, and even
geographical mobility, still seek to employ men.
This *'primary'* labour sector is distinguished by
Garnsey from the *'secondary'* sector where wages, job
security and job content are all inferior.   *'Primary'*
companies only employ females in the worst jobs,
e.g. as clerks or secretaries, because their labour
is judged to be of low quality:

> *It is therefore the lower market value of female*
> *labour which results from the household division*
> *of labour that leads women into inferior jobs,*
> *rather than the prejudice and convention of male*
> *employers and co-workers.*[28]

It has been argued that *'secondary'* workers may be
attracted to their employers if they have the five
characteristics of dispensability, clearly visible
social differences (from other workers), little
interest in acquiring training, low economism and
lack of solidarity - clearly all characteristics
which would accentuate their low status, low pay and
poor future prospects.[29]   Garnsey's hypothesis of
separate *'primary'* and *'secondary'* labour markets of
the lines indicated above has a certain intuitive
appeal and can be supported by reference to certain
occupations from which women are virtually excluded
- e.g. bank managers; it is not, however, entirely
convincing, and certainly to equate *'primary'* with
'male' and *'secondary'* with 'female' would be too
simplistic.   At least some large-scale employers of
women, e.g. the civil service or local education

authorities, do offer the possibility of upward
mobility through a network of job hierarchies and
at least some women do take advantage of this;
since, however, the majority of the women employees
are congregated at or near the base of their respective labour pyramids, may they be said at least in
part to choose not to avail themselves of the
opportunities that exist for career promotion?
This brings us back to the notion of choice to which
reference was made earlier, but such choice has to
be seen in terms of women's domestic and family
situations.

Research into the attitudes of managers towards
women workers found that,

> *managers believed that women were less likely
> than men to possess the important employee
> attributes of good training, education and
> personality, that they were unsuitable for
> skilled or technical jobs, but had greater
> manual dexterity and patience and had an
> aptitude for dull, repetitive work.*[30]

The notion of women's work being inherently of
lower quality than that of men also requires reference back to background factors such as those considered earlier:

> *the ascriptive practices of the educational
> system, which reflect the belief that certain
> manual and intellectual qualities are appropri-
> ate for boys rather than for girls, and the
> prejudice displayed in unions and professions
> which control access to their trades prevent
> women from enhancing their market capability by
> acquiring the sorts of skills that do have a
> market value irrespective of the length and
> continuity of periods of employment.*[31]

In other words, whilst there is no suggestion that
it is in any way women's fault - indeed, quite the
reverse - the mix of all such factors does lead to
the quality of women's work being assessed as of
lower quality than men's.

There are obviously counter-arguments to the
above, i.e. arguments that suggest that in certain
circumstances women may be more, not less, efficient
than men.   Firstly there is considerable evidence
that employers rate women more highly than men for
the kind of work, usually classified as semi-skilled,
where manipulative dexterity, patience and extended

concentration are required. The example most
frequently cited is that of the assembly of intricate
electronics components where women workers are widely
considered to be the most suitable: the much-
referred-to 'chip' has usually been put together by
female hands.

Secondly, and many women might consider more
importantly, there is a range of jobs where the fact
that women have themselves borne and reared children
must enhance the quality of their work in a way that
can never be true of a man. The obvious example
would be nurses, teachers (especially at primary
school level) and social workers. A typical problem
that will confront a social worker will be that of a
young mother suffering from puerperal depression at
home alone with two or three unruly children apart
from the new baby who seems to fret and cry continuously or a single-parent mother working part-time
and worried about harming her children. Perhaps
only a woman who has had children could fully
sympathise with her, i.e. it is doubtful whether any
man ever could. Far, however, from such factors
being universally recognised, the reverse is often
still the case:

> It's absurd that it should be a handicap in
> a career in obstetrics to have had a baby and
> to have been a mother. [32]

And thirdly reference must be made to part-time work.
After marriage and childrearing many women seek to
return to work on a part-time basis, for obvious
reasons. What evidence exists relating to part-time
work suggests that *pro rata* it is much more productive to employers than full-time work: a half-time
teacher or social worker or secretary typically does
more than 50 per cent of the work done by a full-time
person. There is an inevitable tendency for a full-
time worker not to be able to work intensively for
the whole day or week whereas a part-time worker
frequently can and does do so. A full-time worker
will typically work the prescribed hours, e.g. 9 to
5 p.m., but anecdotal evidence suggests that a part-
time worker is frequently less concerned about leaving promptly at, for example, 12.30 p.m. and may
stay on for a short while to finish the task in
hand. All of this will tend to raise her marginal
product.

On balance, therefore, the evidence regarding
whether female workers are less productive than males
is not clear-cut. Doubtless many are, largely due

to the kinds of jobs in which they find themselves
but for at least some others the reverse may be true.
There is certainly no evidence that on average women
would not be as productive and efficient as men did
not their educational background, lack of training
opportunities, interruption of career (perhaps more
than once) and commitments to home and family, all
operate against them.   Overall, therefore, the case
must remain that as a nation we are substantially
under-investing in the education and training of
women.

THE NATURE OF WOMEN'S WORK

The *type* of work done by a large proportion of working women has been described by such epithets as
degrading, soul-destroying and monotonous.   Frequently the work requires only a low level of skill, has
to be done within a specified time and carries little
or nothing in the way of intrinsic reward: all this
is especially true of work on production lines in
factories, where the moving conveyor belt dictates
what is to happen and when, but it is also true of
other typically female jobs such as shop assistants,
who in modern supermarkets are increasingly little
more than shelf-fillers, and secretaries or clerical
workers in offices.
     Work on a production line has been described in
graphic detail by Ruth Cavendish:[33]

> *All in all there was quite a lot to do in the*
> *one minute allowed for each UMO.   It was*
> *impossible to keep up unless the trays came at*
> *regular intervals and difficult even then.*
> *On the Maxi, after torque checking, I attached*
> *three metal clips, three screws and the*
> *resister.   This job was excruciating at first;*
> *by 10 a.m. my neck and back were in agony from*
> *straining forward to press on the airgun and I*
> *didn't know how I would get through the day.*
> *I often put the clips in wrong, as two went one*
> *way round while the third went the opposite way,*
> *and I was slow with the screws.   You had to*
> *hold the three screws in your left hand, and*
> *the airgun in your right, twiddle the screws*
> *onto the magnetic head of the gun, and then*
> *screw them down.   Obviously it was quicker if*
> *you had the next screw ready in your left hand*
> *and didn't have to put down the airgun in*
> *between each.   My left hand was so inflexible*

141

> for the first few weeks that I had to do it all
> with my right hand which took at least six
> times as long, but otherwise I would never have
> managed to get the screws in at all ...
> Most days I was worked so hard that I couldn't
> look up at all, or had to work extra specially
> fast so that I would have time in between one
> tray and the next to unwrap a piece of chewing
> gum, or take a sip of tea ...
> The nuts, screws and basic mechanisms were
> black and greasy and the bench was covered in
> dust, so you had to spend most of the breaks
> cleaning your hands so as to avoid smearing
> black grease on your food.

To have to do seven operations in one minute *allows
just over eight and a half seconds for each operation*
and this continued for the whole of the working day.
Small wonder that each evening the writer reported
returning home physically and mentally exhausted.

The impression that Ruth Cavendish gives
throughout her book is confirmed by Pollert's
study[34] of women workers at a tobacco factory for
whom

> work was essentially unskilled, boring,
> repetitive, alienated, something to be
> endured.

What most angered the women was

> not primarily pay, but becoming machines - and
> insults to dignity: being 'us nits, working',
> while men stood by doing nothing; or being
> 'taken for granted'.   Exploitation - being
> tied to a machine - was sensed, but resented
> most bitterly when turned into belittlement or
> insult to their intelligence.

In the factory,

> the atmosphere was thick not just with tobacco
> but with male stereotypes about the women.
> Not all men were hostile; but the crux of
> their attitude was that the woman's place was
> in the home, or in 'feminine' jobs such as
> nursing.   As factory workers they were awkward,
> superfluous, or downright problems.

Pollert's conclusion,

> *that women workers are workers in a man's*
> *world ...*

seems obvious but the author continues:

> *... yet they also create their own ... they*
> *remain separate, women importing their own*
> *world, living in it, and maintaining a dual*
> *existence*

provided, that is, that they can continue at work,
but this has become less and less certain:

> *... the key problem facing women workers now*
> *is the right to work itself.*

Such first-hand, anecdotal, accounts of women working
on factory production lines or in similar situations
bring home all too clearly the realities of the working conditions that women have to endure.
Clerical and secretarial work by women office
workers does not readily lend itself to such graphic-
al accounts but with the exception of the physical
manual labour, the questions of drudgery, boredom
and relatively low pay recur just as strongly with
regard to such work:

> *Women - or rather girls, for the great majority*
> *are under twenty-five - will, at present, accept*
> *routine jobs that are unlikely to lead anywhere*
> *... they are willing to put up with tasks that*
> *are intrinsically dull and for the same reason*
> *they are not unduly anxious for promotion.*[35]

This is why,

> *so much of clerical work is being taken over*
> *by women.*

An up-to-date postscript would have to comment that
many of those same office jobs previously taken over
by women are now disappearing with the introduction
of modern technology and the advent of the electronic
office.

PART-TIME WORK AND EARNINGS

The brief reference above to part-time work needs
amplification. The reasons that lead many women to
seek to return to work on a part-time basis after

childbirth and/or child-rearing are self-evident:
with continuing family and home commitments women
can manage part-time work much more easily than a
full-time job.   Rather little information exists
about part-time work, in the sense that there has
been very little relevant research.[36]   Part-time
work, however, is associated with low pay, inferior
conditions of employment and low status relative to
full-time work.[37]

The great majority of part-time jobs are held
by women, over one-third of all working women work
part-time (conventionally defined as less than 30
hours per week), and Elias and Main found that 85
per cent of female part-time employment was concentrated in the service sector, i.e. an occupational
structure quite unlike that for women in full-time
jobs.   The National Training Survey[38] showed that
during the years when there are in the family home
children aged 5 to 15, that is when the women are
between aproximately ages 30 and 45, around 50 per
cent of working women work part-time.   Much the
largest concentration of part-time working women
(nearly 40 per cent of the total) is in the occupational category *'other personal services'*, i.e.
*'waitresses, bar staff, counter hands, domestic
helpers, school meals assistants, caretakers,
cleaners, attendants'*:   merely from this listing of
such part-time jobs, the low status, the menial and
unskilled nature of the work, the low pay, the lack
of training or educational qualifications and the
small possibility of advancement through some form
of career progression, are all immediately obvious.

A particularly important finding by Elias and
Main related to 'skill down-grading':   of part-time
women in *'other personal service'* jobs, around 20
per cent had previously had a full-time job in some
higher status occupation group and around 38 per cent
had qualifications relating to teaching, nursing or
clerical/commercial.   Quite apart from the perspective of the women themselves who have had to take
such work at levels clearly below their qualifications
and capabilities, from the perspective of national
economic efficiency there is clearly a waste of
expensively-produced skill and expertise which it
would be in the national interest to put to fuller and
more efficient use.   Part-time women workers receive
little training, tend not to belong to trade unions
and, since they are often employed on a casual hourly
basis, they often do not qualify for sickness,
maternity, or pension benefits or holidays with pay.

Just in case there might be any room for

optimism regarding future trends, Elias and Main conclude:

> *The problems we have highlighted in this report are unlikely to resolve themselves with time. To the contrary, we believe that such problems are likely to become more acute. Over the last two decades, educational participation levels amongst women have been rising. More young women now hold some form of post-school leaving qualifications than at any other time. Furthermore, we have experienced a widening of the acceptability of women in a range of occupations which were previously the exclusive domain of men. Young women are encouraged to plan careers, fostering expectations which twenty years ago would have been viewed as quite unrealistic. On the other hand, there has been no major social reorganisation of the division of domestic responsibilities within the family. The role of motherhood will, therefore, still necessitate the need for part-time employment amongst women. We anticipate that the growth of part-time employment will continue in the low pay, low skill, low status sector of the market.*

Low pay is a persistent problem relating to all work done by women, even though the male/female earnings gap has gradually decreased over time, and decreased substantially between 1974 and 1976 due to the coming into force in December 1975 of the 1970 Equal Pay Act. Women's earnings have generally reached about two-thirds of men's earnings,[39] and on an hourly wage rate basis the figure is now around three-quarters. Since then there has been rather little change. The typically low pay of part-time workers was considered above: for full-time women workers, the New Earnings Survey of 1981[40] showed clearly the very considerable differences in earnings at different levels, as in Table 6.3, on which comment is superfluous. Whilst the monetary figures quoted in the table are now out-of-date, the principles remain valid: in round terms a female three-quarters of the way up the female earnings league table earns about the same as a male only one-quarter of the way up the male earnings league table.

Many explanations have been given for women being relatively so poorly paid, including discrimination, sexism, lack of dependability and many of the other factors considered previously. Shirley

Table 6.3: Full-time Male and Female Workers and
Earnings

Earning less than (£ per week)	Male (%)	Female (%)
50	0.4	5.1
60	1.1	15.3
70	3.4	30.7
80	7.9	46.8
90	15.0	59.8
100	24.0	70.0

From this point on the male proportion starts to
increase rapidly.

Dex[41] shows that the main body of theoretical writ-
ings relevant to women's low pay has centred on the
question of *Segmented Labour Markets*, one variant
of which, that by Garnsey, was referred to previously.
All such theories are shown to be unsatisfactory in
varying degrees, partly because they do not take
account of the post-war mushrooming of jobs for
women in public sector employment where relatively
greater equality has been achieved, and partly
because they treat all women as homogeneous and do
not allow - because they never could do - for the
many variations in work-home-family situations in
which women find themselves.

FUTURE PROSPECTS

What of the future? Abstracting for the moment
from the current situation of economic recession and
persistent large-scale unemployment, which have
certainly affected the employment of women more
severely than that of men, what trends can be seen
as having most influence on the future on the working lives of women? Two in particular have
received much attention. Firstly the micro-chip:
microprocessors have now come into use in a wide
variety of fields and it is confidently forecast
that before long no aspect of human activity will
remain totally unaffected by this new technology.
To cite just one example, a single micro-chip in an
electronic sewing machine replaces 350 standard
parts: similar stories can be told from telephone-

switching to food-mixers.   Already there has been a
marked decline in female employment on assembly lines
and further substantial losses of such jobs seem
inevitable, in practically every industry, the losses
probably totalling hundreds of thousands.[42]

The effects on work in offices, too, is already
considerable, as indicated previously, and this is
bound to develop further.   Secondly, and closely
related to the above is the question of '*de-skilling*'
as relatively skilled jobs (such as pattern designing
and cutting in the clothing industry or compositing
in printing) are replaced by relatively unskilled
operations.   The notion of '*de-skilling*' has been
around for more than a decade[43] but in its newest
impetus it seems likely to be particularly applicable
to jobs done by women.   The most serious effect for
women of the introduction of new technology is
undoubtedly the decline in the number of jobs but in
addition it is already bringing in its train
restricted promotion and concentration in de-skilled
work.[44]   It has also been suggested that the
increased use of VDUs, word processors and other
electronic gadgetry may lead to a considerable
increase in home-working which has been a predominantly female-centred, low-paid, area of the labour
force in which many women have felt compelled to
engage as their only chance of gaining employment.

For those women - a gradually increasing number
- who will be able to take advantage of educational
opportunities to enter professional-type careers, it
may well be that the constraints on their working
lives may gradually lessen with the extension of such
facilities as maternity leave, creches and nursery
schools, often by large employers, and with the
gradual lessening of sexual discrimination in such
careers.   But for the less fortunate women - the
great majority - in low-status jobs, for all the
reasons considered above the prospects do not look
at all good.   It therefore looks to be a strong
possibility that the next few years will see an
increased polarisation between the 'haves' and the
'have-nots' in female labour markets.

NOTES

I am grateful to Dr Jane Littlewood for helpful
comments on an earlier draft of this chapter.

  1.   See in Chapter Four.
  2.   See in Chapter Three.

3. e.g. Maria Hirszowicz, *Industrial Sociology* (Martin Robertson, 1981). There have elsewhere been suggestions that female writers are particularly at fault in this respect, e.g. by Carol Adams and Rae Laurikietis, *The Gender Trap* (Virago/Quartet Books, 1976), p.46.

4. S. Hill, *Competition and Control at Work* (Heinemann, 1981).

5. Deidre Sanders with Jane Reed, *Kitchen Sink or Swim?* (Penguin, 1982).

6. Quoted in Adams and Laurikietis, *The Gender Trap*.

7. Sanders with Reed, *Kitchen Sink or Swim?*

8. National Council for Civil Liberties, *Womens Rights* (NCCL, 1973).

9. Sue Sharpe, *Just Like a Girl* (Pelican, 1976).

10. P. Mahoney, *Schools for the Boys?* (Hutchinson, 1985).

11. V. Hannon, 'Education for Sex Equality: What's the Problem?', in D. Rubinstein (ed.), *Education and Equality* (Penguin, 1979).

12. Hannon, 'Education for Sex Equality'.

13. *Ibid.*

14. G. Joseph, *Women at Work, The British Experience* (Philip Allan, 1983). (The labour force is a wider term than the working population including, for example, those wanting to work but temporarily unemployed.)

15. S.R. Parker *et al.*, *The Sociology of Industry* (Allen & Unwin, 1981).

16. Joseph, *Women at Work*.

17. *Ibid.*

18. *Ibid.*

19. W.W. Daniel, *Maternity Rights: The Experience of Women* (Policy Studies Institute, 1980).

20. Joseph, *Women at Work*.

21. M. Woodhall, 'The Economic Returns to Investment in Women's Education', *Higher Education*, Vol.2 (1973) and reprinted in C. Baxter and others (eds), *Economics and Education Policy* (Longman, 1977).

22. J. Mincer and S. Polachek, 'Family Investments in Human Capital: Earnings of Women', *Journal of Political Economy*, Vol.82, No.2, Part 2 (1974) and reprinted in A.H. Amsden (ed.), *The Economics of Women and Work* (Penguin, 1980).

23. B.N. Seear, *Re-Entry of Women to the Labour Market After an Interruption in Employment* (OECD, 1971).

24. Jean Martin and Ceridwen Roberts, *Women and Employment, A Lifetime Perspective* (OPCS and Department of Employment, HMSO, 1984).

25. In a radio broadcast in the form of a letter to her daughter, BBC Radio 4, August 1985.
26. Sanders with Reed, *Kitchen Sink or Swim?*
27. Hill, *Competition and Control at Work.*
28. E. Garnsey, 'Women's Work and Theories of Class Stratification', *Sociology*, Vol.12, No.2 (1978).
29. R.D. Barrón and G.M. Norris, 'Sexual Divisions and the Dual Labour Market', in Diana Barker and Sheila Allen (eds), *Dependence and Exploitation in Work and Marriage* (Longman, 1976).
30. A. Pollert, *Girls, Wives, Factory Lives* (Macmillan, 1981). See also, A. Hunt, *Management Attitudes and Practices Towards Women at Work* (OPCS, HMSO, 1975).
31. Hill, *Competition and Control at Work.*
32. 'Anne', quoted in Sanders with Reed, *Kitchen Sink or Swim?*
33. Ruth Cavendish, *Women on the Line* (Routledge & Kegan Paul, 1982). ('UMO' = 'unidentifiable mechanical object', an acronym used by the author to avoid identification and possible legal proceedings.)
34. Pollert, *Girls, Wives, Factory Lives.*
35. E. Mumford and O. Banks, *The Computer and the Clerk* (Routledge & Kegan Paul, 1967), quoted in F. McNally, *Women for Hire* (Macmillan, 1979).
36. P. Elias and B. Main, *Women's Working Lives: Evidence from the National Training Survey* (Institute for Employment Research, University of Warwick, 1982).
37. J. Hurstfield, *The Part-time Trap: Part-time Workers in Britain Today* (Low Pay Unit, 1978).
38. Reported extensively in Elias and Main, *Women's Working Lives.*
39. Susan Lonsdale, *Work and Inequality* (Longman, 1985).
40. As quoted in Lonsdale, *ibid.*
41. Shirley Dex, *The Sexual Division of Work* (Harvester Press, 1985).
42. Joseph, *Women at Work.*
43. Dex, *The Sexual Division of Work,*
44. Jackie West, 'New Technology and Women's Office Work', in J. West (ed.), *Work, Women and the Labour Market* (Routledge & Kegan Paul, 1982).

Chapter Seven

THE FINANCE OF EDUCATION

As in all other comparable countries, the education
service in the UK grew remorselessly in size throughout the twentieth century until the late 1970s, and
the financing of that service also grew in both size
and complexity during the whole of that period and
especially after the Second World War.   From the
financial point of view, education has been likened
to a vast machine which now requires funding to the
extent of close on £14,000m. (in England and Wales
for 1983/84, the last available year for which
statistics have been published).

STUDIES OF EDUCATIONAL EXPENDITURE

Any commentary on the development of educational
expenditure in the UK has to start with the pioneering work of the late Professor Vaizey.   In retrospect it seems remarkable that no attempt was made
to study educational finance trends in the UK before
Vaizey published the result of his pioneering inquiry
in 1958[1] and then with Sheehan produced a follow-up
study 10 years later.[2]   Vaizey encountered a number
of difficulties with the use and interpretation of
the statistics then available but after making
various adjustments was able to express education
expenditure as a percentage of net national income
at factor cost;   this led, in his own words, to the
'*melancholy conclusion*' that the figure for 1955 was
less than that for 1932, and that over the period
1945-1950 the percentage was lower than for most pre-
war years.   When viewed against the background of
the 1944 Education Act, the claim of '*secondary
education for all*' for the first time and the
intensive post-war school building programme, these
conclusions must be seen as quite astonishing even in

150

in spite of all the economic and social problems the
country faced before and after the outbreak of war
in 1939.   To quote monetary values is problematic:
these can only be compared over time if they are
corrected to real values via a suitable (educational)
price index, and for earlier years the latter did not
exist and had to be computed.   Nevertheless, it
could be shown that total expenditure per child year
in England and Wales in 1955 amounted to £45.40.
At current prices total outlay on public expenditure
had grown from £84.6m. in 1921 to £410.6m. in 1955,
with the largest increase occurring in the years
after 1946;   at constant (1948) prices, the growth
from £128.1m. for 1921 to £300m. for 1955 represented
a real growth of 134 per cent, or 3.9 per cent per
year.   Expenditure rose fastest in those years when
the numbers of children rose fastest and the peaks of
expansion coincided with years of high economic
activity.
   Three highly critical conclusions were:

(1)   that in secondary schools expenditure per
      school child year had risen little since
      1938 (but the school life of the average
      child had lengthened by one-third);
(2)   70 per cent more was spent on the education
      of a grammar school pupil than on that of
      his or her secondary modern counterpart;
      and
(3)   there were probably grave differences in
      levels of expenditure per child in
      different geographical areas but the
      extent of these was unknown.

   It seemed that year-to-year fluctuations of the
economy had little effect on the level of educational
expenditure in real terms but they did affect its
rate of growth over time;   this operated as a gloss
on the secular trend of rising real expenditure - in
real terms total spending on education for 1955 was
twice that for 1938 and showed an increase of 66 per
cent over 1946.   Capital expenditure in real terms
did not exceed the 1932 total for the next 20 years.
   A breakdown of the total figures into functional
headings showed a striking fall in the percentage
devoted to teachers' salaries (69 per cent in 1921,
52 per cent in 1955) whereas the largest percentage
increases related to the school health service, to
meals and milk, and to heating and lighting.   Transfer payments grew from some 8 per cent of the total
in 1921 to around 14 per cent in 1938, but then fell

to around 10 per cent in 1955, the fluctuations
relating primarily to loan charges and to teachers'
superannuation payments and not to grants to pupils.
A number of separate calculations were also made for
each of primary, secondary and further education,
and secondary education was shown to be taking an
increasing share of the total education budget over
time; here also emphasis was laid on the lack of
some of the requisite statistics.

Finally, Vaizey forecast that the trends most
likely to affect the level of expenditure in future
years would be:

(i)   rising prices;
(ii) relative changes in teachers' salaries;
(iii) change in population and rise in percent-
      age of children in state schools;
(iv) rising educational standards;
(v)   raising of school leaving age;
(vi) increased demand for higher education;

and these have all been verified by the events of the
ensuing 20 years, although inevitably new problems
also arose, especially in the 1970s.

In their follow-up study, Vaizey and Sheehan
were able to report that the rapid expansion of
education after 1955 had been accompanied by a long
overdue expansion of the official education
statistics. By the mid-1960s, the education service
was taking some 5.0 per cent of gross national product and 18.9 per cent of total public expenditure.
From 1955 to 1965, whilst the number of secondary
pupils rose by 50 per cent real expenditure on them
more than doubled, the greater part of the increase
going to non-academic secondary pupils. The proportion of total educational expenditure devoted to
the secondary sector also rose, to 28 per cent by
1965 (it had been 17.7 per cent in 1920). Expenditure on secondary teachers' salaries as a proportion
of the total continued to fall, from 67 per cent in
1955 to 60 per cent in 1965, whilst the proportions
devoted to salaries paid to non-teachers, and to
'things' both rose. Total real expenditure on
public education rose by 50 per cent over 1955 to
1965 and as a percentage of gross national product
rose slowly but surely each year; over the
same period capital expenditure rose by 180 per cent
in real terms. A critical commentary on the
inequality of educational finance was provided by a
reference to the heavy weighting given to older
pupils in the rate support grant (RSG) calculations,

the effect being that the most prosperous localities received the largest grants; Tower Hamlets and Hounslow, for example, had very similar population grants for children under 15 (respectively £47,380 and £43,775) but their supplementary grants were respectively £493,699 and £806,139 - despite the fact that Hounslow would have many more children in private schools and hence being educated at no cost to the rates, and fewer children with educational disadvantages.

The calculation of the relationship between education expenditure and Gross National Product was continued in a previous work by the present writer:[3] this showed that the percentage continued to increase steadily until the peak year of 1975 when total education expenditure amounted to 7.0 per cent of GNP, after which there was a gradual decline, a decline which has continued in subsequent years: by 1983/4 the figure was less than 6 per cent. This decline was in percentage terms, educational expenditure continuing to grow in monetary terms to reach the vast total of around £14,000m. mentioned above.

EXPENDITURE IN REAL TERMS

Whether education expenditure continued to grow in real terms, i.e. in monetary terms after allowing for the effects of inflation, is a more complex matter. Inflation has to be allowed for via a suitable price index and an educational price index is computed each year by the Department of Education and Science; however, all price indices are necessarily no more than approximations and undue reliance should not be placed on their accuracy. The DES itself has always readily acknowledged this.[4] In the 1970s this point became particularly important: in the words of the DES,

> *The estimate of changes in educational expenditure in real terms is dependent on the accuracy of the price index, which, in turn, depends on the completeness of reporting by the spending authorities of changes in component prices. While the possible errors in the index which result from incomplete or delayed reporting seem unlikely to be significant when overall prices change relatively little, this may not be true during periods of rapid price change: the error margin in the price index could become significant in relation to the underlying*

153

> *real change in volume of education expenditure
> in such circumstances, and the effects would
> be even more noticeable when the cumulative
> effect is calculated. Estimates of volume
> change should therefore be interpreted with
> especial caution for years of rapid inflation
> from 1973-74 onward.*

Until the financial year 1973-4 the annual increase
in educational expenditure in real terms was often
of the order of 5, 6 or 7 per cent - it in fact
averaged just over 5.8 per cent from 1961-2 to
1973-4 inclusive. Then came a dramatic change:
from 1974-5, in the wake of the oil crisis, not only
did inflation escalate to reach the unprecedented
level of 26 per cent but any increase in GNP in real
terms was non-existent for the next few years; concomitantly measured increases in education expenditure in real terms fell to very low levels, 0.4 per
cent in 1974-5, 1.5 per cent in 1975-6, 0.6 per cent
in 1976-7. As above, the degree of approximation
involved renders problematic any attempt to calculate
whether education expenditure had in fact increased
in real terms. Subsequently the combined effects
of the worsening state of the national economy, the
successive cuts in public expenditure (including the
curbs on local authority expenditure) imposed by
both Labour and Conservative governments and the
implications of the falling numbers of pupils in
schools due to the low birth-rate, all conspired to
produce a much more depressed scenario. Far from
it being possible now to debate whether education
expenditure is falling *in real terms*, the most recent
annual White Papers on public expenditure have made
it clear that education expenditure is to fall *in
monetary terms* (with the consequence that there must
be a much more marked fall in real terms). This was
clearly shown by the figures for education expenditure by local authorities in England (i.e. leaving
aside expenditure in Scotland and Wales and that by
central government, on universities, etc.) included
in the 1985 White Paper:

(£m.)	1984/5 Budget	1985/6 Plan
Current	11,154	10,920
Capital	280	272

The figure for capital had in fact been falling
steadily since the peak of £472m. for 1980/81,

indicative of the fact that fewer new schools or extensions to schools were being built. Education continues to dominate the finances of local authorities, comprising some 44 per cent of their total recurrent expenditure, but in the expenditure of central government it is now dwarfed by the seemingly ever-increasing commitments of the Department of Health and Social Security and the Ministry of Defence. Local authority education expenditure now comprises some 8.5 per cent of all public expenditure, a significant fall from the figure of just on ten per cent for 1977-8.

STATISTICAL DATA

When Vaizey was conducting his path-breaking research he had great problems with the data then available. As he wrote later, '*The state of official statistics at that time was scandalous*'. Subsequently, no doubt thanks at least in part to his criticisms, matters improved and the Department of Education and Science eventually arranged with HMSO to publish annually six separate volumes of educational statistics, including one on finance and expenditure. Regretfully, when the education cuts were starting to bite in the early 1980s, these publications were discontinued, although they have now been resurrected in a broadly comparable form but published by the DES itself and not by HMSO.[5] There have even been some improvements in the published educational expenditure statistics in that these are now available on a regional basis, derived from the grouping together of returns from the relevant LEAs, which was not previously the case. One can for example read that one London borough, Brent, has *over five times* as many awards to students in higher education as another, Barking, just a few miles away.

In other respects, however, the situation has deteriorated. An example of the latter would be the figures for total education expenditure, for which it is remarkably difficult to follow through the trends over time: up to 1980-81 these are published for England and Wales but from 1981-82 for England only. The Department of the Environment publishes statistics of local authority expenditure[6], including education, for England and Wales, but compiled on a somewhat different basis; that therefore leaves other expenditure, including by central government, in Wales not accounted for and needing to be extrapolated. As may be imagined, none of

this makes life any easier for the would-be
researcher.   It also means that in order to
arrive at the grant total of nearly £14,000m for
1983-4 one has to proceed as follows:

(£m.)

Local authorities in England and Wales	12,160	*(Source: Department of the Environment)*
Central government - England	1,339	*(Source: DES)*
Central government - Wales	400	(extrapolating)
	13,899	

It is difficult to see the logic of the change
adopted in 1981-2, for which the DES gives no explanation and which can scarcely be saving very much
money since the relevant statistics must be available
somewhere within the government machinery.

Expenditure by Level of Education
This same fact again makes life difficult when one
wishes to consider the breakdown of total education
expenditure over the different levels of the service,
as in Table 7.1, and for the same reason it is
difficult to know what interpretation to place on
the figures given there as regards any trends over
time.   Table 7.1 does show, as would be expected,
that secondary education is much the most costly
sector, accounting for some 35 per cent of the
expenditure total shown.   The percentage spent on
primary education appeared to decline, as smaller
age-cohorts of pupils worked their way through primary schools, with a relative adjustment in favour of
further and adult education, influenced particularly
by the increased numbers of young people enrolling
in colleges.
     The rather different total figure given in
Table 7.1 for 1983-4 as compared with that quoted
above relates to the different method of compilation,
as mentioned previously: the figures in the right-hand
column are for England only.   The reference in the
last line of the table to 'and related' expenditure
covers various maintenance grants and allowances,
especially to students in higher education, transport and certain forms of assistance to needy
families.

Table 7.1:   Expenditure by Level of Education

	1977-8 (England & Wales)		1983-4 (England only)	
	£m.	%	£m.	%
Nursery schools	26.8	0.4	43.4	0.4
Primary schools	1,678.0	27.4	2,792.4	25.3
Secondary schools	2,192.0	35.7	3,927.6	35.6
Special schools	246.7	4.0	518.5	4.7
Further and adult education	990.8	16.2	1,938.9	17.6
Training of teachers – tuition	34.0	0.5	51.2	0.5
Universities	667.4	10.9	1,206.2	10.9
Other	297.0	4.8	554.5	5.0
Total education expenditure	6,132.7	100.0	11,032.9	100.0
Total education and related expenditure	7,042.6		12,526.2	

Source: Statistics of Education - Finance and Awards (Department of Education and Science, 1986).

Table 7.2 shows the results of dividing the amounts of total recurrent expenditure by numbers of pupils/students (full-time equivalent in the case of part-timers) both in current monetary terms ('out turn') and after correction to allow for inflation ('real terms') over the period from 1980-81 to 1983-84.   Even allowing for the comment made previously regarding the degree of approximation involved in making such adjustments, we can see that in real terms over that period expenditure per pupil or student continued to increase, albeit by quite small and sometimes very small amounts, for each of nursery, primary, secondary and special education, remained constant for further education excluding polytechnics but declined significantly for polytechnics (17 per cent) and marginally for universities (2 per cent). This makes it clear that the prime cause of

Table 7.2: Unit Expenditure by Level of Education

Net recurrent expenditure per FTE pupil/student (£) (England)		1980–81	1983–84
Nursery	out turn	990	1,230
	real terms	1,215	1,230
Primary	out turn	545	730
	real terms	670	730
Secondary	out turn	770	1,015
	real terms	945	1,015
Special	out turn	2,455	3,265
	real terms	3,020	3,265
Further education	out turn	1,815	2,230
(excluding polytechnics)	real terms	2,230	2,230
Polytechnics	out turn	2,930	2,990
	real terms	3,605	2,990
Universities (GB)	out turn	4,065	4,895
	real terms	5,000	4,895

Notes: (1) Within further education, unit expenditure for
non-advanced further education declined marginally.
(2) Within secondary education, unit expenditure for
16+ pupils declined from 1980–81 to 1981–82 but
then recovered.

Source: *Statistics of Education - Finance and
Awards (Department of Education and Science,
1986).*

decreasing total expenditure is in the case of schools
the declining number of pupils but in the case of
higher education the effects of successive government
cuts.
The finding that expenditure per pupil at school
has continued to increase may seem surprising in view
of the considerable volume of recent media publicity
relating to schools' financial problems. The recent
financial treatment meted out to polytechnics is
shown in sharp focus by the above figures, whereas
the universities, whose public protests have been
even more vociferous, have in fact suffered a decline
in unit expenditure which, whilst real, does not

remotely match that borne by the polytechnics. The difference between the unit cost figures for the polytechnics and the universities is a more complex matter, relating as it does to the degree of allowance that has to be made for the latter's more extensive commitments to research, and has been the subject of much public debate, but whatever allowance has to be made for research it could not match the unit expenditure differential of nearly 64 per cent in 1983-4 indicated by the figures in Table 7.2.

THE SYSTEM OF EDUCATIONAL FINANCE

All of the above relates to the method or system through which educational finance is distributed, a system that has been described as so cumbersome and so frequently altered that it is often poorly understood, including by those whose working lives are crucially affected by it.[7] Many studies of educational organisation, management and policy have either given little attention to educational finance or have ignored it completely.

Britain has what may be described as a unique system of government control of education since whereas the Department of Education and Science is the responsible arm of central government it leaves the day-to-day running of most of the education service to the 100-plus Local Education Authorities. The question of the delicate and changing relationship between the DES and the LEAs is complex and often absorbing, with the balance between them changing over time, but we must leave the reader to explore this elsewhere.[8] The DES itself is directly responsible for only a small proportion, usually around 10 per cent, of educational expenditure, and even for this expenditure many of the detailed policy decisions are taken not by the DES but by, for example, the University Grants Committee. For the remaining 90 per cent of expenditure the responsibility lies with the LEA even though, as we shall see below, the major source of the relevant finance again comes from central government: the DES has no direct say in this expenditure but is instrumental in laying down or helping to lay down a long list of educational and other requirements which may be said to predetermine how a large part of the money is spent.

Most prominent among these would be the national Burnham salary scales on which teachers are employed: experience in other countries varies from that in the USA, where there are no national salary scales for

teachers and where salaries may vary widely between
different localities, to that in France where all
teachers in state schools are the direct employees
of the Ministry of Education. Another notable
example would be the mandatory grants for students
in higher education, for which eligibility, amount
and operation of parental income scale are all
prescribed by the DES: the LEA is therefore in the
position of having to pay out grants over which it
has effectively no control, and with a requirement
which may be said to be open-ended.

There is a wide range of questions - such as
secondary school re-organisation, the development of
a core curriculum, policy relating to the 16-19 age
group, the revision of governing bodies, the
expansion of nursery education or the raising of
the school-leaving age - on which the DES enunciates
educational policy, sometimes backed by the force of
law, sometimes merely set out in Departmental
circulars, and expects the LEAs to follow its lead.
This they normally do, with only relatively rare
disagreements, which in quite exceptional cases have
had to be settled in a court of law, not always in
favour of the Secretary of State.

Clearly all such matters have expenditure connotations and the trend over the period since the
1944 Act has been for more and more such requirements
to be laid on the shoulders of LEAs, further limiting
their financial freedom, whilst it still remains true
that the LEAs retain the responsibility for the final
expenditure decisions. Thus whenever children have
been injured in schools as the result of, for example,
faulty glass doors or imperfect surfaces in playgrounds, it has always been the LEA that their
parents have been able to sue, never the DES. When
all such aspects are considered it is small wonder
that the complexities of the relationship between
the DES and the LEAs have baffled many foreign
observers and it may be said that nowhere is this
complexity more marked than in the case of educational expenditure.

The total relationship between the LEAs and
central government is, however, yet more complex:
as units of local government (save in the case of
the Inner London Education Authority) with wider
responsibilities than their major portfolio education,
the authorities come under the financial control of
the Department of the Environment (the successor to
the Ministry of Housing and Local Government) and
through it indirectly the Treasury. The Treasury is
the senior Department of central government which has

particular responsibility for the conduct of macro-
economic policy, an important part of which is the
control of public expenditure.

It is the Treasury, under the Chancellor of
the Exchequer, which gives final authorisation for
all economic policy measures including for example
the interest rate changes which are announced
periodically by the Bank of England. The Treasury
also monitors control over those other government
departments responsible for major areas of expenditure - sometimes dubbed the 'spendthrift' departments. One of the major developments over the last
20 years has been that the Treasury, in line with
one of the major recommendations in a report published by a team of visiting American economists,[9] has
sought to play an increasing role in and to exercise
tighter control over the supervision effected by the
Department of the Environment of the expenditure
plans of local authorities. Such control can be
made immediately effective because the major source
of local government finance, perhaps 60 per cent of
the total, comes from central government grant, the
balance being raised by the rating system which is
the only form of taxation open to local government
and over which the central government has again come
to exercise increasing control.

The pattern of Treasury/Department of the Environment involvement in recent years has been as
follows:

(i)   The annual White Paper on Public Expendi-
      ture specifies for each service the govern-
      ment's intentions relating to expenditure
      over the ensuing period of three years
      (formerly five) in the light of the govern-
      ment's estimates of what the country can
      afford and of government policy relating to
      that service. The forecasts for education
      will include the government's assumptions
      relating to such matters as the numbers of
      pupils in schools, pupil-teacher ratios
      (and therefore the numbers of teachers to
      be employed), higher education and capital
      expenditure.

(ii) The education expenditure budget is *cash-
      limited*, as are those for many other,
      although not all, government services.
      This means that once the total amount of
      money provided for a service has been
      specified, it will not normally be increas-
      ed subsequently, even to allow for

161

inflation. The implication of this is
that if, for example, annual salary settle-
ments are higher than the government had
anticipated, the balance of the cost has
to be found from elsewhere within the
education budget, e.g. by reducing expenditure on books or materials. From the
point of view of central government, therefore, this operates as a very tight and
effective form of financial control, but
from the point of view of the local authorities it makes their financial planning
very difficult.

(iii) Guidance will be given to local authorities
regarding their maximum permitted expenditure during the year, usually via the
specification of a maximum rate of
increase (usually quite low) over the
expenditure of the previous year. Individual authorites which exceed this rate
of increase have in recent years had
imposed on them a financial penalty, known
as 'rate capping', under which they have
forfeited part of their grant from central
government. The tendency has been for
such rate-capping to be applied to, i.e.
for part of central government grant to be
withdrawn from, those Labour-controlled
councils in more deprived areas who have
tended to overspend and whose education
services may be said to have been in greatest need. This has to be seen in the
context of the succession of 'cuts' which
have been applied to education under both
Labour and Conservative administrations
but with increasing severity since the
return to power of the present Conservative
government in 1979.

THE RATE SUPPORT GRANT

Central government grants to local authorities have
existed in some form or other since the nineteenth
century but the present system may be said to date
from the introduction of the Rate Support Grant
(RSG) in 1967. It is based on a block grant to
each authority, supplemented by additional specific
allowances for nominated activities, notably urban
aid and the police. The amount each authority
receives derives from a complex formula which tries

to take account of the wide variety of circumstances in which the authority finds itself, including, for example, population, number of children of school age and a variety of other educational variables, number of elderly people and product of a penny rate (which in Sutton, Surrey, raises about double what it would in South Tyneside). The needs element and the resource equalisation element in the formula attempt to lessen the wide inequalities between local authorities in different parts of the country, but they have never succeeded in doing this very effectively. To cite just one aspect of a large problem, affluent authorities such as Surrey or Sussex have high staying-on rates and therefore large numbers of pupils to be catered for in the sixth forms of their schools (even after allowing for the fact that they will have larger proportions of each age cohort in independent schools) and each such sixth-form pupil attracts additional grant. This is clearly needed if the education is to be provided and yet it aggravates the problem of inter-authority inequality. The grant also includes a domestic rate relief component in order to reduce the rating bills of local householders.

Since 1981/2 the annual calculation of the RSG has supposedly been simplified. For each authority its Grant Related Expenditure (GRE) is first assessed, much on the lines indicated above but intended to give a clearer picture of each authority's requirements. In reality even more variables are now included than previously and whether there has really been much simplification or whether the purpose of the change was overtly political is rather a moot point:

> The criticisms of complexity and influences of political whim levelled at the needs element remain. The rationale may be clearer, but, intentionally, by adding so many additional factors to the calculation understanding has not been assisted. In addition, by adjusting variables and dominating the whole process of calculation, government retains control and is enabled to pursue its political objectives. Indeed that was a powerful motivation when initiating the change.[10]

The concept of GRE has, however, introduced some normative notion of what *ought* to be spent because it includes a notional unit cost for each service; this in turn is related to the Grant Related Poundage (GRP)

163

for each authority to determine how much grant it should receive. The importance of all this for the financing of education, much the largest of the services provided by local authorities, is obviously crucial and educational needs play a major role in the annual grant negotiations.

There have been a series of attempts to reform the whole system of local government finance over the last 30 years or more but most have foundered on the fact that central government has been unwilling to give local authorities additional powers to levy local taxation. Britain has less local taxation than most other countries but it does not seem likely that this will change. The Conservative government is on record as saying that it would like to abolish the rating system but no obvious successor has emerged; the government would also like to reduce local authorities' dependence on the annual grant but in view of their heavy commitments it is not easy to see how this could be achieved. One possibility that has been mooted is that part or all of the financing of education, possibly teachers' salaries for example, might be taken away from local authorities and be paid directly from the DES, but local authority organisations have always opposed what they see as a possible diminution of their power. There have also been arguments relating to an earmarked block grant for education, separate from the remainder of local authority finance, including a proposal from the Society of Education Officers.[11] Whether the education service would really benefit from either of such major changes must depend on the details of any scheme and on whether the total level of finance would increase or decrease. Drawing on the experiences of other countries, there does not seem to be any particular merit in regarding education as essentially a local authority service, yet this perhaps typical British compromise has, for all the criticism it has attracted, generally worked well for more than 40 years and great care would have to be taken over the implementation of any radical change.

Leaving aside the Inner London Education Authority which is a special case deriving its finance by precept upon the London borough authorities, each LEA exists within the wider framework of either a County Council or a Metropolitan District Council and the relationship between the LEA and its parent authority is complex. At its simplest level the former may be seen as having the largest spending requirement in respect of the financial income

raised or received by the latter, but at a more
involved level the LEA may be seen as having to
persuade the latter of the need for the various
elements of the service.   The main vehicle for
doing so will be the annual education budget which
will be drawn up by the Chief Education Officer and
his staff for presentation to the Education Committee,
consisting cf elected members, and then onward presentation to the full Council (probably via a Finance
or General Purposes Committee), through its Chief
Executive.

In addition, therefore, to all the national-
local negotiation referred to previously, there now
takes place a great deal of what might be called
local-local negotiation centring on the preparation
of the education budget.   This budget will include
within it financial provision for the implementation
of all the LEA's policies and it therefore embodies
key priorities.   Necessarily, however, the greater
part of the expenditure represents a continuation of
the local education system from the previous year and
in that sense is outside the LEA's immediate control
but budget choices and the determination of educational priorities do take place at the margin.

CRITICISMS OF THE SYSTEM

Finally, it is interesting to note that when Chief
Education Officers or the equivalent have commented
publicly on the system for financing education in
this country, they have almost always been very
critical, particularly in terms of what they have
seen as their lack of freedom to get on with doing
the job they were appointed to do.   Thus one Chief
Education Officer wrote:

> ... *the over-riding impression is of a*
> *precarious, indirect, insensitive and cumber-*
> *some method of financing education.   In any*
> *severe cutback of grants to local authorities*
> *education must perforce suffer most, whatever*
> *plans the Secretary of State has in mind for*
> *the service*[12]

whilst Mr P. Newsam, the then Education Officer of
the Inner London Education Authority, attacked
'*mismanagement, inefficiency and unwise spending in*
education', described the financing of education as
'*a stupefyingly inefficient business*' and commented,
'*we don't really want more money.   All we need is*

to be able to stop wasting the money we've got'.[13]
Another similar comment read:

> *The present system does not encourage head
> teachers to be cost conscious except within
> narrow limits and along well-trodden paths
> ... the present methods of allocating non-
> teaching staff to schools can be wasteful,
> frustrating, and tend to inhibit experiment
> or change ... head teachers and the teachers'
> professional associations, administrators in
> the education department, the authority's
> treasurer and his staff, must show a greater
> willingness than has generally been evident
> in the past to think, plan and work together
> as trustful partners in a common enterprise.*[14]

In the 1980s that background of frustration
with the workings of the system combined with the
effects of successive annual cuts in public expenditure produced an extremely difficult situation for
Chief Education Officers and their staffs.   Small
wonder then that they reacted sharply to the new
series of annual reports on the state of the
education service issued by Her Majesty's Inspectorate, one arm of the DES.   This reaction seems to
have stemmed partly from the critical tone of the
reports, which will be dealt with in more detail in
the next chapter, and partly from the fact that these
were entitled *'Report on the Effects of Local
Education Authorities' Expenditure Policies'* whereas
from the point of view of the LEAs it was the *central
government* that had to bear responsibility for the
admittedly deteriorating situation.   This brings us
on to the question of the resources actually available to schools, which is dealt with in the next
chapter.

NOTES

1.   J. Vaizey, *The Costs of Education* (Allen &
Unwin, 1958).
2.   J. Vaizey and J. Sheehan, *Resources for
Education* (Allen & Unwin, 1968).
3.   J.R. Hough, *A Study of School Costs* (NFER,
Nelson, 1981).
4.   See comments in *Statistics of Education*,
Vol.5, formerly published annually (Department of
Education and Science, HMSO).
5.   *Statistics of Education* (five volumes

annually) (Department of Education and Science).

6. *Local Government Financial Statistics* (annually) (Department of the Environment, HMSO).

7. W.F. Dennison, *Educational Finance and Resources* (Croom Helm, 1984). Other material in this section also draws on this useful book.

8. See e.g. M. Shipman, 'The United Kingdom', in J.R. Hough (ed.), *Educational Policy, An International Survey* (Croom Helm, 1984).

9. R. Caves (ed.), *Britain's Economic Prospects* (Brookings Institute, Allen & Unwin, 1968).

10. Dennison, *Educational Finance and Resources*.

11. Society of Education Officers, Occasional Paper No.2, 'Education Block Grant: How It Could Work', Supplement to *Education*, 25 June 1982.

12. D. Birley, *The Education Officer and his World* (Routledge & Kegan Paul, 1970).

13. P. Newsam, 'Mismanaging of the Schools', *The Guardian*, 27 March 1979.

14. R. Burton, 'Education Finance at Local Level', in G. Taylor (ed.), *The Teacher as Manager* (National Council for Educational Technology).

Chapter Eight

SCHOOL COSTS AND RESOURCES

The previous chapter leads on directly to a consideration of the inequalities in levels of expenditure
between LEAs and, even more crucially, between
individual schools, i.e. to school costs and
resources.   Although some attention had previously
been paid to inter-LEA inequalities, in retrospect
it seems remarkable that no major study of costs and
resources at the level of individual schools in
England and Wales appeared until a previous work by
the present writer was published in 1981.[1]

PREVIOUS RESEARCH

Within the UK, much the most serious earlier attempt
at such research took place in Scotland, by Cumming,[2]
over 15 years ago, its principal findings being as
follows:

(i)   clear evidence for economies of scale for
       primary schools;
(ii)   *no* clear evidence for economies of scale
       for secondary schools *'because of the
       paucity and variety of secondary schools'*;
(iii) teachers' salaries per pupil in secondary
       schools were approximately double those in
       primary schools, due both to their better
       qualifications and to smaller class sizes;
(iv)   *'no obvious connection exists between unit
       outlays on salaries/wages and size and
       type of secondary school'*;
(v)   expenditure per head on educational equip-
       ment in secondary schools was nearly 3½
       times that in primary schools;
(vi)   calculations to allocate teaching costs
       over various school subjects resulted in

the finding that average teaching costs *per pupil period* varied from the high of classics (£6.40) to the low of modern studies (£1.54) whilst on a *per pupil* basis the range was from £36.70 (classics) to £3.83 (music);

(vii) a number of problems implicit in such calculations were admitted, for example:

(a) no data was collected on how the age or experience of teachers might affect the results and this '*could affect the figures by 100 per cent*';

(b) '*it would be easy to dispute the allocation of the responsibility allowance element of a teacher's salary to the head "school adminis-tration" (as opposed to teaching costs)*'; and

(c) statistics for some schools were distorted by cyclical items occurring in the period studied - e.g. the painting of schools on a 5-year cycle.

Studies at LEA Level

Other relevant research in the UK is fragmented and is mostly at the level of LEAs rather than of individual schools.   One of the most detailed pieces of research at LEA level was that by Eileen Byrne[3] who studied the allocation of educational resources within three authorities, the cities of Lincoln and Nottingham and the county of Northumber-land, over the 20-year period to 1965.   All three authorities had differential schemes for school allowances, to provide additional money for older and more intelligent secondary pupils, yet three-quarters of all heads were shown to disapprove of such differentials for pupils under or over 16. The study found '*inherent inequality*' throughout the school system in connection with patterns of expenditure and the allocation of resources: that grammar schools should have higher expenditure per pupil for such items as teachers' salaries and capitation was only to be expected, yet, more sur-prisingly, a similar differential was also found for the maintenance of buildings.   Within a school, GCE and CSE groups tended to be '*subsidised*' by other classes;   smaller schools, rural schools and second-ary modern schools, typically could offer only a limited range of subjects and less adequate facilities.   Over time it seemed doubtful whether

nominal monetary expenditure had risen quickly enough
to maintain the same real expenditure per pupil and
at times of, for example, large salary increases for
teachers, the LEAs pruned other areas of expenditure
to compensate.   There was clear evidence of considerable problems and inconsistencies arising out
of centralised directions from the Ministry of
Education, later the Department of Education and
Science.   The Ministry issued a steady stream of
recommendations urging desirable educational developments of various kinds whilst not allowing LEAs any
extra grants or even sometimes approvals for building work to go ahead;   even in 1974 the Department
insisted on a level of overcrowding of 15 per cent
in all secondary schools before permitting new
building.   Frequently optimistic public statements
relating to expansion of, and improvements in, the
educational service, were accompanied by cuts in
expenditure and grants in real terms.   The Ministry
constantly overrode the wishes of LEAs on a variety
of matters, so that from the point of view of the
LEA it seemed that rather little real local autonomy
remained, and control by the Ministry seemed to have
increased over time.

Regarding the three LEAs studied, Lincoln for
many years seemed preoccupied by its grammar schools,
for instance in the way it concentrated capital
expenditure on them, to the detriment of secondary
modern schools (in which pupils were banned from
taking external examinations right up to 1962);
Nottingham, on the other hand, had developed bilat-
eral schools by the late 1950s, spent relatively more
than other authorities on secondary modern pupils and
was so concerned to raise standards that over time
its rate of increase of secondary school expenditure
was greater than the rate of growth of pupil numbers
(as would, of course, be the case with many other
LEAs).   Northumberland was shown to be a poorer
authority than either Lincoln or Nottingham, with
only 15 per cent of pupils in grammar schools, GCE
performance rates well below the national average
and many pupils leaving school underachieving by
national standards;   yet the authority appeared to
favour prestige innovatory projects at the expense
of basic standards and often refused to co-operate
with central government suggestions, as when the
county instructed its planning committee to refuse
planning consent to prefabricated huts designed by
the Ministry of Works to cope with the raising of
the school leaving age.   There was again substantial
imbalance in spending in favour of grammar school

pupils, also in favour of schools in new buildings
or with new head teachers, both of which fared
better than average for additional resources.

Overall, Eileen Byrne reported that, whilst no
single identifiable pattern of resource allocation
could be deduced, it seemed clear that inequalities
between areas had widened, not narrowed, over time,
including since the 1974 re-organisation. A *'cycle
of deprivation'* arose from the fact that additional
resources each year were allocated on a percentage
basis, so that those areas poorly equipped in the
1940s were effectively discriminated against;
building programmes never matched the increases in
number of pupils and most schools remained severely
overcrowded. Even rating revaluations were shown
to favour the richest areas most, because of their
higher incidence of industrial property, and as a
consequence their future financial problems were
eased. A major conclusion was a call for much more
information and research relating to expenditure and
resource allocation patterns on the part of local
education authorities.

The latter point was reiterated strongly by the
only other study to investigate in depth the provision of educational resources by individual LEAs,
that by Byrne, Williamson and Fletcher.[4] Their
objective was to, *'Measure the precise contribution
which system inputs make to variations in rates of
educational attainment'* and they proceeded to
identify 69 separate variables, to represent *'total
material environment'*, *'LEA's policy'* and *'educational attainment'*, which were then applied to a
number of LEAs.

The latter evidenced wide disparities: Merthyr
Tydfil and Wigan were both relatively poor areas
with low rateable values but whereas levels of
educational expenditure and achievement were high in
the former they were low in the latter, Wigan being
an example of a predominantly working-class authority taking an elitist view of its grammar schools
and spending heavily on them. Solihull, a prosperous and mainly middle-class suburb of Birmingham
had more than twice as many children in private
schools as the national average but even so the LEA
schools had exceptionally high involvement by the
parent-teacher associations in the life of and the
provision of additional resources (for example,
swimming pools) for the schools, and the schools
recorded high levels of educational attainment.
This was in contrast to Blackpool whose above-average
social-class composition was not reflected in high

171

success rates in education due to the local authority's policy of keeping down the local rate, and
therefore the level of educational expenditure.
Evident disparities within the area of one LEA were
also noted, a particular example being Bristol.
The study found, *inter alia*, that poor provision in
primary schools was strongly associated with poor
provision in secondary schools, and that various
indicators of educational attainment were much more
positively correlated with measures of *'social class
plus provision plus environmental factors'* (R^2 =
c.0.70) than with measures of social class alone
R^2 = c.0.35).   Some 30 years after the 1944 Education Act, concluded Byrne, Williamson and Fletcher,
far from providing equality of opportunity, our
schooling system evidenced a considerable degree of
territorial injustice and sustained political pressure would be needed to effect any substantial improvement.

Practically no other studies of educational
expenditure, wholly or partially at the local authority level, appear to exist.   One comparison of
education services of a relatively deprived London
borough (West Ham) and a rather more affluent Berk-
shire town (Reading) contained much descriptive
material but little or no information regarding
expenditure or resource allocation, save for a
reference to the, *'need for more sophisticated and
rigorous studies of ... costs and effectiveness'*.[5]
In each case the system was shown to be well if
rather autocratically administered by powerful
Education Department officials, with little or no
active local participation.   Boaden[6] examined the
needs, dispositions and resources of county boroughs
for a number of their services, including education;
and found wide variations.   The amount spent on
education in the county boroughs per 1,000 population, for example, varied from £17,263 to £28,093,
but not in the way that might be imagined: some
'poor' authorities spent highly on education and
vice versa and there were no clear patterns of
correlation between expenditure on education and
expenditure on related social services such as the
welfare and children's departments.   Expenditure,
as shown by simple correlation calculations, tended
to be higher where the borough had a lower social-
class composition, was relatively poorer or was
Labour-controlled, but the correlations are only of
the order of 0.5 or less.   Since these three independent variables (and others quoted) are obviously
strongly inter-correlated, partial correlations were

calculated to control for the effect of each in turn
but the only clear conclusion that was not intuitively obvious appeared to be that social class composition exerted no independent effect.

Pratt, Burgess *et al.*[7] used the expenditure and
other educational statistics for each LEA published
annually by the Chartered Institute of Public Finance
and Accountancy (CIPFA). These list for each LEA,
and for each of the primary, secondary, special
schools and further education sectors, expenditure
on such headings as teachers' salaries, non-teachers'
salaries, repair and maintenance of buildings, books,
educational equipment and various other headings,
together with total net expenditure. Unfortunately
it is widely agreed that the potential usefulness of
the CIPFA statistics is greatly diminished by the
fact that the basis on which they are prepared is not
standardised from one LEA to another, quite apart
from the fact that some LEAs are unable to provide
all the information requested. Further, even with
the figures that are published, considerable care in
interpretation is needed and the reader needs to be
aware of the sometimes intricate conceptual and
measurement problems involved and of the adjustments
that may be necessary before meaningful conclusions
can be drawn. Particularly this is true regarding
inter-authority comparisons: the heterogeneity of
LEAs' accounting practices in fact bedevils almost
any attempt to do serious research in the field of
school costs at LEA level: the accounting system in
use by LEAs have in the past varied widely although
they have gradually become more standardised in
recent years. Some LEAs still do not know how much
one of their schools costs to run although in this
respect the situation has greatly improved since most
LEAs have computerised their systems of accounts and
record-keeping.

Pratt, Burgess *et al.* found wide disparities
between the levels of expenditure by different LEAs
and subsequently found that those disparities largely
continued unchanged three years later.[8] Particularly
revealing was the finer detail included in the
accompanying case studies of three LEAs, Doncaster,
Bootle and Wiltshire. Regarding Bootle, for example,
the authors write:

> *The real trouble in Bootle's case is that*
> *resources must be spread very thinly. By our*
> *resources index it is one of the poorest auth-*
> *orities in England and Wales. Thus there is*
> *very little margin for error and, when mistakes*

are made, the effect is often drastic - and tragic. When the plans for establishing Educational Priority Areas were announced by the government, the Bootle council failed to apply on the grounds that no one school within the authority could be singled out as being much worse than any other. The result was that Bootle lost some valuable government aid.

Vandalism is a problem in many of the authority's schools. Windows are the obvious targets, and some schools seem to undergo attacks of window-smashing several times a term. The authority cannot replace the windows quickly and, on many buildings, vast rows of plyboard wait patiently to be replaced. Litter also seems to be ubiquitous. Even at one of the newer primary schools the grounds were covered with a fine layer of small bits of paper, broken glass and other refuse.

The lessons of Bootle are clear: nothing short of massive outside help will turn the tide. After more than 100 years of progressive legis- lation in education, Bootle still struggles with its appalling problems. And Bootle is not alone. All over the North of England there are authorities suffering from the same or similar problems. There are many auth- orities that do not have enough money to ensure that adequate facilities are waiting for pupils at newly reorganised schools, or can't afford to provide for all their pupils kept on by the new school-leaving age. There are local auth- orities which cannot even afford to pick up the broken glass from outside a primary school.

The CIPFA statistics were subsequently used by Hough (1981) to show that in 1975-6 net expenditure per pupil varied from £366 (Leeds) to £594 (ILEA), i.e. some 63 per cent more, although allowance would obviously have to be made for higher costs in central London. Harrow, for example, spent over 60 per cent more per pupil on teachers' salaries than Leeds whilst ILEA spent *over twelve times as much* on educational equipment as Rochdale and Bed- fordshire spent *nine times as much* on books as Durham. Predictably most northern LEAs were able to spend less on education than their typically more affluent southern counterparts but it was a surprise that an authority with one of the most favourable pupil-teacher ratios was Newcastle-on-Tyne (15.8) whilst one of the least favourable was the Isle of Wight (19.5, i.e. nearly 25 per cent worse). Overall the levels of inter-LEA inequalities had remained much the same over the years, as indeed they have continued to do until the present day. Mention should also be made of one more recent study of inter-LEA inequalities, that by Lord, where the emphasis was on cost-effectiveness and 'value for money'.[9]

EVIDENCE FROM OVERSEAS

As may be imagined, in contrast to the lack of hard evidence relating to school costs and resources available for the UK, much interesting work has been carried out in other countries.

For anyone embarking on a serious study of educational costs one of the most interesting of all the items of reading available to date is a volume by Coombs and Hallak[10] which, whilst containing some data relating to developed countries including the UK, refers primarily to education systems in developing countries overseas. The book contains many words of caution for administrators in such countries setting up or expanding education systems and urges them, in terms which also seem relevant to this country, to identify and collect a variety of reliable cost data. Thus when Coombs and Hallak write: *'all budget figures and statements of expenditures should be used with extreme caution and discernment'* and *'cost analysis has become imperative ... but is ... still in a relatively primitive state'*, it would be difficult to exonerate the UK from the criticisms implied. When we find the authors urging developing countries to make detailed studies of comparative costs for different types of secondary schools, such as different sizes of school, single sex or co-educational, selective or comprehensive, rural or urban, it is difficult not to be struck by a feeling of irony in that for the UK, which has had a system of compulsory education for over 100 years, no such studies exist. Thus Coombs and Hallak write that, for the countries in which they are interested, it is usually,

> *impossible to tell, for example, how much was*
> *spent for first graders as against second*
> *graders, or for learning to read and write as*
> *against learning arithmetic, or for what goes*

175

> *on inside the classrooms as against other*
> *school costs ... these shortcomings reflect*
> *the fact that education budgets were originally*
> *designed to serve the purpose of appropriations*
> *bodies and auditors, not the needs of edu-*
> *cational planning and management ... cost*
> *analysis ... has now become essential ...*
> *budgetary accounts will have to be modified*
> *and amplified.*

From the many other aspects of school costs discussed
in this book particular mention may be made of the
effect that inflation (which is typically a far more
serious problem in developing than in developed
countries) was found to have on educational spending:

> *budgets and salaries almost invariably lag*
> *behind the general rise in prices and wages,*
> *thereby robbing education's real purchasing*
> *power and reducing its ability to attract*
> *and hold good teachers and administrators.*

Finally, a last quotation may serve to illustrate
the conviction of Coombs and Hallak that a certain
hard-headedness of attitude, concomitant with paying
more attention to economic criteria, may be highly
desirable in education systems:

> *... the romance and nostalgia which adults*
> *often feel for the one-room village school can*
> *impose heavy penalties on their children's*
> *education and on the public purse.   A pre-*
> *requisite for being able to afford good schools*
> *is that they be of at least the minimim size*
> *that is economically and pedagogically viable.*

The book was accompanied by a further three volumes
of case studies relating to school costs, which contained a total of over 30 separate detailed studies
drawn from developing countries all round the world.
    Of experience in other countries, much the most
interesting relates to the long period of attempts
in the USA to alter the legislative arrangements for
allocating funds and resources between school districts and between individual schools, summarised as:

> *a frenetic period of litigation to overturn*
> *those state school finance systems which pro-*
> *duced wealth-related disparities in per pupil*
> *spending among districts within a state.*[11]

Although there had been some previous litigation, nation-wide interest in inequalities in the financing of schools was raised by the case of *Serrano v. Priest* before the California Supreme Court in 1971 in which the court decided that the quality of a child's education could not be a function of the wealth of his parents and neighbours without violating the Fourteenth Amendment to the Constitution of the United States, which refers to the *'fundamental rights'* of US citizens.   In 1973, however, in the case of *San Antonia Independent School District v. Rodriguez*, the United States Supreme Court reversed the above decision: it held that education was not a *'fundamental right'* under either the Fourteenth Amendment or any other part of the US Constitution and that plaintiffs could only rely on any provision in the constitution of each state which might prescribe that the provision of education was an obligation on that state.   Just one month later, in the case of *Robinson v. Cahill*, the New Jersey Supreme Court ruled that inequalities in the financing of schools must cease in that they did violate the state constitution which required the provision of *'a thorough and efficient system of free public schools'*.

By February 1974, 59 such cases had been filed in more than 30 states.   In the period of 18 months following the Rodriguez case, seven states were ordered by their state courts to revise their school finance systems;   thereafter the pace slowed but in the ensuing four years this situation was repeated in a further four states;   both litigation and related legislative reforms have continued ever since.   This is not the place to consider all the legal niceties involved but a number of relevant economic issues do arise.   Firstly, how equal do school expenditures in different districts have to be, i.e. what degree of variation is permitted? The California State Court ruled: *'the state may not ... permit ... significant disparities in expenditures between school districts ... disparities must be reduced to amounts considerably less than $100 per pupil'*.   Why $100?   Is this figure inflation-proof, or will it need to be revised annually?   How is 'considerably' defined?   Secondly, would equalisation of annual expenditure in dollars be a good thing and would it necessarily induce greater equality of educational provision?   The New York Supreme Court accepted the submission of the four largest cities in New York State that it would not: these cities argued that they faced a combination of

177

exceptionally high costs and an above average proportion of disadvantaged students for whom high
levels of expenditure were required.   The Court
held that the school systems must seek to equalise
educational output rather than input, such output
being defined as: 'that educational opportunity
which is needed in the contemporary setting to equip
a child for his role as a citizen and as a competitor
in the labour market'.

The problems involved in interpreting and/or
enforcing by law such a vague statement seem on the
face of it to be insurmountable.   A somewhat similar, if more specific, approach was adopted by the
Seattle, Washington, Court which suggested that
standards of schooling in Seattle must be raised to
at least the average for the rest of the state: on
one calculation this would have required expenditure
on education in Seattle to be raised immediately
from $47.3m. to $72.8m. (for 1975-6).   Other
courts (in New Jersey and Texas) have held that a
minimum adequate standard of education must be provided in all districts, above which variations may
be permitted, whilst the California Supreme Court
held: 'that parent-taxpayers of children in some
school districts may not be required to pay significantly higher tax rates than parent-taxpayers in
other school districts'.

New laws have been passed in many states to
include such measures as maximum tax rates, maximum
revenue levels, ceilings on the annual rate of
increase in per pupil expenditure, or changes in
measures of district wealth, and in most of these
states further lawsuits have followed to challenge
the new measures.   (One commentator illustrates the
clash of interests by showing that in many states
traditionally such issues have been decided by
referenda, in which only property owners have been
permitted to vote.)   The ensuing position has become
extremely complex, with considerable variations from
one state to the next and few states left unaffected.
One report argues strongly that in many states the
education statistics available do not enable one to
identify whether inequality exists in any meaningful
sense, and, if so, to what extent: 'most states do
not have the capability to conduct a systematic
analysis of their own school finance programme'.

To seek to equalise educational expenditure at
the level of school districts might seem a daunting
enough task but in a further, highly publicised law-
suit, *Hobson v. Hansen*, before the Washington D.C.
Court, the issue was that of unequal levels of

expenditure between individual schools within a
district (i.e. instead of district school boards
suing the state, a board found itself being sued by
a parent). This case was also noteworthy in that
prominent economists were invited to present the
economic and statistical arguments to be put forward
by each side. Regrettably, however, the Judge had
to find not only that parts of their report were in
such technical language that they could not be read
or understood by laymen but also:

> *the studies by both experts are tainted by a
> vice well known in the statistical trade -
> data shopping and scanning to reach a pre-
> conceived result; and the court has had to
> reject parts of both reports as unreliable
> because biased.*

Differences in per-pupil spending in the public
school system of Washington D.C. were, of course,
viewed by the plaintiff and the bodies supporting
him as an aspect of racial segregation: the under-
privileged schools containing largely black children
were shown to have worse pupil/teacher ratios, less
well qualified and less well paid teachers, and lower
expenditures per pupil, than other schools. A major
counter-argument put forward by the defence was that
since substantial economies of scale existed in the
larger schools, no conclusions regarding inequality
of educational provision could be drawn. To these
and other points (for example that predominantly
white schools had older and longer-serving teachers
who were naturally on higher salaries), the court
ruled that *'dollars count unless proven otherwise'*
and the defendants were largely unable to prove their
assertions to the satisfaction of the court.

The court considered that expenditure on such
items as heating or vandalism might vary widely for
a number of good reasons and even such items as
teaching materials, text books and field trips were
considered problematical so no order was made about
any of these; for teachers' salaries and benefit
expenditures, however, the court ordered that, in the
district of Columbia, *'expenditures ... in any
single elementary school ... shall not deviate by
more than 5 per cent from the mean per-pupil expenditure for all teachers' salaries and benefits'*. As
a consequence the school board has had subsequently
to embark on a programme of transferring some of its
more highly paid teachers to some of the more under-
privileged schools.[12]

Such great interest has developed in these
questions in the USA that specialist centres have
been set up at a number of university campuses and
elsewhere to make detailed studies of the area of
educational finance. *The Journal of Education
Finance* regularly publishes the results of such
studies.

There have been many other studies of various
aspects of educational finance in different countries,
especially the USA, but space does not permit a complete review of these here. For a comprehensive
bibliography, the reader is referred to Hough (1981).

INTER-SCHOOL DIFFERENCES

Reverting to the UK, research into school costs and
resources at the level of individual schools in
England and Wales may be said to have commenced with
the research reported in Hough (1981), since previously no major work existed. That research made a
detailed study of the costs and resources over a
period of three years of the schools within the areas
of four LEAs who had agreed to co-operate with the
project. The initial intention was to concentrate
on secondary schools but considerable data relating
to primary schools also became available. After
emphasising the problems involved in defining costs
and in any attempts to make such comparisons, the
main finding was the remarkably wide variation in
the levels of expenditure per pupil between apparently comparable schools within each of the four
LEAs. Leaving aside definition problems and concentrating on recurrent expenditure per pupil, within each LEA expenditure per pupil at the '*most
expensive*' secondary school was almost always at
least twice as much, and occasionally three times or
even four times as much, as at the '*least expensive*'
school. Even if it might be thought that looking
at the extremes of the range of school costs in this
way might be unrepresentative, the large standard
deviations (expressed as percentage of the mean unit
costs) showed that within each LEA's secondary
schools wide variations existed throughout.

Even when each LEA's secondary schools were
subdivided into apparently homogeneous groups, whilst
the variations in levels of expenditure per pupil
were less extreme, they were still considerable and
it still often happened that within a homogeneous
group of schools one 'cost' twice as much to run as
another, with again standard deviations often being

of the order of 10 per cent.   As might have been
expected there was a clear pattern of significantly
higher expenditure per pupil in grammar and technical
schools than in secondary modern schools, in upper
schools than in high schools, in comprehensive 11-16
schools than in middle schools and in comprehensive
11-18 schools than in comprehensive 11-16 schools.
Less expected was the finding that in one of the
LEAs in one of the years studied, expenditure per
pupil in comprehensive schools overtook that in
grammar schools and subsequently forged further
ahead.

Primary schools had, as expected, substantially
lower levels of expenditure per pupil than secondary
schools and in some of the LEA areas these would have
been even lower but for the fact that they were bol-
stered up by the very small rural primary schools
which existed and which were very expensive to run
in per pupil terms.   These schools had the highest
maximum unit cost figures, in one case as much as
seven times the level of expenditure per pupil in
the 'cheapest' school.   Throughout, primary schools
evidenced wide variations, broadly comparable to
those in secondary schools.

Much the largest single item constituting
recurrent expenditure in a school obviously relates
to teachers' salaries and this item was found to
comprise some two-thirds of the total, often more
when 'on-costs' were included.   To some extent,
although not uniformly so, the percentage was higher
in grammar schools or upper schools, presumably
reflecting the more highly-qualified and highly-paid
staff and/or favourable pupil/teacher ratios in such
schools.   Of the four LEAs, one consistently devoted
a greater proportion to teachers' salaries whilst
one other consistently did the reverse.

An examination of correlation coefficients
between constituent items of recurrent expenditure
per pupil found much the strongest positive relationship, up to a correlation coefficient of 0.92, to
exist between teachers' salaries and non-teachers'
salaries, i.e. salaries of other staff in each
school.   The implication was that where a school had
a highly-qualified and highly-paid teaching staff
and/or favourable pupil/teacher ratio, it also had a
high level of support staff, and vice versa.   No
other constituent item evidenced such a strong and
consistent pattern but expenditure per pupil on such
items as fixtures and fittings, books and periodicals,
rent and rates (reflecting size of building space and
land area) and equipment, all tended to show positive

181

association with expenditure per pupil on teachers'
salaries, albeit with smaller coefficients and lower
levels of significance than the item of non-teachers'
salaries discussed previously. For most of the
other constituent items of expenditure, any pattern
of correlation was weak or even non-existent. It
should perhaps be emphasised that all such comments
have nothing to do with the fact that, for example,
grammar schools have always tended to be better
staffed and better equipped than secondary modern
schools: all of the comments regarding the correlation coefficients refer to patterns of association
within homogeneous sub-groups of schools.

Finally, the same research examined the question
of economies of scale or size in schools. This is
a concept with a long history in the field of industrial economics where, almost universally, large-
scale production can be shown to be more cost-
effective per unit than that on a smaller scale, and
where it is sometimes possible to demonstrate an
'optimum' (in the sense of lowest cost) size. More
recently the same notion has been applied to schools,
particularly in the USA, where the evidence for
economies of size is considerable but uneven and
inconclusive, and where calculations of 'optimum'
size have produced results which have varied widely
from around 900 pupils to around 2,500 pupils.
(American schools are, of course, typically larger
than those in the UK or Western Europe.) It cannot
be emphasised too strongly that all such studies have
always related solely to cost, i.e. to recurrent
expenditure per pupil, and have not been able to take
account of any possible variations in the *quality* of
education, or indeed of any other educational factors,
found in schools of different size. This is obviously a considerable limitation and it implies an
immediate caveat in connection with any possible
attempt to make use of evidence of economies of
size in schools for the purposes of educational
policy.

All such studies have always focused on recurrent
expenditure per pupil, data relating to capital costs
almost always being unavailable on an individual
school basis. In any event the use of capital-type
data would always be problematic: present payments
for school buildings and other fixed investments
embrace both servicing charges and repayment of principal and these will vary widely according to the age
and type of building, what cost limits were in operation at the time of construction, prevailing rate of
interest, whether the debt was borrowed at fixed or

fluctuating interest rate, and over how long a
period the debt is being amortised. LEAs have
indicated that their total borrowing comprises a
number of loans contracted at different dates and at
varying rates of interest and they would have no way
of apportioning some part of these to individual
schools. Nevertheless it can be said with confidence that economies of scale do operate at the
capital level. The DES has indicated that it
expects per pupil construction costs typically to be
lower for schools of larger size and has always fixed
cost ceilings for school buildings on that basis, the
rationale being that communal facilities, such as a
hall or gymnasium, are less costly on a per pupil
basis in larger schools. Where, therefore, evidence
for economies of size can be found from examination
solely of recurrent operating costs, the result must
understate the total scale effect.

The statistical problems relating to calculations of economies of size are complex and are
explored in detail in Hough (1981). Suffice it to
say here that the main findings from this research
were:

(i)   There was very clear evidence for economies
       of size in primary schools, with the
       largest schools having the lowest per pupil
       average costs; no minimum point emerged.
(ii)   When secondary schools within each LEA
       were viewed as complete groups there was
       usually (but not always) quite strong
       evidence of economies of size but the
       evidence for 'optimum size' was not clear.
(iii) When secondary schools were divided into
       (relatively) homogeneous sub-groups, some
       of these groups provided clear evidence of
       economies of size and minimum cost sizes
       but others did not.
(iv)   Where an 'optimum' size of school was
       indicated, it usually lay within the
       range of 800 to 1,000 pupils.

The results of follow-up research, published
subsequently by Hough and Warburton,[13] confirmed the
above findings regarding inter-school differences
but also extended them to consider disaggregated data
at the within-school level. Examination in turn of
each of teachers' salaries, other salaries and other
(non-salary) expenditure found these to be highly
correlated in per pupil terms: a school favourably
treated in respect of any one such element tended

183

to be favourably treated in respect of all of them,
and vice versa.   Since teachers' salaries comprised
much the major element of recurrent expenditure, an
attempt was made to disaggregate this into *basic
teacher cost* (derived essentially from the pupil-
teacher ratio), *scale cost* (to represent the
'above-the-norm' element) and *incremental points
cost* (to represent years of experience).   The
differentials between schools were found to relate
not to the first of these (since pupil-teacher ratios
vary relatively less than other variables) but
strongly to the latter two: the more privileged
schools with their high levels of expenditure clearly
have teachers who are placed relatively highly on the
Burnham salary scales and who are more experienced
teachers in that they have more years of accumulated
increments up their respective scales.

Mention should be made of the one serious
attempt to review the cost implications of running a
school made by a practising headteacher, Brian Knight
of Holyrood School, Chard, Somerset, an 11-18 comprehensive school with some 1,125 pupils.   Initially,[14]
the total current costs of the school for one year
were sub-divided over a number of headings and,
after a number of gross assumptions had been made,
were eventually allocated over the principal teaching
subject areas (English, science, etc.).   The basis
for such allocation lay primarily in the salaries of
the teachers concerned, with no allowance for such
factors as variations in class sizes or in the sixth
form/lower school mix for different subjects.   Even
such items as telephone charges and school meals were
'charged' to the various subject departments.   In
the circumstances, to quote from the conclusions,
that on average a pupil-period cost £12, that a
humanities lesson cost some 25 per cent more than one
in foreign languages, or that lessons in design were
easily the most expensive, may be misleading, particularly if any attempt were to be made to use these
figures to draw comparisons with figures from other
sources.   After examining each cost heading in turn,
Knight concluded that, within the framework of the
existing educational and political system, there was
little hope for effecting any significant savings in
the costs of running the school.

Subsequently,[15] Knight published an authoritative
volume on the management of school expenditure from
the point of view of headteachers and educational
administrators.   After exploring in detail all
aspects of a school's budget, Knight proposed a programme for action to bring about both greater under-

standing of the whole field of school expenditure and resources and also greater adaptability and flexibility in using the funding already available. This is much the best book of its kind to have been published to date.

CRITICISM BY HMIs

Finally, interest in school costs and resources has come to prominent national focus not because of any academic research but because of the decision of Her Majesty's Inspectorate, a branch of the Department of Education and Science, to publish from 1981 onwards annual reports which were effectively to monitor the effects of successive cuts in educational expenditure; these cuts originated from central government and it therefore seemed misleading to entitle the reports, *Report on the Effects on the Educational Service in England of Local Authority Expenditure Policies*.[16] These reports, which indicated all too clearly the serious effects that the cuts in expenditure were having on schools, gradually became sharper and more critical in tone, as is indicated by the following extracts from the report published in 1985:

> *There are many schools with insufficient numbers of books; others with old stock which cannot be replaced; and many which are having to choose between the replacement of old stock and the purchase of the books needed to intro- duce new courses and examinations. Both schools and FHE face the continuing difficulty of replacing ageing capital items of equipment, particularly in practical subjects or where technological change is most rapid. The problem is much more acute in schools than in FHE but in the longer term less complex, demanding and costly. However, the picture is patchy, caused in part by the continuing wide variations in the capitation made available to schools; the growing differences in parental contributions to schools; and the funding made available through specific national curriculum develop- ment projects such as TVEI, ESGs and the LAP projects.*
>
> *It is clear that the disparities in provision both between and within LEAs and institutions are increasing. The variations in PTRs,*

capitation, parental contributions, and the
selectivity of funding deriving from schemes
such as the TVEI and the ESGs, all contribute
in various ways to the differences in provision
observed for similar pupils and for those of
different ages and ability groups.   In general,
in terms of levels of resources, the 11-16 age
group is less well provided for than are the
16-19 year olds, while the 16-19 year olds are
better provided for in NAFE than in schools.
In quite a number of authorities this latter
situation arises in part from the economies
and diseconomies of scale, particularly in the
size of teaching groups which in NAFE generally
tend to be larger than similar groupings in
many sixth forms where they are often so small
as to be educationally unsatisfactory and
financially costly.   These groupings are often
a consequence of falling rolls and failure to
take school places and schools out of use.

The condition of much of the accommodation
used by pupils, students, teachers and lecturers
continues to deteriorate.   Last year's report
warned that without urgent attention the cost
of putting things right would become prohibitive.
There has been no such improvement.   In fact
there has been no improvement overall in the
state of school buildings since 1981, and the
current programmes of maintenance in many LEAs
suggest that the situation is likely to continue
to worsen.   The quality of the furniture available is also now becoming of concern as schools
find it increasingly difficult to replace worn,
inappropriate items.   In some schools and
colleges, the conditions in which teaching and
learning take place adversely affect the
quality of pupils' and students' work and do
nothing to encourage their sense of enjoyment
and pride in their school or college.   In many
more the environment is shabby and uninviting
and does little to stimulate learning or to
impress parents or other visitors.   The cost
of attending to these problems, added to those
arising in some authorities from vandalism and
arson, is mounting and has now reached proportions where it is difficult to see how on
present funding the education service can prevent further decline let alone reverse the
situation.

*It is the schools sector where there is cause
for most concern. It is getting by and providing satisfactorily for most pupils in many
places by robbing Peter to pay Paul; doing
less; or with the help of sizeable contributions from parents. There are sharp polar-
isations in provision between schools in
different parts of the country and within the
same LEA. Where hard decisions about
priorities have to be made at LEA level it
tends to be building maintenance, redecoration
and furniture replacement programmes that
suffer. At school level it is the least able
in all types of school and top junior and
early year secondary pupils who appear to bear
the brunt of reduced or inappropriate provision.
In addition many schools are finding it increasingly difficult to replace old books, equipment
and furniture; to implement curricular change;
and to respond to planned changes in assessment
and examination procedures.*

When such comments are viewed against the
tradition of reserved and cautious, non-critical,
tone often used by the DES or HMIs in their reports,
the implications seem all the more dramatic. They
make it clear that the questions discussed in this
chapter are of the greatest importance for the future
of education in this country.

We may conclude this chapter with a comment made
by Maureen Woodhall in 1972 but still valid today:

*The most obvious area for research by the
economist is the whole question of educational
costs (but) even after more than a decade of
research activity ... cost analysis ... remains
one of the most fruitful areas of research ...
it is hoped that the sophistication of information on costs will again be increased, particularly by means of detailed studies of
institutional costs.*[17]

In the intervening period much light has been
thrown on problematic questions relating to school
costs and resources but much still remains to be
done. For the overwhelming majority of the 100+
LEAs in England and Wales, for example, no studies
of the costs and resources of their schools have ever
been published. This must represent a serious gap
in our knowledge about a vital aspect of the
educational system.

Studies of the inputs going into schools must represent only one side of a complex mechanism, and must lead on to and need to be complemented by data relating to the educational outcomes achieved. This linkage will be explored in the next chapter.

NOTES

1.   J.R. Hough, *A Study of School Costs* (NFER, Nelson, 1981).
2.   C. Cumming, *Studies in Educational Costs* (Scottish Academic Press, 1971).
3.   E. Byrne, *Planning and Educational Inequalities* (NFER, 1971).
4.   D. Byrne, B. Williamson and B. Fletcher, *The Poverty of Education* (Martin Robertson, 1975).
5.   D. Peschek and J. Brand, *Policies and Politics in Secondary Education, Case Studies in West Ham and Reading*, Greater London Papers No.11 (London School of Economics, 1966).
6.   N. Boaden, *Urban Policy-Making Influences on County Boroughs in England and Wales* (Cambridge University Press, 1971).
7.   J. Pratt, T. Burgess, R. Allemano and M. Locke, *Your Local Education* (Penguin, 1973).
8.   J. Pratt and T. Burgess, 'Change for the Better?', *The Guardian*, 25 November 1979.
9.   R. Lord, *Value for Money in Education* (CIPFA, 1984).
10.   P. Coombs and J. Hallak, *Managing Educational Costs* (Oxford University Press, 1972).
11.   Lawyers Committee for Civil Rights under the Law, *Summary of State-Wide School Finance Cases since 1973* (Lawyers Committee for Civil Rights under the Law, Washington D.C., 1977).
12.   For an up-to-date account of such developments, see S. Carroll and R. Park, *The Search for Equity in School Finance* (Ballinger, 1982).
13.   J. Hough and S. Warburton, 'U.K. Research into School Costs and Resources', *Economics of Education Review* (1986).
14.   B. Knight, *The Cost of Running a School*, Occasional Paper No.6 (Scottish Centre for Studies in School Administration, 1977).
15.   B. Knight, *Managing School Finance* (Heinemann, 1983).
16.   Annually since 1981 (Department of Education and Science).
17.   M. Woodhall, *Economic Aspects of Education* (NFER, 1972).

Chapter Nine

INPUT-OUTPUT ANALYSIS

We face a pervasive ignorance about the
production function of education, that is,
the relationship between school inputs, on
the one hand, and school outputs as
conventionally measured by achievement
scores, on the other.

These words of Professor Marc Blaug[1] were written in
1970 but, after a long period of attempts to investigate that relationship, they still remain largely
true today. Of all the fields of study referred to
in this book, the one covered in this chapter has
remained the most intractable. After many years of
research into this question, still remarkably little
is known about which combination of which inputs into
schools will be most likely to give rise to more
successful educational outcomes.

Input-Output Analysis refers to the search for
relationships between resources of all kinds
(education and other) going into schools and the
outcomes, again widely defined, being achieved in
schools; as a field of study it has developed
extensively in other countries, especially the USA,
and has more recently been of considerable interest
in the UK. The rationale for such studies was
always clear: if ways could be found of spending
money and using other resources in schools more
effectively, then perhaps there could be significant
improvements in the outcomes of the educational process even without committing any additional
resources.

The origins of such an approach may be traced
back to economists specialising in industrial studies
who have in the past devoted much time and effort to
calculating '*production functions*', mathematical
expressions (of ever-increasing complexity) showing

the relationships between industrial raw materials
or inputs and finished products or outputs, usually
based on repeated statistical testing.   It was
perhaps inevitable that there should eventually be
attempts to extend the production function analogy
to other institutions such as schools where the
'production process', if it may be so termed, will
necessarily be more difficult to identify.

PROBLEMS OF DEFINITION

It will immediately be apparent that a particular
problem arising in the case of all such attempts at
educational input-output studies must be how to
frame suitable definitions of variables to represent
educational *'inputs'* and *'outputs'*:   the former may
encompass some mix of the money being spent, aspects
of the teaching staff or materials supplied, and
socio-economic variables to represent family and home
background.   The definition of schools' *'outputs'* is
even more problematic, for obvious reasons: many
schools would be hard put to specify all the things
that they are trying to achieve, or trying not to
achieve, for all of their pupils and to embrace all
of these within a mathematical relationship would
usually be impossible;   often some of the data that
would ideally be required either does not exist or
cannot be made available.   This point is particularly problematic in respect of those pupils who are
at the lower levels of intellectual ability or
academic achievement in schools.   The most readily
available indicator of school achievement is usually
the results of external examinations: for all its
faults as a statistical variable this does at least
give some indication, on an objective and comparable
basis, of the educational standard being achieved by
those pupils who take such examinations but these
tend to be the more able and more successful pupils.
For the less able pupils, schools may be aiming to
achieve a variety of outcomes of diverse kinds but
the search for any statistical or other indicators
that would encompass these has proved largely
fruitless.   In the case of both inputs and outputs,
therefore, it is inevitable that not every aspect of
the lives of the schools will be included and the
equation specifications are bound to be incomplete
in at least some respects.

EVIDENCE FROM OVERSEAS

Much research of an input-output nature has been
carried out in other countries, especially the USA,
but the results are far from conclusive. In the
words of the President's Commission on School
Finance,

> *research has found nothing that consistently*
> *and unambiguously makes a difference in student*
> *outcomes.*[2]

In so far as relationships between resources and
performance have been identified, it appears that
differences in physical resources are rather
unimportant and that teacher characteristics,
especially verbal ability, have more consistent
effects. This at least was one of the conclusions
of the Coleman Report[3] which has been termed the
largest and most comprehensive study ever made of
the USA school system. Unfortunately, from the
point of view of any movement towards equalisation,
the report found that all the within-school
factors considered had much less effect on variations
in children's verbal achievement than did the
children's own background and attitudes. In the
words of one commentator:

> *The Coleman Report stands as a benchmark for*
> *a number of reasons. More than any other*
> *study, it provided an impetus for theorists*
> *of all orientations to become more involved*
> *in what had previously been a very specialised*
> *and obscure branch of educational research -*
> *input-output analysis. Because of its indict-*
> *ment of school effectiveness (whether that*
> *indictment was well founded or not) it also*
> *stimulated greater interest in other areas of*
> *school research and functioning.*[4]

This finding gave rise to much subsequent comment,
criticism and further research, which tended to be
characterised by the question, *'Does school make any*
difference?' The notion that, as Coleman had
implied, it might not, was to prove profoundly dis-
turbing to educational researchers from a wide
variety of backgrounds, particularly when broadly
similar conclusions emerged from a number of other
large and reputable pieces of research. A study of
educational expenditure in large cities of the USA
described the extreme inequalities involved, with,

for example, taxable property per head in San Francisco being worth around four times as much as in Philadelphia but, in spite of many ambitious statistical calculations, was able to identify practically no clear relationships between educational expenditures and any other relevant variables applying in all the 15 cities studied.[5] Similarly, a subsequent study of high schools in one large city, Chicago, found little in the way of very clear relationships between school inputs and outputs: out-of-school variables appeared as more important than in-school variables and within the latter there was some evidence that teachers were a more important influence than buildings, but it was noted that many of the relationships investigated were not statistically significant. The authors also commented:

> *What is disturbing is that ... so little careful assessment is made of the contribution of additional resources devoted to one or another purposes ... little attention has been paid to educational productivity ... an absence of research that attempts to measure the relationships between costs and educational outputs of particular programs.*[6]

There have, however, also been some reverse findings. Thomas[7] studied the relative effects on the verbal scores of Negro students of (i) within-school variables and (ii) socio-economic background variables. He found, contrary to Coleman, that the former - and particularly those relating to specific teacher attributes - did have important effects. Similarly, Klitgaard and Hall[8] looked at whether certain schools consistently produced exceptionally good results on reading and mathematics achievement tests, after due correction had been made for socio-economic background. After describing the notion that no clear relationship could be found between student learning and within-school variables as *'perhaps the most counter-intuitive finding in public policy research in the past decade'* the authors assessed those schools whose scores were one standard deviation or more above the mean. They calculated variation due to chance via the binomial distribution and then compared this theoretical chance distribution with the actual distribution via a chi-square test. Contrasting results were found for different groups of schools; for Michigan rural schools, for example, *'the chi-square tests showed*

*more consistently overachieving schools than chance
alone would allow'* and there was a tendency for the
same schools to re-appear as *'exceptional'* in
successive years.   For other groups of schools,
however, the conclusions were the reverse.

A similar aim of hoping to relate school inputs
to performance may be found in the report by Tuckman[9]
of research into 1,001 public sector high schools
completing questionnaires for the US Census Bureau,
a further 6,700 replies not being usable since
information on one or more variables were missing.
The variables, *'percentage of teachers with 10 or
more years of teaching experience'* and *'percentage of
students who are male'* were found to always have
significant effects on school performance, but
'percentage of teachers with masters degrees' was
not significant.   Overall students' home and social
background variables were shown to have much greater
effects than within-school variables, the effect of
the latter frequently being to reinforce the former.
A pessimistic conclusion as to what schools could
achieve was reported by Barnow[10] who conducted a
detailed study of primary schools in Pennsylvania
and concluded, *'The effects of the school inputs have
been statistically insignficant although usually of
the expected sign'.*   Marco[11] calculated correlation
coefficients between 30 separate within-school
variables for 70 schools but had to conclude that any
attempt to assess school effectiveness by such a
method was highly problematical.

Many other attempts to relate school input and
output variables were reported in the extensive literature review given in Cohn (1975)[12] which may be
described as the most comprehensive work on this
subject to have been published.   Cohn reviewed the
many relevant USA studies from the point of view not
so much of their results but more of their method-
ologies which varied widely, particularly with regard
to the input and output variables used.   The former
ranged over various expenditure indicators, data
relating to teachers' experience, verbal ability,
teaching loads, educational qualifications, race and
job satisfaction, age, condition and utilisation of
buildings and textbooks, science laboratory and
other facilities.   Output variables used included
pupils' aptitude and achievement tests of various
kinds, pupils' expectations and 'attitudes to life',
'school holding power' and parental attitudes.

The complexity of the statistical manipulations
involved in some of these studies is almost beyond
belief: Coleman, for example, used 93 separate input

variables and had data relating to some 645,000
individual students.   Cohn commented that in so far
as a unified conclusion could be drawn from such a
large and varied body of research, it had to be on
rather unsatisfactory lines: some school components,
such as teacher experience, salary and facilities,
had been shown to be significant positive influences
in a number of places and at a number of times but
not all studies had found this to be so.   No one
variable had been found that *consistently* and
unambiguously made a difference in students' outcomes
and the author concluded: '*We have no clear idea of
why a practice that seems to be effective in one case
is apparently ineffective in another*'.

INPUT-OUTPUT IN THE UK

Following and doubtless influenced by the USA experience, interest has grown in input-output analysis in
the UK and a number of significant studies have now
appeared.   One of these, which has become known as
the Rutter Report and which related to secondary
schools in Inner London, has received wide publicity
in educational circles and in the national press.
Its principal findings have been summarised as
follows:

> *First, secondary schools in Inner London differ
> markedly in the behaviour and attainments shown
> by their pupils.   This was evident in the
> children's behaviour whilst at school, the
> regularity of their attendance, the proportions
> staying on at school beyond the legally enforced
> period, their success in public examinations,
> and their delinquency rates.*
> *Second, although schools differed in the
> proportion of behaviourally difficult or low-
> achieving children they admitted, these
> differences did not wholly account for the
> variations between schools in their pupils'
> later behaviour and attainment.   Even when
> comparisons between schools were restricted to
> children who were quite similar in family back-
> ground and personal characteristics prior to
> secondary transfer, marked school variations
> remained.   This meant that children were more
> likely to show good behaviour and good schol-
> astic attainments if they attended some schools
> than if they attended others.   The implication
> is that experiences during the secondary school*

years may influence children's progress.

Third, the variations between schools in different forms of 'outcome' for their pupils were reasonably stable over periods of at least four or five years.

Fourth, in general, schools performed fairly similarly on all the various measures of outcome. That is, schools which did better than average in terms of the children's behaviour in school tended also to do better than average in terms of examination success and delinquency. There were some exceptions to this pattern, but it appeared that in most schools the different forms of success were closely connected.

Fifth, these differences in outcome between schools were not due to such physical factors as the size of the school, the age of the buildings, of the space available; nor were they due to broad differences in administrative status or organization. It was entirely possible for schools to obtain good outcomes in spite of initially rather unpromising and unprepossessing school premises, and within the context of somewhat differing administrative arrangements.

Sixth, the differences between schools in outcome were systematically related to their characteristics as social institutions. Factors as varied as the degree of academic emphasis, teacher actions in lessons, the availability of incentives and rewards, good conditions for pupils, and the extent to which children were able to take responsibility were all signficantly associated with outcome differences between schools. All of these factors were open to modification by the staff, rather than fixed by external constraints.

Seventh, outcomes were also influenced by factors outside teachers' immediate control. The academic balance in the intake to the schools was particularly important in this connection. Examination success tended to be better in schools with a substantial nucleus of children of at least average intellectual ability, and delinquency rates were higher in those with a heavy preponderance of the least able. Interestingly, however, while the balance of intake was significantly associated with pupil outcome, it did not appear to have any comparable influence on school functioning, as reflected in our school process measures.

> *Eighth, this effect of balance in the
> intake was most marked with respect to delin-
> quency, and least important in the case of the
> children's observed behaviour in the classroom
> and elsewhere about the school.*
>
> *Ninth, the association between the combined
> measures of overall school progress and each of
> the measures of outcome was much stronger than
> any of the associations with the individual
> process variables. This suggests that the
> cumulative effect of these social factors was
> considerably greater than the effect of any of
> the individual factors on their own. The
> implication is that the individual actions or
> measures may combine to create a particular
> ethos, or set of values, attitudes, and behav-
> iours which will become characteristic of the
> school as a whole.*
>
> *Tenth, the total pattern of findings
> indicates the strong probability that the
> associations between school process and outcome
> reflect in part a causal process. In other
> words, to an appreciable extent children's
> behaviour and attitudes are shaped and influ-
> enced by their experiences at school and, in
> particular, by the qualities of the school as
> a social institution.*[13]

The above extract indicates the considerable
range of variables used by Rutter, not all of them
directly educational. The report's findings have
not gone without challenge, indeed two small
volumes[14] were subsequently published to criticise
its methodology and results; Rutter has, however,
generally been regarded as very significant, both in
this country and in the USA where it has attracted
wide interest, particularly because its outcome runs
directly contrary to the Coleman notion that 'school
makes no difference'.

The Rutter Report, published in 1979, may be
said to have been the start of serious interest in
educational input-output analysis in the UK and it
provided the stimulus for other research work in
this field. Firstly Gray *et al.*[15] published the
results of a large-scale survey of some 20,000 former
pupils at most of Scotland's secondary schools,
including such measures as '*truancy*' (the percentage
of pupils who admitted being persistent truants from
school), '*satisfaction*' (the percentage of pupils
who assessed their last year in school as being
'worthwhile'), '*belting*' (the percentage of pupils

who were 'often' belted) and *'O-grades'* (successes
in external examinations), as well as five separate
measures of *'intake'* (including percentage of school-
leavers with middle-class fathers).   The authors
described their approach as *'illustrative and explor-
atory'* and commented, *'We do not pretend that we have
reached final and definitive answers'.*
     Secondly, Steedman[16] produced for the National
Children's Bureau an analysis of longitudinal data
collected by the National Child Development Study
and based on the lives of some 4,400 pupils;   this
study was largely confined to the selective versus
non-selective schools controversy, an emotive issue
which regrettably, from the point of neutral and
objective research, has been the aspect of such work
which has received the most extensive media coverage.
Steedman concluded:

> *The task here, to describe progress in compre-
> hensive and selective schools to the limited
> extent that progress can be judged with examin-
> ation results, was almost impossible.*

Thirdly, Marks *et al.*[17] analysed the external examination results from 2,100 schools in 57 LEAs and
related these to the social class composition of the
LEA.   As with Steedman, the main objective was to
pursue the controversy over selective versus non-
selective schools in terms of their respective examination results.   Marks's research was subsequently
subjected to considerable criticism, not least by
Gray and Jones.[18]   A particular point at issue was
that Marks related statistics of socio-economic
disadvantage to educational *success*, which led Gray
and Jones to comment:

> *It goes without saying that levels of disadvant-
> age in an LEA are by no means always the mirror-
> image of levels of advantage.*

According to one report, the DES was critical of the
Marks approach, particularly with regard to their
measures for social class which were seen as
inadequate.[19]   A plethora of comment and criticism
followed in the educational and national press.[20]
     The DES itself became interested in such work
and its statisticians sought to relate at LEA level,
inter alia, levels of educational expenditure to the
external examination results achieved.   The results
showed that whereas social background provided a
statistically significant explanation of variations

in the levels of examination successes of school
leavers, school based variables, including the
expenditure variables, did so only to a much less
degree.   This included the variables representing
teaching and non-teaching expenditure, teacher turnover and pupil grammar school attendance.[21]   Mention
should also be made of work by Wilby[22] published in
The Sunday Times: he gave each LEA an *'input'* score
based on six measures of educational and social
handicap, including socio-economic status, overseas
origin of head of household, large families, one
parent families, overcrowding in homes and free
school meals.   This was then compared with the
'output' of each LEA, as measured by the proportion
of school leavers passing respectively one or more
A-levels, five or more O-levels and no external
examinations, to assess the *'value added to or
subtracted from'* their children by LEAs.   This in
turn was related to the average per pupil unit costs
for each LEA and, after an analysis in which it was
made clear that he was not unaware of the many
difficulties raised by such a simplistic approach,
Wilby felt able to conclude: *'on average high spending does get better results'*.   For a good survey of
some of the practical problems arising with all such
work, the reader is referred to Shipman.[23]

ANALYSIS FOR INDIVIDUAL SCHOOLS

Almost all such studies in the UK were conducted at
the level of inter-LEA comparisons, never at that of
individual schools.   Not until 1986, when the
results of the Loughborough-based research by Hough
and Warburton were published, was there any information at all regarding inter-school comparisons of
an input-output nature within the area of one LEA,
i.e. relating to a broadly homogeneous group of
schools.   A number of writers[24] have called
attention to the fact that research at LEA-level may
conceal wide divergencies at the level of individual
schools and have urged the need for studies to be
carried out at individual school level, thus permitting inter-school comparisons.   In the words of
Professor Goldstein, *'it is such lower level relationships which are of real interest'*.   The Economics
Division of the DES had previously sought to make a
study at the level of individual schools but had had
to use sample data, collected for another purpose,
relating to 59 secondary schools scattered over seven
LEAs;   this included no in-school data at all except

for the pupil-teacher ratio, and concentrated on
socio-economic background factors for the school
catchment areas, thus obviously imposing severe
limitations on the results.[25]

Hough and Warburton[26] were able, as an extension of their work on school costs and resources, to
relate within one LEA (a large county authority with
a mix of 11-18 comprehensive schools, 9-13 middle
schools and 13-18 upper schools), data on level of
expenditure per pupil in each secondary school to
statistics of external examination successes,
especially at O-level.   At the same time data
derived from the National Census of 1981 became
available for this county, notably the Small Area
Statistics (SAS) for enumeration districts (EDs) of
which there are nationally some 13,000, each comprising around 150 households.   Using the standard computer programme SASPAC, which permits ready analysis
of SAS data, and with the help and advice of county
officials, it proved possible to aggregate SAS data
in such a manner that this could be reconciled with
the LEA's school catchment area.   Broadly this
could be done for the whole of the county with the
exception of the county town where transportation
movements were so complex that reasonably clear
school catchment areas could not be defined, whereas
for the remainder of the county very little pupil
movement took place across catchment area boundaries.
Even the implementation of the 1980 Education Act and
increased parental choice of schools had made very
little difference to this situation, probably largely
because of the distances involved.

Some schools also had to be excluded for other
reasons;   the part of the county with middle schools
leading on to upper schools gave rise to complications
and could not readily be compared with the 11-18
school pattern, Roman Catholic schools typically drew
pupils from wide areas and had no easily-identifiable
catchment area boundaries and for some other schools
data was incomplete.   After all such adjustments
there remained a list of 30 comprehensive schools
with which it was possible to proceed.   For these
schools it was possible to use SAS data aggregated to
catchment area level to compile a socio-economic
profile of the catchment area for each school.

From the many census variables available the
following were selected:

SOCL1	proportion of head of households in social class 1 (Registrar-General's classification)
SOCL2	ditto for class 2
SOCL3N	ditto for class 3 non-manual
SOCL3M	ditto for class 3 manual
SOCL4	ditto for class 4
SOCL5	ditto for class 5
RESDEG	proportion of residents aged 18 or over with degrees and/or professional or vocational qualifications
ECONACT	proportion of persons aged 16+ economically active
SEEKWK	proportion of persons aged 16+ seeking work
OWNOCC	proportion of all households owner occupied
COUNC	proportion of all household council houses
1+CAR	proportion of all households with one or more cars

The first seven indicators listed above (SOCL1 to RESDEG inclusive) are taken from the Census's representative 10 per cent sample of SAS, the remainder from the 100 per cent Census data.

The researchers spent some time with the LEA officials discussing possible alternative 'output' indicators other than external examination results, such as staying-on rates, rates of entry to higher education, rates of truancy and absenteeism and indicators for vandalism. Eventually, for various reasons, it proved impracticable to use any of the these. Results of GCE A-level examinations posed problems because although all the schools were nominally 11-18 comprehensive, a number of them had only acquired sixth-forms relatively recently and had as yet no tradition of A-level successes. Eventually, therefore, school 'output' had to be measured via GCE O-level successes per fifth-form pupil in each school. Regrettably the manner in which the LEA kept the data meant that it was not possible to include some indicator to represent the grade of pass at O-level, e.g. via a suitable weighting system (as is commonly done for A-level scores of entrants to higher education). This may be seen as a limitation but it does follow accepted procedure elsewhere. Passes at CSE grade 1 were included and counted as equivalent to passes at GCE O-level. This information was available for three successive years, 1979, 1980 and 1981 labelled

OLEV79, OLEV80, OLEV81, respectively.   Statistics
of O-level and CSE examinations taken by pupils in
sixth-forms were held separately by the LEA and
were not included.

The cost data used related to the total recurrent expenditure per pupil in each school for each
of the three financial years 1978/79, 1979/80 and
1980/81.   These therefore included all recurrent
expenditure in these schools and were not limited to
those specific to the fifth-form classes taking GCE
and CSE examinations.   Capital expenditures were
not included: apart from any other reasons, the LEA,
in common with most other LEAs, did not apportion
capital expenditure on a school-by-school basis.

Whereas the recurrent cost data for each of the
three financial years could be related to the record
of examination successes at the end of the relevant
school year, the Census data all referred to 1981,
the year of the National Census: however, socio-
economic variables such as those listed above are
usually considered to change over time only very
slowly.

The data was processed through the standard
MINITAB programme to produce multiple regressions in
which each of the dependent variables OLEV79,
OLEV80, OLEV81 (proxies for 'outputs') was regressed
in turn on the unit costs input for the respective
year together with the socio-economic profile data,
i.e. the equation tested was of the form:

$$OLEV = a_1 + a_2 UC + a_3 SOCL1 + a_4 SOCL2 + a_5 SOCL3N$$

$$+ a_6 SOCL3M + a_7 SOCL4 + a_8 SOCL5 + a_9 ECONACT$$

$$+ a_{10} SEEKWK + a_{11} OWNOCC + a_{12} COUNC$$

$$+ a_{13} 1+CAR + a_{14} RESDEG$$

With such a large number of independent variables the
problem of which to include in the final equation(s)
was solved via stepwise multiple regressions: the
'best' independent predictor, i.e. the one causing
the highest R^2, was selected by the programme for
inclusion in an initial one-variable linear equation,
then the second strongest predictor was added, etc.,
until the best six predictors had been included.
The inclusion of each additional independent variable
should always increase the total prediction power, as
indicated by $100R^2$, but decrease the F-test value due
to the loss of one further degree of freedom.

201

However, changes in the coefficients of already-included variables and their statistical significance cannot be predicted in advance and may be erratic, even to the extent of changing sign.

The Results

The results of the stepwise multiple regressions, as generated by MINITAB, are shown in Table 9.1. Those variables not shown in each of the three matrices have already been discarded by the programme as being of less interest than any of the variables shown. Underneath each coefficient the t-test result for statistical significance of individual variables is shown in parentheses (since the t-test table for 5 per cent level = 1.96, a useful standard rule-of-thumb is that t⩾2 indicates statistical significance). Of the three sets of results shown, those for OLEV79 are clearly the weakest: overall statistical significance at the 5 per cent level, as indicated by the F-test result, ceases on the inclusion of the fourth independent variable, UC7879; the statistical significance of individual coefficients, as indicated by the t-test results, occurs only twice in the case of ECONACT, three times for SOCL2 and not at all for any of the other variables, and the highest $100R^2$ shown is only 36.7. Thus some 73 per cent of the variation in O-level examination results is not explained by the longest of the six equations shown. From this equation set only ECONACT and SOCL2 emerge as meaningful predictors, a finding very much in keeping with the literature relating to the influence of social class on educational success.

For both OLEV80 and OLEV81 the results are more satisfactory in that the equations are always overall statistically significant and the $100R^2$ from the full equations are 48.6 and 47.5 respectively. In each set SOCL2 emerges as much the most important predictor and is almost always statistically significant (as indicated by t-test result) for OLEV80 and always for OLEV81. No other independent variable is ever statistically significant with the sole exception of UC8081 in the full equation for OLEV81.

With regard to any possible causal mechanism or linkage between unit expenditure per school and O-level successes, the regression results are confusing in the extreme: for 1979 the coefficients are always positive (suggesting that more expenditure per pupil in each school is associated with better examination successes), for 1980 they do not appear at all, and

Table 9.1: Inputs and Outputs: Stepwise Multiple Regressions

(i) <u>1979</u>

	ECONACT	SOCL2	UC7879	SOCL1	SOCL3N	RESDEG	$100R^2$	F
OLEV79 = 12.441 -	0.167 (2.19)*						16.1	4.78*
10.553 -	0.153 (2.09)*	+ 0.040 (1.87)					26.7	4.37*
4.740 -	0.118 (1.54)	+ 0.053 (2.28)*	+ 0.007 (1.36)				32.1	3.63*
5.587 -	0.124 (1.58)	+ 0.060 (2.23)*	+ 0.006 (1.18)	- 0.056 (0.53)			33.0	2.71
2.744 -	0.109 (1.28)	+ 0.058 (2.13)*	+ 0.009 (1.20)	- 0.074 (0.66)	+ 0.058 (0.54)		33.9	2.16
3.715 -	0.121 (1.40)	+ 0.023 (0.51)	+ 0.009 (1.17)	- 0.122 (0.99)	+ 0.035 (0.32)	+ 0.169 (0.94)	36.7	1.93

(ii) <u>1980</u>

	SOCL2	SOCL1	ECONACT	SOCL5	SOCL4	COUNC	$100R^2$	F
OLEV80 = 0.826 +	0.040 (3.11)*						27.9	9.69**
0.749 +	0.034 (2.17)*	+ 0.043 (0.69)					29.3	4.98*
5.695 +	0.033 (2.20)*	+ 0.034 (0.57)	- 0.077				38.2	4.74*
5.759 +	0.026 (1.50)	+ 0.003 (0.04)	- 0.069 (1.57)	- 0.055 (0.94)			40.6	3.82*
4.533 +	0.040 (2.16)*	+ 0.012 (0.18)	+ 0.070 (1.66)	- 0.076 (1.30)	+ 0.063 (1.68)		47.6	3.76*
4.650 +	0.043 (2.21)*	+ 0.022 (0.32)	- 0.075 (1.73)	- 0.100 (1.40)	+ 0.059 (1.52)	+ 0.008	48.6	3.15*

(iii) <u>1981</u>

	SOCL2	UC8081	SOCL1	SOCL4	SEEKWK	SOCL3N	$100R^2$	F
OLEV81 = 1.038 +	0.035 (3.35)*						31.0	11.2**
2.196 +	0.324 (3.05)*	- 0.02 (1.01)					33.7	6.12**
2.231 +	0.033 (2.57)*	- 0.002 (0.95)	- 0.003 (0.06)				33.9	3.91*
1.740 +	0.046 (2.95)*	- 0.003 (1.39)	+ 0.002 (0.04)	- 0.047 (1.41)			39.2	3.55*
1.804 +	0.040 (2.44)*	- 0.002 (1.04)	- 0.023 (0.38)	- 0.051 (1.50)	- 0.036 (0.93)		41.6	3.01*
3.31 +	0.038 (2.32)*	- 0.003 (1.34)*	- 0.026 (0.45)	+ 0.039 (1.14)	- 0.067 (1.57)	- 0.067 (1.49)	47.5	3.00*

* significant at 0.05 level.
** significant at 0.01 level.

for 1981 they are always negative (suggesting the reverse of the above). However since the coefficients are always very small - never exceeding 0.009 - and they are never statistically significant except in the one instance cited previously, we can only say that no meaningful conclusions can be drawn regarding linkage between expenditure per pupil and external examination success at the level of individual schools. This would also seem to point to the need for further studies to be conducted at even more disaggregated levels, e.g. by isolating expenditures within a school actually devoted to the fifth-form pupils taking the O-level examinations. It scarcely needs to be said that such research would be both complex and costly.

It is worth recalling some of the limitations applying to the above analysis that were indicated previously, perhaps particularly relating to the desirability of including a wider range of *'output'* variables if this were feasible: no one doubts that comprehensive schools have other objectives than merely external examination successes but the practical problems involved in encapsulating these are not easy to overcome. Data relating to one set of 30 schools within one LEA cannot, in any event, be said to constitute a conclusive test and it would be interesting to replicate similar analysis elsewhere. The practical problems outlined above serve to show how difficult it is to do such work.

In summary, input-output analysis relating to education, and particularly relating to secondary schools, has developed significantly in recent years, originally in the USA and subsequently in the UK. It has now become a noteworthy addition to the available literature relating to education. It seems likely that it will further develop, with gradual refinement of techniques and methodology, over the next few years and will in time make a significant contribution to major questions of educational policy.

NOTES

1. M. Blaug, *An Introduction to the Economics of Education* (Penguin, 1970).
2. H. Averch *et al.*, *A Critical Review and Synthesis of Research Findings: A Report to the President's Commission on School Finance* (Rand, 1972).
3. J.S. Coleman *et al.*, *Equality of Opportunity, Summary* (Government Printing Office, Washington D.C.,

1966.
    4. E. Cohn, *Input-Output Analysis in Public Education* (Ballinger, 1975).
    5. H. James, J. Kelly and W. Garms, *Determinants of Educational Expenditures in Large Cities of the United States* (US Office of Education, 1966).
    6. J. Burkhead, T. Fox and J. Holland, *Input and Output in Large-City High Schools* (Syracuse University Press, 1967).
    7. J. Thomas, *The Productive School* (Wiley, 1971).
    8. R. Klitgaard and G. Hall, 'Are There Unusually Effective Schools?', *Journal of Human Resources*, Vol.X, No.1 (Winter 1975).
    9. H. Tuckman, 'High School Inputs and their Contribution to School Performance', *Journal of Human Resources*, Vol.6, No.4.
    10. B. Barnow, *The Productivity of Primary Education in Pennsylvania*, Working Paper No.4 (University of Pittsburgh, May 1975).
    11. G. Marco, 'A Comparison of Selected School Effectiveness Measures Based on Longitudinal Data', *Journal of Education Measurement*, Vol.2, No.4 (Winter 1974).
    12. Cohn, *Input-Output Analysis in Public Education*.
    13. M. Rutter *et al.*, *Fifteen Thousand Hours - Secondary Schools and their Effects on Children* (Open Books, 1979), and reprinted in T. Bush *et al.* (eds), *Approaches to School Management* Harper & Row, 1980).
    14. B. Tizard *et al.*, *Fifteen Thousand Hours, A Discussion* (University of London Institute of Education, 1980) and E. Wragg *et al.*, *The Rutter Research* (University of Exeter, School of Education, 1980).
    15. J. Gray *et al.*, *Reconstructions of Secondary Education: Theory, Myth and Practice since the War* Routledge & Kegan Paul, 1983).
    16. J. Steedman, *Examination Results in Selective and Nonselective Schools* (National Children's Bureau, 1983).
    17. J. Marks *et al.*, *Standards in English Schools* (National Council for Educational Standards, 1983).
    18. J. Gray and B. Jones, 'Disappearing Data', *The Times Educational Supplement*, 15 July 1983. Criticisms also appeared in the *TES* of 1 July 1983 and 8 July 1983.
    19. H. Goldstein, 'Different Standards, Different Interpretation', *The Guardian*, 1 November 1983.

20.   For example, P. Venning, 'NUT Joins the War
of Words on Standards', *The Times Higher Education
Supplement*, 21 October 1983;   W. Berliner, 'Joseph
Hides DES Report on Research "Flaws"', *The Guardian*,
14 October 1983.
21.   DES, *School Standards and Spending*,
Statistical Bulletins Nos 16/83 and 13/84.
22.   P. Wilby, 'Where School Money is Spent',
The Sunday Times, 18 September 1983.
23.   M. Shipman, *In-School Evaluation* (Heinemann,
1979).
24.   Including Professor H. Goldstein, 'The Sums
that Don't Add Up', *The Guardian*, 7 February 1983.
25.   J. Darlington and B. Cullen, *Pilot Study
of School Examination Performance and Associated
Factors*, Working Paper No.75 (Government Economic
Service, 1984).
26.   J.R. Hough and S.J. Warburton, 'Input-Output
Analysis at School Level', in T. Simkins (ed.),
Research in Education Management (Sheffield Polytechnic, 1986).

Chapter Ten

HIGHER EDUCATION AND THE CUTS

The importance of the crucial relationship between
national economic performance and the country's
system of higher education recurs throughout this
book.   Efforts to quantify or specify precisely the
nature of that relationship have largely been unsuccessful but it can scarcely be doubted that economic
growth and competitiveness are closely related to
large numbers of our brightest young people having
the opportunity to become educated to the highest
levels.   The system of higher education in the UK,
consisting as it does of the semi-autonomous universities and the LEA-controlled polytechnics and
colleges, unevenly scattered throughout the country,
follows no ideal or theoretical model.   It has grown
higgledy-piggledy under various influences and at
various times and, for all the criticisms that are
levelled at it, has achieved an outstanding repu-
tation internationally.   At its best it offers
degree-level education second to none in the world.

EXPANSION

Until about a decade ago the dominant theme in
higher education in the UK, as indeed in all other
comparable countries, was one of expansion: this
expansion had developed ever since the ending of the
Second World War but it was particularly marked after
the publication of the Robbins Report on higher
education[1] in 1963 and the White Paper recommending
the establishment of the polytechnics[2] in 1966.
Throughout the country, new institutions were established, new buildings constructed, new courses
developed, additional staff recruited and large
numbers of extra students enrolled.   Overall the
system coped remarkably well with this quite

dramatic and rapid expansion. For many of the
academic staff who began their teaching careers in
large numbers during this period, it was difficult
to see any end to this process, which was common to
the universities, the new polytechnics and colleges
of various kinds. Throughout, Britain had relatively fewer students in higher education than any of her
competitor countries and the overwhelming emphasis
was on the need to catch up with the latter. Even
though it seemed obvious that the country needed
more and more, and better, graduates if national
economic performance was to recover, only in retrospect does it seem surprising that so few observers
were aware, or commented publicly, that such a process of expansion could not continue for ever.

By various indicators, including that of total
numbers of students on all courses, higher education
has continued to expand to this day. However since
around 1973 the rather emotive term that has been
increasingly applied to parts of the system or to
the provision of available finance, or to the numbers
of young people qualified, ready and willing to continue their education after school, has been *the
cuts*. In various ways parts of the system of
higher education in the UK, and eventually the whole
of that system had to face up to the fact that, for
a number of reasons, inexorable expansion could not
continue. When one considers the country's deteriorating economic performance and relative disadvantage
in respect of higher education when compared with
other countries, what follows in the remainder of
this chapter represents a melancholy story.

THE COLLEGES OF EDUCATION

The change when it came applied initially to the then
colleges of education, and came suddenly and, for
many people, quite unexpectedly, even though, as was
shown in the section on the demand and supply situation for schoolteachers, the combination of the
demographic fact of a quite dramatic fall in the
birth-rate with the nation's continuing disappointing
economic performance made it inevitable. The
colleges of education, being largely monotechnic
institutions, were obviously very vulnerable in the
event of any marked changes in the numbers of
teachers that the nation needed or felt it could
afford to employ and it was not surprising that they
should suffer cuts in student numbers long before
any other type of institution. What was surprising

was that the DES seemed to react so slowly, if at all, to the steadily accumulating evidence regarding the downward trend in the birth-rate. As late as 1970, by which date the birth-rate *had already been falling for six years*, the DES proposed that the numbers of students in the colleges of education should continue to grow from the figure of some 114,000 set for 1972 to around 130,000 for 1981, almost a decade later. Yet in December 1972 the rather ironically entitled White Paper *Education: A Framework for Expansion*,[3] whilst envisaging that the total number of students in higher education should continue to grow to 750,000 by 1981 (a figure which was, as we shall see, considerably less than that of 830,000 suggested by the DES in 1970), outlined that the numbers on teacher-training courses in public sector colleges must be cut from the figure of 114,000 quoted above to some 60,000-70,000 for initial teacher training plus a further 15,000 for in-service and induction programmes by 1981. This may be seen as the beginning of the era of cuts in student numbers, staff and finance, and of the closure of courses, buildings and whole institutions, which has now become all too familiar.

Why was the DES so slow to react? This is a question that has been much debated in subsequent years, the answer apparently lying in the fact that all the officials and ministers concerned had been accustomed for so many years to concentrate their minds on growth and expansion that psychologically it was extremely difficult to effect the about-face required. It is worth quoting in full the comments made subsequently by Mr Hugh Harding, the then Head of Teacher Training Branch in the DES:

> *The birth-rate had been falling since 1964 and the teaching force was increasing at a rate of 15,000 to 20,000 teachers a year. Rising teacher numbers were on collision course with pupil numbers destined presently to fall. Even if the result was merely to stabilize the teaching force, in due course some 50,000 fewer teacher training places could be needed. The expansion programme, however, had attained its own momentum. In 1967 the Department was promoting a further capital programme to expand, as they said, capacity from 100,000 to 110,000 places, ignorant of the fact that the system could, with a little crowding up, already accommodate 112,000 students. As late as 1970 Education Planning Paper No.2 gave fresh*

> *currency to the myth that 130,000 places would
> be required in due course ...*
>
> *Teachers Branch whose responsibility it
> was, were well content with a growing teaching
> force, the problem was some years ahead, and
> they were preoccupied with pressing and import-
> ant problems of teachers' pay. Teacher Train-
> ing Branch regarded the problem as more urgent,
> but had no direct responsibility and insuf-
> ficient leverage to get the work put in hand
> elsewhere. The difficulty was compounded by
> the fact that the two branches reported to
> different Deputy Secretaries and that later,
> planning fell within the remits of two differ-
> ent planning committees ... the failure to
> initiate public discussion of the impending
> problems was the cause of much trouble later ...*
>
> *I think there can be little doubt that,
> had work on teacher supply projections been
> continued between 1965 and 1971, the signifi-
> cance of successive projections of births would
> have been more fully recognised, our analysis
> more sophisticated and the 1972 White Paper
> proposals pitched at lower levels.*[4]

In the above comments, the word '*momentum*' has
particular significance and shows how difficult it
is to change the assumptions behind on-going official
policy. The impression given is that it is rather
like trying to stop an ocean liner steaming at full
speed. The final sentence quoted is also significant, indicating as it does that when the first
intimation of a reduction came in the 1972 White
Paper, in terms of numbers it was inadequate.

There has also been some confusion over the
workings of the James Committee, whose report
entitled *Teacher Education and Training*[5] was published in January 1972. It seems that the Committee did
discuss, probably at some point during 1971, statistics showing that, due to the declining birth-rate,
fewer new teachers would be needed,[6] but the report
contained only the briefest of passing references to
this possibility. One critical commentator has
suggested that the reason for this was that either
the committee did not understand the implieations or
they were so worried about the seriousness of the
latter that they declined to include them more
publicly.[7]

Whatever the truth behind the decision not to
publicise this issue in the report in January 1972,
it figured prominently in the educational headlines

after the White Paper was published in the following
December; this led on to the period in which
colleges of education faced the prospect of becoming
non-viable institutions and had, often with rather
undue haste, to seek a merger with a local polytechnic, university or other college. The years
1973-75 are castigated by Hencke as *'The Drift
through Chaos'*[8] whilst the preoccupation of the
colleges became, in the words of one research thesis,
'death or transfiguration'.[9]   Uniquely within British higher education, the numbers of students on
teacher-training courses were and still are con-
trolled directly by the DES; in respect of no other
aspect of the system is this true in quite the same
way.   Therefore the DES could effect reductions in
the numbers of student places on such courses by
simple edict, which would take immediate effect.
Gradually, very gradually, the full implications of
the continuing decline in the birth-rate became
clear to the DES and on no fewer than four occasions
between 1974 and 1977 successive Secretaries of
State announced reductions in the numbers of places
in colleges of education, down to 45,000 (from the
previously-announced expected high, never actually
achieved, of 130,000); by 1982 the figure would be
as low as 27,000.
     The reduction in teacher-training places was
concentrated almost entirely in the colleges of
education where control was easiest and mainly
affected the three-year and four-year 'long' courses.
As was shown in Chapter Four, the annual intake on to
such courses fell from just over 37,000 in 1972 to
under 7,500 by 1981.   Even so, by 1976 there were
reports of some newly-qualified teachers having
difficulties in finding teaching jobs, a far cry from
the severe teacher shortages of the previous 30 years.
By 1982, further reshaping and reductions in secondary training led the DES to propose that a further 16
institutions (later reduced to 13) should cease
initial teacher training and that some of these,
including some that thought they had re-organised
themselves very successfully over the previous decade,
should close.   From this and the next round of DES
proposals, which included suggestions that some of
the smaller voluntary colleges should close, final
decisions dragged on into 1986.   By then such
colleges had had a full 14 years of continuing cuts
and uncertainty and for the smallest colleges their
futures still looked far from secure.
     For the colleges of education, there seems
little doubt that the worst experiences they had to

face were at the start of the process of cutting-
back, presumably because none of the people involved
had any experience of conducting such an exercise.
Hencke says there was '*total confusion by all the
participants with the possible exception of the
Department officials*'.   He shows how the DES gradually became more and more severe in its attitudes
to LEAs' proposals, and he is particularly scathing
of the secrecy, amounting almost to an obsession,
which the DES insisted on maintaining throughout the
exercise: '*the colleges' figures were guarded by
the Department as though they were front line bases
defending Britain from nuclear attack*'.

Faced with the dramatic reduction in numbers of
student places required after 1972, the monotechnic
colleges clearly could not continue to exist as such:
in the ensuing re-organisation not one of the 155
colleges emerged unscathed, the great majority
effecting mergers with polytechnics, other colleges,
or universities or developing into diversified
institutions offering a range of degree and sub-
degree courses with a predominant 'liberal arts'
emphasis.   Only 14 colleges had to close altogether
at the time (causing dramatic advertisements to
appear in national newspapers on the lines of the
one that read '*For Sale - The College of Education
at Milton Keynes*') although others suffered a rather
similar fate later by a slower process (e.g. Madeley
College of Education, which was absorbed into North
Staffs. Polytechnic before the site was eventually
closed down and some of the courses transferred
elsewhere).   One story that caught the headlines
was that of the college where the new library was
still being built when the notice of closure of the
college arrived.

There has been much criticism of the experiences
which the colleges had to suffer, not least by Hencke,
writing in 1977:

> *The last five years in the history of teacher
> training have been a story of missed opportun-
> ities, shabby compromises, failed policies, and
> a trail of chaos through the public higher
> education system.*

Whilst it may be true that the DES '*failed to
devise a coherent strategy for teacher training*'[10]
it can scarcely be doubted that the eventual outcome
was in at least some respects beneficial and was
even handled generously by the government.   The
diversified institutions which have emerged, offering

a much wider range of courses and with a larger
proportion of their work at degree level, are undoubtedly stronger than their predecessors and have
now achieved considerable standing in their own
right; their graduates go out to a much wider range
of occupations than the previous concentration on
teacher training. None of the academic staff from
the former colleges had to face the prospect of
redundancy (as increasingly did their counterparts
in industrial or commercial firms), all either finding posts in the new institutions, being offered
alternatives by the LEA, or taking early retirement
on the generous pension terms offered by the
'Crombie' scheme. Most of the buildings and other
facilities continued in educational or suitable
alternative use, and in that sense waste was mini-
mised.

The colleges of education as such had ceased to
exist. In terms of planning the system of higher
education, however, their demise did not lead to
identifiable savings since the reductions in the
numbers of student places on teacher-training courses
were more than offset by the proliferation and growth
of other degree courses. Such was the combination
of momentum and inertia in the system. There was
no identification of national needs or priorities
(other than that the country would need fewer
teachers) but there were buildings and other
facilities to be utilised, academic and other staff
to be employed and seemingly as many student places
of a 'liberal arts' nature would be filled as could
be provided. Hence one end result of the story
outlined above was a further accentuation of the on-
going trend, noted in Chapter Four, away from
science and engineering.

In more recent years, it has, as was seen in
Chapter Four, become more convenient to the DES to
reduce the relative importance of the 'long' three-
and four-year teacher-training courses, whether
denominated as certificate or degree courses, in
favour of the one-year PGCE course, now being extended to 36 weeks. Educational arguments have consistently favoured the former courses but the latter
have gained popularity with planners on account of
their flexibility and potential for rapid change.
Over 50 per cent of new teachers now train via this
route, in contrast to only 15 per cent in the early
1960s. The division of places between universities
on the one hand and polytechnics and colleges on the
other has largely become a political decision, with
the DES now aiming at approximate equality between

the two sectors in their planning decisions.

STUDENT NUMBERS

If the years outlined above were traumatic from the point of view of the colleges of education, they were also difficult in other respects, one notable one being the numbers of students *opting* to enter higher education (as distinct from the downward demographic trend due to the birth-rate statistics, which could be predicted with little difficulty). Speaking at a Council of Europe Symposium in Oxford in April 1974 Mr Edward Simpson, Deputy Secretary at the DES responsible for higher education, described the period since the publication of the December 1972 White Paper as *'a planner's nightmare'*.[11] Professor Williams comments that there was *'an all-pervasive air of disaster just around the corner'*.

As we have seen, higher education in the UK has always proceeded largely on the basis of providing places to cater for student demand - indeed this was enunciated as the core principle in the Robbins Report that *'Courses of higher education should be avilable for all who are qualified by ability and attainment to pursue them and who wish to do so'* - with rather little reference being paid to national economic or industrial needs. That demand was high and ever-increasing throughout the period from 1945 to around 1972: the percentages of each successive age-cohort seeking to enter firstly sixth-forms and then higher education were rising steadily each year and particularly sharply from 1966 onwards.

By the time, however, of the White Paper *Education: A Framework for Expansion*, published in December 1972, the DES was starting to suspect that these unprecedented increases could not go on for ever and indeed that White Paper embodied in its statistical workings a forecast of a *decline* in the percentage of the age-cohort passing two subjects at GCE A-level and therefore liable to go on to higher education. This revised forecast passed largely unnoticed at the time but it is an example of the DES reacting remarkably swiftly to changing statistical evidence, in considerable contrast to the way the Department reacted so slowly on the teacher-training question, as outlined above. The first-hand evidence came with the statistics relating to 1972 school-leavers which were not published until 1974 and which the DES must still have been in the course of assembling in the autumn of 1972 when the White

Paper was being written. However, it seems likely that officials were also influenced by the fact that the increases recorded in each of 1970 and 1971 were considerably smaller than had been the case for the previous three years or so, as shown in Table 10.1.

Table 10.1: Percentage of Age-Cohort Obtaining Two or More A-Levels[12]

1966	9.6
1967	10.9
1968	11.9
1969	12.7
1970	13.3
1971	13.9
1972	13.9

The DES may also have been influenced by the fact that of all school-leavers with two GCE A-levels a gradually increasing proportion were girls - just on 45 per cent by 1972 - and the trend was still for far fewer girls to seek to go on to full-time higher education than boys. And of those who did so large numbers chose teacher-training courses where competition for places was bound to become more intensive as the number of places available started to decline. Also the expansionary effect of the recommendation of the Anderson Committee implemented in 1962, that maintenance grants should be available as of right to all students who had secured two or more A-level passes, had by then worked its way through. Then in late 1973 came the oil crisis and the economic crash and by 1974 it was clear that applications for university entrance through UCCA were no longer rising at the rate that had previously been expected.

Which of the above considerations was uppermost in the minds of the DES statisticians we shall probably never know. Also, as with all such statistical series, it is always a problem for forecasters to decide what weight to place on the possibly aberrant figures of the last year or two and what weight to attach to what were previously thought to be long-term trends. Suffice it to say that whereas the DES revised *upwards* almost annually its forecasts of the percentages of young people that would be obtaining two A-levels by the early 1980s, from the 13.3 per cent suggested in Robbins (1963) to 22.7 per cent by 1970, after an ominous silence in 1971, by 1972 the Department produced a *lower*

estimate for 1981 of 19.7 per cent, and then further
revised this downwards on two occasions in 1974,
firstly to 18.2 per cent and then to 16.0 per cent.
    The above figures, both the actuals and the
forecasts, must relate primarily to the decisions
taken by young people at about age 16 to enter sixth
forms, or their equivalents in colleges of further
education, in preparation for A-levels.   At the risk
of labouring the point, it should be clear that the
percentage doing so was still rising but at a slower
rate than had previously been expected;   by around
1973 it began to look as if a virtually stable level
had been reached.   That decision taken at about age
16 then had to be related to the decision taken two
years later, after the successful acquisition of two
A-levels, whether or not to enter higher education.
Robbins largely assumed that a high proportion of
18-year-olds would choose to do so and the then
statistics showed this to be true of over two-thirds
of the eligible candidates.   By 1973 this proportion had fallen alarmingly to under 62 per cent
and was still falling.   It was the interaction of
these two indicators that led the DES to revise
downwards the estimate of total full-time students
in higher education in the early 1980s from the
figure of 830,000 given in *Education Planning Paper
No.2* (1970) to the target of 750,000 in the 1972
White Paper, a reduction which again aroused little
comment at the time;   and it was not long before
observers were suggesting that a figure of considerably less than 700,000 would be more realistic.[13]
(In the event by 1981 there were some 687,000 students
in higher education, including some 170,000 on part-
time courses in polytechnics and colleges.)   All of
this was, of course, *before* the effects of the lower
birth-rate could be felt: since the decline in the
latter began in 1964, its incidence on higher
education would only become apparent, slowly at
first and then cumulatively, after 1982.
    Clearly then in at least some sense young people
were becoming less attracted by what higher education
had to offer.   What were the causes of this dissatisfaction?   No one can say with any certainty but it
seems likely that it stemmed from a combination of
factors.   The worsening economic situation but still
fairly ready availability of suitable jobs for 16-
year-old and 18-year-old school-leavers must have had
their impact, although these would be more marked from
the onset of the oil crisis in 1973.   It is also
possible to show, as Professor Williams has done with
great care, that not only were salaries of non-

graduates rising more rapidly than those of graduates, but also the purchasing power of students' grants had not only fallen in real terms, i.e. when compared with the retail price index, but had fallen even more rapidly in relative terms when compared with the wages earned by those of their contemporaries who were at work. There was also some, although rather limited, incidence of graduates starting to have difficulties in securing suitable jobs after obtaining their degrees. In respect of each of these indicators, there were slowly developing trends that were to become more pronounced in future years. To what extent 16-year-olds or 18-year-olds, or their families, were aware of such evidence is of course another matter and is one on which we have no reliable information. We can only hypothesise that there may well have been some link, presumably either via general impressions gained from the mass media or via reports from former alumni filtering back through schools.

In more recent years, the percentage of qualified young people, in the sense of having two or more A-levels, at first fluctuated and then stabilised, in considerable contrast to the previous trend for the percentage to rise steadily year by year. Not until the 1980s did the percentage again appear to be rising, albeit rather slowly. Presumably by then the incidence of large-scale youth unemployment had become the major factor. The DES's latest projections as given in the Green Paper *The Development of Higher Education into the 1990s*, are that the numbers of first degree home graduates (university and CNAA) in Great Britain will be as follows:

1986-87	99.7
1987-88	99.5
1988-89	100.5
1989-90	100.5

After 1990 numbers are projected to fall steadily, by around 33 per cent by 1996, due to the decreasing size of the relevant age population.

THE POLYTECHNICS AND COLLEGES OF HIGHER EDUCATION

From their inception in the late 1960s the polytechnics saw more rapid growth than any other sector of higher education, as new courses were developed and students recruited in large numbers, particularly in the categories '*social, administrative and business studies'* (much the largest), *'music, drama, etc.'* (the second largest) and, to a slightly less extent, *'engineering and technology'*. In their early years the 30 polytechnics seemed to have almost no limitations placed on their rates of growth and student numbers escalated rapidly. Almost all their degree-level students were on courses validated by the Council for National Academic Awards which alone had the power to award degrees outside the universities. The same is true of those degree courses which sprang up in the much smaller Colleges and Institutes of Higher Education and so statistics of CNAA degrees awarded include the latter, but they are overwhelmingly dominated by the polytechnics. These statistics are the most reliable single source for the purpose of establishing trends over time, even though they exclude all the work at sub-degree level.

By 1970 only 2,910 first degrees were awarded by the CNAA, just on 70 per cent of these being in the categories *engineering and technology* and *science* from which the polytechnics derived their main roots. Since many of these courses replaced others previously in existence, especially external University of London degrees, there had by that date been rather little genuine growth. The next nine years saw unbridled expansion to reach 23,401 by 1979, with now less than 28 per cent being in engineering and technology and science: the growth occurred primarily in the social science and arts subject areas. If one takes the published statistics at face value, there was then a slight contraction to a total of 22,751 in 1980. The most probable interpretation, however, is that in 1980 a number of awards were delayed until 1981, apparently causing the 1980 figure to be lower than expected and the 1981 figure (at the very high 34,550) larger. Further the method of publication by the CNAA changed in 1981. By 1982 the figures were supposedly back to 'normal', with a total of 29,323 first degrees (i.e. *over ten times* the figure for 1970), of which less than 27 per cent were in the engineering and technology and science categories.[14] Since, however, the comparable figures for 1983 were 25,566 and for 1984 34,496, which again look quite erratic, it is difficult to have confidence in them as indicators of trends over time. A more reliable indication is given by the statistics of students enrolled on CNAA first degree courses in recent years, as shown in Table 10.2. Whilst total student numbers in 1984-5 were higher than ever before, these figures show clearly the progressive

Table 10.2:   Students Enrolled on CNAA First Degree
Courses

	All students		First year students	
	Number	% change	Number	% change
1981-82	138,000	-	52,808	-
1982-83	152,882	10.8	56,821	7.6
1983-84	164,965	7.9	57,781	1.7
1984-85	167,926	1.7	56,707	-1.9

deterioration with the total student intake for
1984-85 being actually below that for the preceding
year.   Needless to say, some individual polytechnics
or colleges had had falls in their student numbers
in earlier years.
     The story of the development of the polytechnics
and colleges over the last five years or so is dominated by the work of the *National Advisory Body for
Local Authority Higher Education*, known colloquially
as NAB.   Following the issuing by the DES of a
Green Paper on *Higher Education in England Outside
the Universities* in July 1981 and a hectic period of
discussion and consultation, the Secretary of State
announced in December 1981 that a new national body
would be set up and would start work almost immediately, its remit being '*to advise on the distribution of
the advanced further education pool and on academic
provision in local authority institutions of higher
education*'.   Since courses were validated and
degrees awarded by the CNAA, clearly a major function
of the NAB would be to control, or strictly to advise
the Secretary of State on the control of, student
numbers in institutions.   That some form of central
control of higher education outside the universities
was necessary had been apparent for some years -
unbridled growth at the rates indicated above and
haphazard as to its location or subject composition
clearly could not be allowed to continue for ever;
there had been various other proposals for centralised control under both Labour and Conservative
administrations but in the end these had come to
nought.   A particular virtue of NAB was that its
two-tier structure enabled it to include political,
external and professional educational representation,

thus giving considerable credence to its work from the outset.

NAB's field of reference embraced the work of some 350 institutions (eventually more when the voluntary colleges were brought within its ambit) but inevitably much of its time has been taken up with the 90 or so polytechnics and colleges that provide the greater part of public sector higher education and virtually all degree-level work outside the universities.

NAB began by not only reviewing the total shape and size of the system of higher education for which it now found itself responsible but also setting up study groups to examine and report upon specific subject areas, early ones selected being pharmacy, art and design, some areas of engineering, agriculture and teacher training. These reviews were to be at least partly trans-binary in nature since each sub-committee was to include university representation and to pay at least some attention to similar provision in universities. Eventually in 1985, two fully trans-binary reviews were set up, for Continuing Education and for Library and Information Studies, jointly by the NAB and the UGC.

NAB had been in existence for less than a year when it found itself, in late 1982, embroiled in the government's determination to achieve a 10 per cent reduction in resources in real terms for public sector higher education for the two years 1983-4 and 1984-5. NAB was required to produce proposals to give effect to this policy and its initial response was to invite colleges to indicate their own strengths and priorities. Thereafter, institutions were informed of their expected student enrolments and NAB announced that a few courses and a small number of colleges should be closed. All in all the system changed rather little and the outcome was certainly less draconian than many people had feared. The aim of the DES, and at first this was also largely true of NAB, was not in fact to cut student numbers at all but to accommodate as many students as possible, at least as many as before, whilst resources were decreasing in real terms. This was eventually stated clearly in the government's Green Paper *The Development of Higher Education into the 1990s*, published in 1985. In that sense the workings of NAB were not primarily to do with student numbers but with funding, which is dealt with separately below.

NAB subsequently embarked on its second major planning exercise, leading to decisions due to take

effect from September 1987, and based on the assumption that the number of student places in public
sector higher education would have to be reduced by
about 6,800 overall; this seemed a comparatively
small figure but in the event proposals to achieve
it were to prove quite traumatic when they were
published in 1986. These included course closures
and the cessation of degree-level work altogether in
some departments at some institutions - engineering
at Wolverhampton Polytechnic being just one example.
Through the summer of 1986, NAB's proposals and the
colleges' often vehemently expressed replies were
still under discussion and this whole issue was not
the least of the problems confronting the new
Secretary of State. Shortly before the start of
the new academic year, the latter was able to
announce the availability of additional funds that
would mitigate the effects of the NAB proposals.

Looking into the future, the Green Paper makes
it clear that the government expects the total system
of higher education to cope with approximately level
numbers of students to the end of the 1980s, but with
decreasing resources. Thereafter the expectation
expressed in the Green Paper is that the total number
of students in higher education will decline by about
70,000 in the 1990s as the smaller age-cohorts work
their way through. This projection came after the
DES had produced alternative forecasts, depending on
the extent to which higher proportions of successively smaller populations would be likely to be
seeking places in higher education.

These forecasts gave rise to much controversy
from 1984 onwards, with most professional education
opinion believing that the DES was being unduly
pessimistic, in the sense of pitching its estimates
too low. In particular, it seemed quite possible
that the percentage take up of degree-level courses
by girls would gradually rise to approach that by
boys, in just the same way that approximate equality
had been achieved in terms of staying on at school
to age 18 and securing A-level passes. Much will
depend on the course of future events, including the
national situation relating to unemployment, as it
cannot now be doubted that the latter consideration
is uppermost in the minds of many young people when
taking decisions about their futures.

THE UNIVERSITIES

Until the rise of the polytechnics and colleges,
higher education in the UK was largely concentrated
in the universities, which have always been regarded
as the most prestigious sector and treated accordingly.   Student numbers in universities were
increasing steadily before Robbins (1963) but grew
much more rapidly thereafter.   From having only some
50,000 students in 1939, by 1962 universities had a
total of 113,000 on full-time and sandwich courses.
During the 1962-67 quinquennium, the later years of
which were the period of most rapid growth, the
figure increased by 63 per cent to 184,000;   during
the 1967-72 quinquennium growth continued but more
slowly, numbers rising by a further 28 per cent to
235,000, continuing to dwarf the still quite small
polytechnics and colleges.   In the words of one
commentator, universities aimed headlong at expansion, seemingly setting out to recruit as many
students as they could, even to the extent of sometimes accepting lower entry standards, and the UGC
seemed happy to continue to allocate resources
largely according to student numbers.[15]
    The years following the issuing of the 1972
White Paper saw, despite the Paper's title *Education:
A Framework for Expansion*, an end to the period of
unremitting growth.   By the autumn of 1973 there
were in universities close on 245,000 full-time
students, still a small increase (of 1.6 per cent)
over the previous year but nearly 7,000 students less
than had been expected at the time the White Paper
was being prepared one year previously.   The age
participation rate had started to fall and was to
continue to decline for much of the 1970s, contrary
to the White Paper's assumption that it would continue to increase significantly.   Even in the
autumn of 1972, before the White Paper was published,
there had been a small and at the time little noticed
shortfall of 3,000 from the planned total of 243,000,
indicating that neither the 1972 White Paper nor the
economic crisis that followed can be held responsible
for the beginning of the downward trend.   When the
effects of all these factors were combined, however,
it became clear that growth expectations had to be
revised and by 1974 the UGC had adjusted its 1976-7
target downwards by between 8 and 11 per cent from
the original figure of 306,000 full-time students.
This process continued in subsequent years with continuing slow growth but successive downward revisions
of expectations.   The White Paper had envisaged some

375,000 full-time students in universities by 1981
but by the time of the Public Expenditure White
Paper of January 1979 the projection had been
successively lowered to stand at 308,000; in the
event the actual total was just below this figure.

Since total numbers of students necessarily
change only slowly it is also instructive to look at
UCCA's statistics of first-year undergraduates
admitted to universities during the crucial period
from 1979, as shown in Table 10.3.

Table 10.3: First-Year Students Admitted to
Universities

	Home	Overseas	Total	% change
1979	76,631	5,767	82,398	+ 2.3
1980	78,939	5,756	84,695	+ 2.8
1981	74,514	5,827	80,341	- 5.1
1982	72,634	5,118	77,752	- 3.2
1983	69,631	5,229	74,860	- 3.7
1984	71,768	5,663	77,431	+ 3.4

*Source: UCCA, Statistical Supplement to the
Annual Report.*

These figures show clearly that in terms of intakes
expansion continued slowly until 1980.   Thereafter
the number of home entrants declined significantly
each year until 1983 and the number of overseas
students also fell albeit unevenly and with a
particularly sharp drop in 1982.   Not until 1984,
the last year for which figures are available, did
intake numbers recover.   By that date the universities' share of entrants to all degree courses had
stabilised at around 58 per cent.   When courses of
all kinds including those at sub-degree level
(86,000 students in polytechnics and colleges in
1983-4) are considered, however, the numbers of
students in polytechnics and colleges easily exceeded
those in universities.   The latter now had the
minority share of the total higher education system.

If the whole of the present chapter provides
rather melancholy reading, this is particularly true
of the following words of the UGC:

> *The Committee is aware of and regrets the con-
> sequence that many well-qualified students in
> fields other than those to which it felt able
> to afford comparative protection cannot obtain
> university places and will be unlikely to do so
> throughout the whole of the 1980s. The
> Committee's demographic analysis indicates that
> the outcome of the restriction on student
> numbers will be a deterioration in the overall
> participation rate of qualified and willing
> students from the present level of 73 per cent
> to around 60 per cent until about 1990.*[16]

FUNDING

Thus far in this chapter we have largely been considering student numbers, which provide the most
obvious and direct connection with national employment needs. All of the changes in direction considered above, however, have in fact been dominated
by questions of finance. In the end it was because
funding ceased to be available at such generous
levels as previously, or because the provision of
finance could not continue to grow to match the
institutions' expectations, that student numbers had
to grow at slower rates before eventually having to
decline. When the term 'cuts' is used, it is often
taken to refer primarily to this reduction in funding or at least in the rate at which funding was
growing. Such diminution in funding, or lack of
willingness to allow it to continue to increase as
previously, partly related to political decisions
taken by successive governments both Labour and
Conservative: to give priority to expenditure on
defence, for example, at the expense of education is
clearly a political decision. But fundamentally it
related to the continuing deterioration in Britain's
economic performance. Whatever administration had
been in power during the period in question, it can
scarcely be doubted that the erosion of the country's
economic base would have made at least some degree
of tighter control of the finance available for
higher education inevitable.

The Control of Public Expenditure
It was as long ago as 1961 that the Plowden Report
on *The Control of Public Expenditure* commented
adversely on the unplanned growth of public expenditure and called for more effective measures of

control.   Four years later, in 1965, a programme of
reduction in the planned level of public expenditure,
as a component part of deflationary macro-economic
policy, was first instituted by a Labour Chancellor:
in February of that year the government announced
that the rate of increase of expenditure over the
next five years would be curtailed and by July, at
the time of the sterling crisis, actual cuts were
announced in levels of public authority investment.
Fortunately education and particularly higher
education emerged unscathed, and were relatively
little affected by further fiscal restraints over
the next few years.

By December 1973, in the wake of the economic
crisis that had begun the previous month with a
two-thirds rise in the price of oil, to be followed
by a further doubling in the following January, the
annual White Paper on Public Expenditure (Cmnd 5519)
announced more severe cuts, including that one-half
of the usual supplement of universities' recurrent
expenditure for the academic year 1974-5 and subsequent years of the quinquennium would be withheld,
that equipment expenditure would not be supplemented
for one year's increases in prices, and that universities were not to compensate by tailoring their
student numbers.   Further reductions, including
withholding the remaining half of supplementation for
inflation for 1974-5 followed later the same month
as the economic crisis worsened.   That, combined
with the restructuring of the colleges of education,
may be said to have been the start of the long
period of financial cuts applied to higher education
which has continued, in one form or another, to the
present day.   Almost every one of the 12 annual
White Papers on Public Expenditure issued during
those years contained, in varying degree, some form
of financial retrenchment to be applied to higher
education.

By 1975-6 the position in which universities
found themsleves was so serious that the UGC felt
obliged to comment:

> *The year under review marked a conclusive down-*
> *turn in a process of growth of resources which*
> *has continued for about twenty years, and is*
> *unlikely soon to be resumed.   Universities are*
> *now conscious not only of difficult but of*
> *novel problems which cannot be solved by*
> *improvisation.   At the same time the financial*
> *system which permitted and encouraged forward*
> *planning has been seriously damaged by*

> *successive short-term decisions relating to*
> *changing national pressures.   As a result*
> *there is a deep and damaging sense of*
> *uncertainty.*[17]

Worse was to come.   During the same academic
year, 1975-6, the government announced, in the White
Paper *Cash Limits on Public Expenditure* (Cmnd 6440)
its new policy of requiring spending departments to
live within cash limits.   These meant that once an
annual budget had been established it would be
adhered to and there would be no supplementation in
respect of inflation, not even for salary increases.
Cash limits were applied to education, including
higher education, and from henceforth were to constitute a tight and severe financial constraint.
In future, if salaries, for example, were increased
in excess of the norm provided for, which was often
quite low, then the excess had to be found from elsewhere within the budget, i.e. by reducing expenditure
on some other heading.   Each university has had to
operate in this way ever since.   So too, broadly,
have polytechnics and colleges, save that in their
case the LEA could provide some degree of mitigation
from within its budget if it chose to do so.

In the case of the polytechnics and colleges,
dissatisfaction with the method and arrangements for
funding grew during the 1970s, relating especially
to the working of the 'pool' system by which the
cost of advanced further education was not allowed
to fall unduly heavily on the authority responsible
for a college or polytechnic but was spread fairly
evenly, via a formula comprising school-age population and non-domestic rateable value, over authorities throughout the country.   There was obviously
a certain fairness in this system in that an authority which happened not to have such an institution
would otherwise happily see the cost of educating
that part of its 18-plus population fall on other
authorities but critics of this system, including
the Layfield Report on *Local Government Finance*,
considered that it removed any incentive for a
sensible check on expenditure and was partly responsible for the mushrooming of advanced further education.   The component elements within the formula
were modified from time to time in efforts to achieve
a greater degree of equity but as the total cost of
the system escalated with the growth of the polytechnics, the issue attracted increased attention.

The principle that there should be a limit
placed on the total size of the pool, and thus on

advanced further education, instead of allowing a
'free market' where the global sum emerged as the
residual from all the demands made upon the pool by
local authorites, was advocated in the Oakes Report
of 1977; this report emerged from the committee set
up by the DES, and chaired by the then Minister of
State, to investigate the arrangements under which
public sector higher education was managed and
funded.   The proposal was not implemented by the
out-going Labour government but was to prove attractive to the in-coming Conservative administration
after the General Election in May 1979: one of its
first decisions in the field of education was to
limit or *'cap'* (to use the term that has become
widely used) the size of the pool for the financial
year 1980-81.   Henceforth any LEA exceeding a predetermined level of expenditure on higher education
would have to find the balance from the rates - and
this in turn became increasingly difficult to do as
local authority rates became subject to tighter controls and the imposition of financial penalties for
overspending.   There had always been authorities
which supplemented the pool funds from other sources
- probably most at one time did so - and some of the
fortunate ones are still able to do so, but increasingly in recent years such supplementation has had
to be curtailed and in a number of hard-pressed LEAs
it has ceased altogether.

Later the same year, in November 1979, the size
of the predetermined pool for 1980-81 was announced
as £375 million, an overall cut in real terms of
about 9 per cent and with much harsher cuts in the
case of some LEAs.   With the capping of the pool,
clearly decisions would have to be taken centrally
which would be of crucial importance to the whole of
the public sector higher education system and this
factor led on to the creation of the National
Advisory Board, as outlined previously.

With relatively minor changes each year the
capped pool has continued to operate in this way,
usually with an annual cut in real resources, an
important exercise being that referred to above when
the government announced in the autumn of 1982 a 10
per cent reduction in real terms in the funding available for 1983-4 and 1984-5.   In September 1986, however, to the surprise of all concerned, the new
Secretary of State was able to find an additional £54
million in order to increase the size of the capped
pool by 8 per cent - more than the rate of inflation
but needed to cope with the numbers of students.

Two further points relating to the pool have

227

been of importance. Firstly, what *The Times Higher Education Supplement* termed: *'the great war between "access" and the "unit of resource"'*[18] as financial constraint became increasingly more severe in real terms, the polytechnics and colleges became louder in their protests that they could not continue to increase student numbers indefinitely. Staff/student ratios in particular have worsened dramatically in polytechnics in recent years and the Committee of Directors of Polytechnics, amongst others, has protested against the continuation of this trend. Such protests seem to have found a sympathetic ear with the new Secretary of State, as noted above. The second point related to the distribution of the pool, particularly as regards the shares to be allocated respectively to the polytechnics, the colleges and institutes of higher education, and the large number of colleges of further education who each undertake a small amount of advanced work; as might be expected, each of these three sectors has argued its case for an increased share in the diminishing pool. Both of these points seem likely to continue to occupy NAB for some time to come.

To revert to the universities, if their financial situation continued to be serious up to 1979, it was to become much more so after the General Election. Nor was the UGC emerging as a strong defender of the university system:

> *By 1979, the UGC system was in serious disrepair. Its planning mechanisms were in tatters, with the Chairman being able to do little more than react to the twists and turns of the Government's counter-inflation policy. It had sought with some success to keep universities informed of developments but there could be little pretence that it remained a body which carried weight with the DES or Whitehall.*[19]

The situation looked bleak but, to repeat a phrase already used in this chapter, worse was to come. In June 1979 the UGC informed the universities of budget reductions and in the autumn of that year the government announced its decision to withdraw subsidy progressively from overseas students; then in the period December 1980 to March 1981 annual expenditure on home students was to be reduced by amounts totalling 8½ per cent in real terms by 1983-4. The UGC calculated that the cumulative effect of the latter

two measures would be to reduce total resources for
universities by 11-15 per cent by 1983-4. It was
primarily as a response to this process of diminishing resources that the UGC was thenceforth to feel
the need to become more *dirigiste* in its dealings
with universities.

In March 1981 the annual White Paper on Public
Expenditure (Cmnd 8175) provided for further planned
falls in public expenditure including in relation to
universities. Thus was set the scene for the UGC's
letter of 1 July 1981 announcing the universities'
grants for 1981-2 and succeeding years. Before
issuing this letter the UGC had been assembling a
mass of detailed information (not all of it fully
up-to-date) relating to each university and attempting to make value judgements regarding each institution's relative strengths and weaknesses. Only
via such selective guidance did the Committee feel
that best use would be made, over the university
system as a whole, of the reduced level of funding
now available (now estimated to be around 10 per
cent down on average by 1983-4). In assessing the
strengths of subject areas at each university, it
appears that the UGC was influenced by a number of
indicators, including A-level grades of students at
entry, ease in getting jobs on graduation, cost-
effectiveness (especially as indicated by staff/
student ratios), and research standing. It also
seemed that the standing and influence of the Vice-
Chancellor had a bearing on the Committee's deliber-
ations, although the Chairman of the UGC later denied
that they took the view that each institution '*had a
personality rather like a filmstar or something*'.[20]
Nevertheless the cumulative effect of the judgements
relating to the various subject areas was that some
universities - such as Salford, Bradford, Keele,
Stirling and Aston - had to face particularly severe
cuts, whilst others - such as York, Bath, East
Anglia, Loughborough and Leicester - were treated
much more favourably. To many observers these
effects were quite perplexing: why, for example,
should some of the technological universities have
been treated so harshly but others quite favourably?
Since the UGC continued its previous policy of not
explaining the reasoning behind its decisions, no
ready answers were forthcoming.

Over the period 1981-84, the effects of the
July 1981 letter gradually worked their way through,
the most noticeable being the numbers of staff
invited to take early retirement or choosing to leave
to move to other jobs. Staff/student ratios

gradually worsened (although not as dramatically as they did in the polytechnics during the same years) and there was an increasing tendency for vacant Chairs and other posts not to be filled; some deterioration in buildings and other facilities started to manifest itself and library opening hours, for example, typically shortened. However, contrary to the worst fears that had been expressed in 1981, no staff were compulsorily made redundant and no universities went bankrupt. Those universities with substantial cash reserves were able to cushion themselves against the worst of the hardships that had been forecast; it appears that the UGC considered but rejected the idea of bringing the size of cash reserves, and some scale of diminution in same, into their calculations for each institution. It hardly needs to be said that the existence of such reserves provides one of the sharpest distinctions between universities and polytechnics in a period of financial stringency.

There was subsequently much criticism of the 1981 *'Restructuring'* exercise, both in the way it had been conducted and in terms of its effects. The Jarratt Report into the efficiency of universities,[21] for example, made it plain that it felt that much more could have been achieved. Having embarked on the path towards the use of selective judgements, however, when the UGC was enjoined by the government to implement further severe cuts, it continued to use the same principle. In 1985 universities were required to supply the UGC with detailed assessments of each of their departments and subject areas as part of what was dubbed the *'selectivity exercise'*: this was required to effect a further reduction (or *improvement*, as ministers now tended to call it) in funding of an additional 10 per cent by 1990.

When the UGC announced, in May 1986, its decisions comprising, for each university, funding, student numbers and qualitative assessment of each department or subject group in terms of its research, as in 1981 the effects were to be felt very unevenly across the country; Loughborough, for example, was in unit cost terms, i.e. when percentage change in grant is related to percentage change in numbers of students, treated more generously than any other institution. Those departments or subject groups in each university which were rated as *'stars'* (= outstanding) for their research were in future to receive more favourable treatment. At the time of writing each university is wrestling with the combined problems of how to achieve such greater

internal selectivity, how to shed itself of sufficient numbers of staff (and particularly those who
are less productive in research terms) to effect the
savings required, how to tailor student numbers to
meet UGC guidelines for subject areas, and the inter-
active effects between all of these.   The useful
cash reserves mentioned above seem likely to dwindle
or disappear altogether in some institutions and by
mid-1986 there were stories in the educational press
of at least one institution, University College,
Cardiff, now running at a large and increasing financial deficit.

CONCLUSIONS

It was said at the outset that this chapter would
tell a melancholy story.   Considerations of national
needs in terms of the supply of highly-educated
graduates to play their part in the nation's economic
and industrial regeneration, have played some small
part in the story outlined in this chapter.   But it
cannot be doubted that such needs have been given
less importance than the prerequisite of achieving
financial savings.   In all types of institution the
growth of student numbers has been curtailed and
expenditure levels have been reduced in real terms.
The system has coped with these cuts, and will doubtless cope with those currently working their way
through, but at a price.   What has been achieved
has, in some respects at least, been the reverse of
that needed from the point of view of future economic
performance.   From the point of view of the system
of higher education, much depends on whether we have
now reached the end of this long period of retrenchment and financial cuts;   whether the quality of the
education which the students receive has already
declined is a moot point but there can be little
doubt that it will do so if at least level funding
in unit cost terms is not preserved in future years.
     At long last in 1986 there seemed to be grounds
for greater optimism with the advent of the new
Secretary of State of Mr. Kenneth Baker, who seemed
determined to preserve and even expand the size of
the higher education system.   By September
Mr Maurice Shock, chairman of the Committee of Vice-
Chancellors and Principals, was moved to comment:

> *I welcome Mr Baker's announcement of the*
> *conversion of the Government to the expansion*
> *of higher education after years in which the*

> talk and the action have been about nothing
> but contraction.[22]

It now remains to be seen whether such hopes will be
borne out in practice.

NOTES

1. Robbins Report: *Committee on Higher
Education* (HMSO, 1963).
2. DES, *A Plan for Polytechnics and Other
Colleges: Higher Education in the Further Education
System* (White Paper, HMSO, 1966).
3. DES, *Education: A Framework for Expansion*
(White Paper, HMSO, 1972).
4. H. Harding, 'Review of D. Hencke, *Colleges
in Crisis*', *Education* (1975).
5. James Report: *Teacher Education and Training* (DES, HMSO, 1972).
6. L.M. Cantor and I.F. Roberts, *Further
Education Today, A Critical Review*, 2nd edition
(Routledge & Kegan Paul, 1983).
7. D. Hencke, *Colleges in Crisis* (Penguin,
1978).
8. *Ibid.*
9. J. Alcock, 'A Case-History of the Merger
Between Battersea College of Education and the Polytechnic of the South Bank', unpublished MA thesis
(University of London, 1979).
10. Cantor and Roberts, *Further Education Today*.
11. G.L. Williams, 'The Events of 1973-74 in a
Long-Term Planning Perspective', *Higher Education
Review*, Vol.3, No.1, and reprinted in C. Baxter *et
al.* (eds), *Economics and Education Policy*
(Longman/OU, 1977).
12. As quoted in Williams, *ibid.*   Further
statistics for the same period quoted in this
section are taken from the same source.
13. *Ibid.*
14. R. Pearson *et al.*, *Education, Training and
Employment* (Institute of Manpower Studies, Gower,
1984).
15. A. Christodoulou, in 'Proceedings of
Discussion of The Encroachment of Dirigisme on the
Development of Arts and Science', *Journal of the
Royal Society of Arts* (July 1981).
16. University Grants Committee, *Procedure
Leading to the 1981-82 Grant Distribution* (Appendix
to Chairman's letter to Select Committee for
Education, Science and Arts, 2 November 1981).

17.   UGC, *Annual Review for 1975-76*, Cmnd 6750
(HMSO).
18.   'The NAB's Good News' (leading article),
The Times Higher Education Supplement, 5 September
1986.
19.   M. Shattock and R. Berdahl, 'The British
University Grants Committee 1919-83: Changing
Relationships with Government and with the Universities', *Higher Education*, Vol.13 (1984).
20.   Evidence to House of Commons Select
Committee (para. 116).
21.   CVCP, *Report of the Steering Committee for
Efficiency Studies in Universities* (CVCP, March
1985).
22.   M. Dowd, 'Baker Goes for Student Loans and
Sponsorship', *The Times*, 24 September 1986.

Chapter Eleven

EDUCATION VOUCHERS AND STUDENT LOANS

The financing of education is a perennial problem
for the government of the day, in the UK as in all
other comparable countries. As was shown in
Chapter Seven, education is always one of the largest
of all categories of public expenditure and the management and allocation of the vast resources required
is not only a matter of great concern in itself but
also has a strong interaction with various other
aspects of government policy. These twin considerations have in recent years led to a resurrection of
interest in two possible controversial schemes for
altering the existing arrangements for the financing
of education, Education Vouchers and Student Loans,
both of which were studied and discussed in the UK
and elsewhere over 40 years ago and both of which
have been at least partly put to the test in other
countries.
      Both are concerned with the total level of
finance available for education but both also have
wider ramifications. The former relates essentially
to the concept of parental and student choice and to
the interconnection between the state education
system, now attended by perhaps 95 per cent of all
pupils, and the independent school sector. The
latter relates to the attempt to relate considerations of equity to the fact that the highest levels
of educational expenditure are concentrated on a
privileged elite minority who are then fortunate
enough to progress, in the main, to the higher-status
and better-paid positions in society. Each of these
schemes will now be considered in turn.

VOUCHERS FOR EDUCATION

The Education Act of 1944 is widely regarded as the
foundation stone on which the education system of
the UK is constructed and perhaps its best known and
most widely quoted part is Section 76 which specified
that children *are to be educated in accordance with
the wishes of their parents*', although this is
immediately qualified by the addition of the words
'*so far as is compatible with the provision of
efficient instruction and training and the avoidance
of unreasonable public expenditure*'. What may have
been the intention of the original drafters of the
Act when they devised that wording it is now impossible to say but, rightly or wrongly, it gave rise to
considerable expectation on the part of the general
public that they could choose, or at least have a
say in choosing, the schools their children should
attend.

In practice such hopes were largely to be
denied, partly because of the restrictive attitudes
that were typically adopted by Local Education Authorities regarding parental choice, a concept that
LEAs tended to regard with deep suspicion if not out-
right hostility, and partly because a long series of
legal cases brought before the courts by frustrated
parents were almost all decided in favour of the LEA.
In other words, the phrase quoted from the Act came
to have a very restricted interpretation and always
excluded the possibility of parents expressing a
general preference for one school as being 'better'
than another. Parents moving house to live in a
new district, for example, and seeking to live close
to a 'good' school invariable found the LEA officials
unwilling to give advice regarding any such general
assessment. Statistical indicators that might have
helped to form such an assessment, such as external
examination results or numbers staying on at school
beyond the age of compulsory schooling, were rarely
published in any systematic or readily usable way,
even though they were known to the LEA. When one
visiting American parent at a parents' meeting asked
what he said would be a normal and even expected
question in the USA, namely what was the level of
recurrent expenditure per pupil in that school as
compared with that in other comparable schools, he
was rather sharply told that such information could
not be made available (even though, again, it was
well known to the LEA).

Rightly or wrongly, this approach by Local
Education Authorities came to be seen as typical of

235

their attitudes to parents in the years after the
passing of the 1944 Act. Notices reading *'Parents
are forbidden to enter the school playground'* became
common throughout the country and were often seen as
symptomatic of a general approach. LEAs and most
headteachers would deny that relationships with
parents ever deteriorated to the point of reaching
unacceptably low levels but it can hardly be doubted
that many teachers and administrators in the education service felt that education was a matter best
left to the professionals. When, for example, the
Taylor Report on School Governors paved the way for
parents and other community representatives to
receive wide representation on governing bodies for
the first time, the National Union of Teachers far
from welcoming such participation described the
report as *'a busybodies' charter'*. More than one
book was published to advise parents regarding their
rights and how to set about obtaining these, including relating to the matter of choice of school. One
of the most celebrated of these, by Judith Stone and
Felicity Taylor, advised that grounds on which
parents might be able to lodge a strong claim included religious questions, medical reasons (e.g. re.
length of journey to school), preference for mixed
or single-sex schooling, if another child from the
same family is already attending the school in
question, or aspects of the curriculum or facilities,
such as study of a particular foreign language,
*'workshops for a girl who wants to be an engineer or
cooking for a boy who wants to be a chef'*, or in
Wales the use or non-use of the Welsh language.[1]
One of the most interesting disclosures in that book
was the fact, of which all but a privileged minority
had been unaware, that some years previously the
Department of Education and Science had issued to
LEAs a *Manual of Guidance* regarding the settlement of
such problems relating to school admissions.
     From the point of view of the LEAs, the years
following 1944, when free secondary education became
available to all children for the first time, were,
of course, years of unparalleled expansion and overcrowding in schools and it seemed to LEAs that only
by having fairly rigid systems of zoning and catchment area boundaries, by which children were allocated to a particular school according to where they
lived (leaving aside the question of selective allocation to grammar school or secondary modern school
which was determined by the 11-plus examination)
could they fit the maximum number of children into
the inadequate number of school places available and

minimise the inevitable overcrowding in classrooms.
It should also be made clear that desirable egalitarian or other objectives were often being pursued
simultaneously, such as achieving in each school a
reasonable mix of children from differing socio-
economic backgrounds in so far as this was feasible.

Attitudes gradually changed, for example many
schools took down the notices in school playgrounds,
but the situation outlined above may be said to have
largely continued until the coming into effect of the
Education Act 1980, which made it clear that parents
were to be given a greater say in choice of school
(as well as having increased participation on governing bodies); schools were also required to publish
fuller details about themselves, including their
external examination results.   Since numbers of
pupils had already started to fall in primary
schools, and were soon to do so in secondary schools,
the problem of overcrowding quite rapidly gave way
to the reverse problem of surplus school places and
the question of parental choice of school was now
placed in quite a different context.   Nevertheless,
most LEAs sought to retain their zoning or catchment
area boundary arrangements whilst at the same time
complying with the Act by inviting parents to state
their choice of school.   The resulting compromise
has generally worked well save for the cases of
appeals, numbering several thousand each year, when
parents and LEA are unable to reach agreement but a
detailed investigation into the working of this aspect of the 1980 Act over the ensuing five years
found that practical policies relating to the
admissions of pupils to schools varied considerably
from one LEA to another.   The authors concluded:

> The research has clearly shown that the majority
> of LEAs are operating a system which meets the
> legal requirements of the 1980 Education Act.
> However, the fact that the concept which started
> out as parental choice was finally phrased in
> the Act as the right to express a preference
> means that 'choice for all' is still a long way
> off.   Indeed it appears that many parents have
> had their hopes raised by popular misuse of the
> word 'choice', only to be disappointed by LEA
> officers who feel the need to constantly
> reiterate the terminology of the legislation,
> i.e. preference.   While the Act has stimulated
> much lively debate and interest as to the rights
> and wrongs of choice, it does not appear to have
> altered the state of play significantly.   Only

237

> *time will tell if the balance between parents*
> *and LEAs has really shifted to any extent and,*
> *if so, whether it will bring about any*
> *beneficial changes to schools.*[2]

This rather long preamble to the subject of
education vouchers has been necessary to show that
the question of choice of school has been an important issue in the UK educational system for the past
40 years or more.   Throughout that period, the
independent, fee-paying schools, not considered
above, continued to recruit, but with a steadily
declining proportion of each age-cohort (*'private
schools were closing at a rate of almost seventy a
year in the mid-1960s'*[3]) until the early 1980s, when
the trend was reversed and their proportion started
to increase somewhat.

Economic Principles

The concept of the education voucher arose before
the period indicated above, indeed before the 1944
Education Act, and has its origins in a basic principle which lies at the heart of economic analysis,
namely consumer choice.   No-one would seriously
doubt that in the market for, say, marmalade, or
strawberries, or shoes, or throughout the whole of
the vast range of products provided by entrepreneurial initiative and offered for sale on the free
market, the potential consumer has the right to
choose whether he wishes to purchase at the ruling
price, and is free to accept or reject and take his
business elsewhere if he so wishes.   At the other
extreme, it is universally accepted in the UK that
a sick person should be able to receive medical
treatment free, regardless of ability to pay
(although it is worth noting in passing that this is
not so in other countries such as the USA, where
stories abound of people injured in road accidents
struggling to their feet and declining to enter the
ambulance, saying 'I can't afford it').   In
between these two extremes, however, there is a range
of services where it can be argued on the one hand
that they should be provided as a general community
service funded out of taxation or in some other
general way with little in the way of customer
prerogative or choice, or on the other hand that
individuals should have the right to choose how much
or how little they require and to make varying payments accordingly.   Examples are the provision of
water, television, refuse collection or the police

238

services.   In practice, often some compromise
solution is reached; in the case of each of those
just cited, a basic level of service is provided out
of taxation or the equivalent, but additional levels
of service are available on request at additional
cost: e.g. policing outside a football stadium is
provided free by the police authority but policing
inside a football stadium is charged to the football
club.

Now education is a prime example of such an
'in-between' service: in the UK we have become
accustomed to education

(i)   largely being provided by the state,
(ii)   largely being free, save for those who
        'opt out', and
(iii)   with rather little being left to the
        choice of the 'customer',

but there is no reason why these should necessarily
be so and indeed they are often not so in other
countries.   The proponents of the education voucher
see it as a means of changing these aspects and of
re-orientating education towards the 'customer' with
hoped-for consequent improvements in incentive,
efficiency and responsiveness.

An education voucher is simply a piece of paper
(or in the modern technological age it could be no
more than a computerised entry on magnetic tape)
worth the yearly cost of educating a child in a
state school, with presumably differing amounts for
primary, secondary to age 16, and sixth-form.   The
parents can then 'spend' the voucher in exchange for
their child's education at the school of their
choice.   The idea of an education voucher was first
proposed before the Second World War as a way of
resolving what seemed to have become an impasse over
the question of separate, religious, schools,
especially for children of Roman Catholic parents,
but its revival in more recent years has been for the
quite different reasons mentioned above.

Possible Effects

Both proponents and opponents of voucher schemes,
however, are agreed that the effects would depend on
the precise details of any scheme that might be
introduced: *'it is impossible to generalise from a
particular voucher plan as the outcomes are a
function of the very specific arrangements inherent
in any particular plan'.*[4]   First and foremost of

these would be whether independent schools would be included, and it now seems very likely that they would. If they were not, the effects of a voucher system would be confined to the question of parental choice of school, which the 1980 Education Act sought to extend significantly. What has limited that extension of choice, and what would still be a limiting factor in any future scheme, has been the question of what to do when a school is full - i.e. what arrangements to make regarding entry of children to those popular schools where applications for places would exceed the number of places available. At present each LEA has its own policy (or in the case of voluntary schools each governing body has its own policy) which usually relates to some mix of residential location, socio-economic class mix, regard for the position of ethnic minority children, and some 'first come first served' element.

If in any new scheme such policy were to be replaced entirely or largely by a 'first come first served' emphasis it is easy to see that the probable effects would be that the children from white, middle-class families would mainly benefit and the children from working-class or ethnic minority families would lose the safeguard of the protection which the LEA had in effect been giving them. It has also been argued that parents would choose schools for 'wrong', e.g. racist, reasons. Obviously proponents and opponents do not agree on such points. This question of school capacity is crucial: the former Director of the Inner London Education Authority wrote recently, *'If a school is not full, a voucher is not needed, if it is full, a voucher is no use'.*[5]

If, however, independent schools were to be included, as seems most likely, then it is necessary to consider the effects on the balance between the state and private sectors of education, in two main ways:

   (i)   parents already opting for private education would be able to 'spend' their state-financed voucher at the private school of their choice; thus a considerable part of the state education budget might be re-allocated to private schools, causing the latter to expand and reversing the previous long-term trend.

   (ii) more parents would probably choose independent schools in future, thus increasing the above effect.

Those in favour of vouchers would argue that this would not only bring private education within reach of a good number of families previously unable to afford it but would remove the injustice of those families who currently pay for education twice in that they not only pay taxes and rates in the normal way but also pay private school fees. Opponents of vouchers would argue that the main effect would be further to debilitate an already improverished state education system, and that it is not at all clear that private schools would expand in this way: the good private schools have for many years had more applicants than places but have always insisted on maintaining high academic entry standards and rejecting any applicants they consider unsuitable, a luxury not open to state schools which have to cater for all children. Unfortunately in the UK private education has become an emotive issue (so that one writer could refer recently to '*the injustice of wealth as a criterion for education*'[6]) as it has in, for example, France but has never been in the USA, so that it has become difficult for such a debate to be conducted in rational terms.

The longer-term effects which would follow would be that the 'popular' schools would need to expand, construct more buildings, and appoint more staff, whilst the 'unpopular' schools would decline in numbers or even have to close. The advocates of vouchers see such '*market responsiveness*' as highly desirable, with teachers' job prospects and future careers linked directly to their present achievements; opponents point to the inevitable waste and additional expense with spare places available in half-empty schools, and also suggest that teachers would be tempted to re-orientate their teaching in order to produce those results seen as desirable to those middle-class parents who are most likely to exercise influence and choice at the expense, for example, of giving extra attention to disadvantaged or slow-learning pupils.[7] It is also alleged, although as yet there is little evidence of this, that particular problems would arise when notions of popularity changed for whatever reason, so that the school which had been expanding now found itself short of pupils, and vice versa. Hence the comment that a voucher scheme

> *would radically decentralize the administration of education, laying schools open to massive fluctuations in funding and enrolment and teachers to non-professional interference and*

job insecurity.[8]

There are several other possible details of a
voucher scheme which would affect the practical outcomes, indeed one study of the subject enumerated
eight different types of education voucher,[9] the
varying details relating to such questions as whether
the voucher should be full-cost or only partial,
whether there should be some form of preferential
treatment for disadvantaged families, whether transport costs would be included, whether all parents
can re-choose schools each year, whether any private
schools participating would be required to offer
bursaries or scholarships, whether there would be
different-level vouchers to distinguish between high-
cost and low-cost schools, whether the voucher would
be linked in some way with the child's educational
attainment, and what mechanism would be used to
allocate places in those popular schools which are
over-subscribed.   Clearly all of these points would
be important and would require detailed consideration
if a voucher system were to be introduced.[10]

Voucher Experiments

There have now been two major experiments into the
effects of education vouchers, one, survey-based, in
the UK and one practical trial in the USA.   The one
in the UK was conducted by Kent County Council in
one of their educational areas, Ashford, as a pilot
scheme.   Responses from over 1,200 parents were
overwhelmingly in favour of having more information
about schools and greater parental choice and felt
that any voucher scheme should include independent
schools.   Within the state sector some 12 per cent
of parents would have chosen a school other than the
one their child now attended;   in addition to the 9
per cent of children already attending independent
schools, about an additional 7 per cent of children
would have been transferred, depending on the
additional fees required.   The great majority of
the teachers surveyed were, however, against the
scheme.   Adequate transport arrangements would be
a problem and would be expensive but would be
essential for a voucher scheme to work.   Overall
the probable changes were perhaps less dramatic than
might have been anticipated:

> *The general impression that emerges from*
> *responses to this inquiry is that choice of*
> *schools is seen as vital by parents, but that*

> *vouchers would not necessarily be the only or*
> *the most satisfactory means of achieving it.*
> *Freedom of choice, the full information about*
> *schools necessary for such choice, a right of*
> *transfer between schools and subsidised trans-*
> *port where necessary to the chosen school -*
> *these are the critical elements. The decisive*
> *factor in making them possible, with or without*
> *vouchers, would be the availability of surplus*
> *capacity in the schools.*[11]

In Alum Rock, USA, a federally-subsidised
voucher experiment was put into practice in the early
1970s and has since produced detailed reports and
analyses. Most of the points noted above recur but
there was also evidence that both schools and parts
of schools did begin to respond to the increased
competitiveness and independence and become more
parent- and pupil-orientated. However, several
years would have been required for such trends to
develop fully, especially in view of the opposition
of the majority of teachers. As commented above,
it seemed likely that many of the hoped-for benefits
of a voucher scheme could be achieved without the
introduction of vouchers as such:

> *As things now stand, the demonstration is not*
> *much of a test of the original voucher model.*
> *But it could tell us a lot about the effects*
> *of a radically decentralized system with*
> *elements of voucher model financing and direct*
> *parent participation in educational decisions.*[12]

Educational Vouchers and Politics

In recent years the possibility of an education
voucher scheme being introduced in the UK has
received considerable political attention. Such a
scheme obviously has more attraction for the Conservative Party where a number of prominent politicians
are pro-voucher. Dr Rhodes Boyson, for example, in
the House of Commons proposed an amendment to the
Education Bill 1976 to permit local authorities to
undertake practical voucher experiments, but this
was defeated. Dr Boyson was also instrumental in
having the idea of voucher experiments written into
the Conservative Party's draft election manifesto.

To what extent the present Conservative government is pursuing the idea of education vouchers is
not at all clear. There were reports that the
previous Secretary of State, Sir Keith Joseph, was

'*intellectually attracted*' to them but ended up agreeing with his deputy, Chris Patten, who once described them as '*theoretically interesting, practically hopeless*'.[13]   At one stage it was even reported that Sir Keith's Cabinet colleagues found his proposals '*too tame*' and told him to come back with more radical proposals.[14]   Sir Keith's successor as Secretary of State, Mr Kenneth Baker, is currently reported to be reconsidering the whole issue and a series of articles published in the spring of 1986 sought to bring pressure on him to decide in favour of introducing a voucher scheme.[15]

STUDENT LOANS

The second of these topics, Student Loans, is equally controversial and has equally become the subject of much political and press discussion in recent years, after having been the subject of study and analysis by interested academics over a much longer period.

The pressure on educational finance, as on all public expenditure, has become acute over the last decade or more and it is not surprising that successive governments should have sought to re-examine where economies could be made or that renewed interest should have been shown in the system of grants paid to those students in full-time courses of higher education, whether in universities, polytechnics or other colleges.   Since 1962 such grants have been mandatory for courses at degree level but discretionary for courses below degree level, i.e. each student on a degree level course is entitled to receive a grant, but they have been tied to a sliding scale relating to parental income, with the full grant only being paid where the parental income is relatively low (there are also special provisions for mature students, who are assessed independently of their parents' income).   Over time the amount of the grant has usually been raised each year but typically by less than the rate of inflation, so that students' incomes have declined in real terms.   Typically, too, the parental income figures have not been increased adequately to compensate for inflation, so that the contributions that parents were expected to make to the students' upkeep have steadily increased at each relative income level.

By 1985-6 the full student grant stood at around £1,830 per year, with parental contributions increasing significantly above a parental income of around £10,000 per year.   By the time the latter

reached around £20,000, the parental contribution
became 100 per cent and no grant was payable; since
this included both husband and wife where both were
at work, over a considerable range of occupations
this joint figure might be reached. (This would
often be the case, for example, where husband and
wife were both in school-teaching, not the most
highly paid of professions.) All this is quite
separate from course fees which, but for a short
interlude in the late 1960s, have always been paid
in full. It also leaves aside the complex question
of student entitlement to other state benefits such
as Supplementary Benefit, essentially during vacation
periods: as many more students, both in number and
as a percentage of the student population, now claim
such benefits than 30 years ago, and as the cost of
their doing so has steadily increased, the government
has sought to impose a number of restrictions in
recent years.

Since the graduates emerging from such courses
of higher education typically embark on attractive
careers with above-average salaries and typically
progress to achieve good standards of living, social
status and job security (by 1986 starting salaries
for graduates of £10,000 per annum were not unknown),
it was perhaps inevitable that there should be renewed interest in the possibiity of their receiving
repayable loans instead of grants. The loans, which
after a long run-in period should eventually be
largely self-financing, could be provided either by
the government or, for example, through an arrange-
ment with the banking sector, and could be repayable
over some future period to be determined, possibly
10 years or so. It now seems to be a serious
possibility that such a loan scheme, in some form
or other, will be introduced.

There is nothing new about the idea of student
loans, either in this country or elsewhere. In the
UK, before and after the Second World War, at a time
when no mandatory grant system existed and when the
number of students going on to full-time post-school
education was relatively small, loans for students
attending certain courses perceived as fulfilling
particular national need were available from the then
Ministry of Education under a scheme that ran quite
successfully for some years. Other countries have
persevered with student loan schemes, either publicly
or privately funded, for much longer periods.

Arguments for and Against

Since the mandatory grant scheme was introduced in
the UK over 25 years ago, it has been probably the
most generous such scheme available in any country
in the world. Experience in other countries varies
widely, from those where effectively no grants are
available, as in Japan, to those where certain grants
are available but for smaller amounts, as in West
Germany. Many countries have student loan schemes
in various forms, notably the Scandinavian countries,
a number of other countries in Europe, Canada, the
USA, Japan and most Latin American countries, the
funding coming either from government sources or
from banks with the aid of a government guarantee:
indeed a recent thorough study found that Britain was
now one of the few developed countries with no system
of student loans in some shape or form. [16]

The main argument in favour of a system of
student loans to replace, in whole or in part, the
present system of government grants must be equity-
based: if the young people in question will, on
average, progress to enjoy in the future the prosperity referred to above, and if that prosperity may
be said to derive in large measure from the high-
level and very expensive education they have
received, then surely it is only 'fair' that they
should reimburse the state, i.e. their fellow tax
payers, for some part of the cost of that education
(this would never be more than part - even if grants
were to be fully replaced by loans, the greater part
of the cost of providing the students' education
would still be borne by the state). In the
absence of such reimbursement the students' education
is being financed by their fellow tax payers who
mostly have not had the benefit of higher education
and who are, allowing for the passage of time, on
average worse off than they are. In that sense the
argument is not dissimilar to that relating to
deficit financing for British Rail, which means that
those people who travel by train are subsidised by
those who do not. The argument gets compounded,
however, by the question of socio-economic class,
since, whereas some two-thirds of the population of
this country are defined as working-class, some four
out of five of all students in higher education come
from that minority of families defined as middle-
class, i.e. from the remaining one-third. The
development of the welfare state in Britain over the
last 50 years or more has been primarily designed to
protect disadvantaged working-class families with the
aid of resources drawn largely from typically better-

246

off tax payers and yet in the case of student grants, again allowing for the passage of time, broadly the reverse happens and the system may therefore be described as frustrating a major issue of government policy.

Against the above equity-based argument in favour of a loans scheme has to be set what is usually seen as the major disadvantage, namely that such a scheme would be likely to act as a deterrent to at least some potential candiates for higher education. Young people leaving school, so the argument goes, would be worried at the thought of contracting a debt running into thousands of pounds which they might have to try to pay off at a time when they would be setting up home for themselves, contracting a mortgage and taking on major other commitments such as buying a car for the first time; as a result they would be less inclined to enter higher education and this would eventually have serious consequences for the nation's future. Further, sociological studies have shown that one aspect of working-class culture is to have typically shorter time horizons for future planning than is the norm for middle-class families who tend to take a longer-term view of future rewards, hence this dis-incentive or deterrent effect would be strongest in the case of bright young people from working-class backgrounds, arguably just the people whom Britain as a nation needs to encourage to apply to enter higher education in much greater numbers. Recent press reports of graduate unemployment will probably have made this situation worse, even though the statistics show that the overwhelming majority of graduates do in fact continue to get good jobs, much as previously. The deterrent effect could also be strong in the case of girls, who already apply for higher education in much smaller numbers than boys and who face the likelihood of future interruption of career and earning capacity. It has even been argued that for a girl of marriageable age to have a large debt to the Department of Education and Science would be akin to her having a 'reverse dowry' which might spoil her chances of marriage!

Financial Practicalities
The practicalities of financing a system of student loans would be complicated and here we can only out-line the broad principles that would arise. Much would depend on whether loans replaced grants in whole or in part: the latter seems the more likely,

possibly via holding the grant at its pre-existing
monetary level so that it was gradually eroded by
inflation with the loan initially being an additional
'topping-up' option open to those who wished to take
advantage of it.   An alternative suggestion is that
the grant might be restricted to the first two years
of a normal three-year course, with the third year
being loan-financed.   In either of these cases, the
debts students were contracting would initially be
not large and the scheme as a whole would take many
years to develop.   With a more drastic full-loans
scheme, government outlay should at first be
identical with the previous arrangements (unless,
for example, the means test applied to parental
salaries were to be altered or even abolished or the
ending of the distinction between the present mandatory and discretionary awards led to a large number
of students having to be included) and it would be
some years before repayments from the new graduates
substantially reduced the government's overall
financial commitment.

Considerations such as what provision to make
in the case of any students who were unemployed or
sick or disabled, or in the case of married women
graduates giving up work to have children, would
obviously be important.   There would probably be a
low rate of interest on the loan, or possibly even
none at all thus granting a rather hidden subsidy.
There would undoubtedly be defaulters - it is notori-
ously difficult to keep in touch with former students
once they have graduated - and presumably the cost
of these would have to be written off.   If funding
were to be provided by the banks, they would
undoubtedly seek recompense against the relatively
high risks involved as compared with their normal
lending to personal customers, which is usually to
people in established positions with regular incomes.
None of these practicalities would be insuperable,
however, once a decision had been taken in principle
to introduce a loans scheme.

Student Loans in Other Countries

In Britain the debate relating to the possible introduction of a student loans scheme has largely been
conducted in terms of *'grants versus loans'* but most
other countries which have such schemes also have
some form of grants, and large numbers of students
benefit from some mix of the two: this is true, for
example, throughout Canada and the USA.   Most of the
countries that have student loan schemes have under-

gone a period of learning by experience, with the
details of the various schemes being altered considerably over the last 20 years or so, depending on
government policies relating to aiding students from
disadvantaged family backgrounds, keeping down the
burden of debt for graduates, or curtailing the
growth of public expenditure. The authoritative
study cited previously[17] found, after a detailed
examination of student loans schemes in Canada,
Sweden and the USA, that a variety of student loan
schemes can be devised to satisfy any objective of
government policy, that the degree of subsidy involved in a loan scheme is variable and is essentially
a political decision, that default rates need not be
unduly high (and can be largely covered by insurance),
that the deterrent effect on either working-class
students or girls entering higher education need not
be significant, and that loans schemes are popular
both among students and among the general public.
There were found to be no significant savings to
public funds in the short run but these did become
significant in the longer term, an important consideration being that funds were then released to be
available for other purposes.

Overall a combination of grants and loans was
found to have greater opportunities for flexibility
and to be widely regarded as more equitable, than
the present system of mandatory and discretionary
awards.   Particularly noteworthy points were that
the notion that potential students would be unwilling
to contract the large debts required was shown to be
not true in practice and that care was needed over
the ways in which financial assistance in the form of
both grants and loans may be channelled towards or
away from certain groups such as those on low incomes.
In all countries the cost of running loans schemes
has greatly exceeded the original expectations, due
partly to the effects of inflation, partly to the
number of students to be covered, and partly to the
extent of the 'hidden subsidy' involved in giving
loans at low rates of interest.   This report concluded by quoting from the view of the US House of
Representatives Committee on Education and Labor:

> *The student loan program is not an unmixed
> blessing, nor an entirely unmitigated evil*
> (but) *in today's fiscal and educational policy
> circumstances, loans are needed*[18]

although it is worth noting that the findings of an
earlier study were considerably more pessimistic:

> *More than half of the benefits of loan programs*
> *accrue to students from families with over*
> *$7,500 income (in 1968). These benefits are*
> *partly in the form of providing access to*
> *capital markets, and a good case can be made*
> *for creating such access for all income classes.*
> *But the greater accessibility to capital markets*
> *was accompanied in 1968-69 by over $100 million*
> *in subsidies to students whose family incomes*
> *exceeded $7,500. Such subsidies cannot be*
> *defined on egalitarian grounds; they have*
> *nothing to do with capital market accessibility,*
> *and they produce inequities when viewed as forms*
> *of general subsidy to higher education.*[19]

UK Evidence

In the UK detailed opinion surveys found wide dissatisfaction with the existing means-tested grants
system and much stronger support than expected for
the introduction of a system of loans: excluding
'Don't Knows' some 62 per cent of the general public
were in favour of either a loans scheme or a loan/
grant mixture. A particularly interesting finding
was that some 5 per cent of students indicated that
they would have been *more* willing to enrol had there
been a loan scheme, presumably because of the problem that at present many parents fail to make up the
parental contribution. Whether some potential
students had in fact been deterred from enroling
could not, of course, be shown from a survey of the
views of students, nor is there any other obvious
way in which this could be verified.[20]

A more recent study carried out on behalf of
the National Union of Students produced strongly
adverse conclusions, relying on the same anti arguments that have already been cited above, particularly with regard to the deterrent effect:

> *It has become clear from our research that*
> *there is a threshold of resistance by students*
> *from working class backgrounds to taking out*
> *loans that cannot be broken by offering loans*
> *with a greater element of subsidy.*[21]

Student loans were considered and rejected by
the Robbins Report on Higher Education and yet some
years later Lord Robbins himself was converted to be
in favour.[22] Since then, there has been a considerable resurgence of interest.

Political Practicality

From being for some years a subject for study by
academic economists and educationists, student loans
have come into much greater prominence in recent
years and it now seems possible that some form of
loan scheme may be introduced in the near future.
In 1980 the House of Commons Select Committee on
Education invited the authors of the UK surveys
quoted above and also Ms Maureen Woodhall, who has
written widely on this subject, to appear before
them to explain the advantages and disadvantages of
loan schemes.[23]   The Thatcher government reportedly
had considered and rejected the principle of student
loans on three separate occasions by 1984,[24] during
the term of office of Sir Keith Joseph as Secretary
of State.   His successor, Mr Kenneth Baker, probably prompted by severe constraints on the education
budget, soon after taking office showed renewed
interest and set up a review committee to consider
the whole question of student finance.[25]   It was
reported, however, that there was no unanimity
within Conservative MPs in the House of Commons on
this issue.   By September 1986, in a major speech
to university vice-chancellors, Mr Baker announced
that he was in favour of the principle of a mixed
system of loans and grants to replace the existing
means-tested grants system, a major incentive being
to save some of the £500 million cost of the existing
system.   It was predicted that the vice-chancellors
would drop their previous opposition to the principle
of student loans and there seemed a likelihood that
such a scheme would be implemented.[26]

   As with education vouchers, therefore, student
loans have now entered the realm of practical
politics and their implementation has become a
definite possibility.   Major changes in the financing of education now seem likely, influenced particularly by the severe pressure on public expenditure,
and we may well see one or both of these schemes
coming into force, possibly initially in some partial
or experimental form, in the near future.

NOTES

   1.   J. Stone and F. Taylor, *The Parents' School-
book* (Penguin, 1976).
   2.   A. Stillman and K. Maychell, *Choosing
Schools - Parents, LEAs and the 1980 Act* (NFER,
Nelson, 1986).
   3.   H. Glennerster and G. Wilson, *Paying for*

Private Schools (Allen Lane, 1970).

4. 'Education Vouchers Under Test', *Oxford Review of Education*, Vol.1, No.2 (1975).

5. P. Newsam, 'Razor's Edge', *The Times Educational Supplement*, 2 May 1986.

6. J. Wilson, 'Freedom for All', *The Times Educational Supplement*, 14 March 1986.

7. J. Sturt, 'Spoilt for Choice', *The Times Educational Supplement*, 7 March 1986.

8. B. Passmore, 'You Pays Your Money, You Takes Your Choice', *The Times Educational Supplement*, 23 October 1981.

9. A. Maynard, *Experiment with Choices in Education*, Hobart Paper No.64 (Institute of Economic Affairs, 1975).

10. For economic arguments relating to such details, see J. Wiseman, 'Vouchers for Education', *Scottish Journal of Political Economy*, Vol.6, No.1 (1959); G. Horobin, R. Smyth and J. Wiseman, 'Vouchers for Education, Reply and Counter-Reply', *Scottish Journal of Political Economy*, Vol.7, No.1 (1960); reprinted in M. Blaug (ed.), *Readings in the Economics of Education*, Vol.1 (Penguin, 1969).

11. Kent County Council Education Department, *Education Vouchers in Kent* (Kent County Council, 1978). See also, B. Petty, 'Cuts Into Vouchers Won't Go', *The Times Educational Supplement*, 7 March 1986. (Mr Petty was Kent's County Education Officer at the time of the experiment.)

12. D. Weiler *et al.*, 'The First Year at Alum Rock', in C. Baxter *et al.* (eds), *Economics and Education Policy, A Reader* (Longman/OU, 1977). Reprinted from D. Weiler *et al.*, *A Public School Voucher Demonstration, The First Year at Alum Rock* (Rand, 1974).

13. D. Argyropoulos, 'Vouchers Can Damage Your Health', *The Times Educational Supplement*, 7 March 1986.

14. B. Passmore, 'Voucher Plan Too Tame: Sir Keith Told to Think Again', *The Times Educational Supplement*, 11 February 1983.

15. Articles by K. Hartley, G. Tullock, J. Barnes, E. West and R. Homan in *Economic Affairs* (April-May 1986).

16. M. Woodhall, *Student Loans: Lessons from Recent International Experience* (Policy Studies Institute, No.605, 1982).

17. M. Woodhall, *ibid*. For an earlier summary of the main arguments see also M. Woodhall, 'The Arguments for and Against Loans', in Baxter *et al.* (eds), *Economics and Education Policy*.

18.   Quoted in L.D. Rice (ed.), *Student Loans: Problems and Policy Alternatives* (New York College Entrance Examination Board, 1977).

19.   R.W. Hartman, 'The Distribution of Benefits of Student Loans', in Baxter *et al.* (eds), *Economics and Education Policy*.

20.   A. Lewis, C. Sandford and N. Thomson, *Grants or Loans?*, Research Monograph No.34 (Institute of Economic Affairs, 1980).

21.   A. Gaines and N. Turner, *Student Loans: The Costs and Consequences* (National Union of Students, 1985).

22.   Lord Robbins, *The Taming of Governments*, Readings 21 (Institute of Economic Affairs, 1979).

23.   'Student Loans Would Win Support from Public', *The Times Higher Education Supplement*, 23 May 1980.

24.   D. Jobbins, 'Loan Rangers Report Back', *The Times Higher Education Supplement*, 20 September 1985.

25.   S. Boseley, 'Loans May be Next Lesson in Economics', *The Guardian*, 4 August 1986.

26.   M. Dowd, 'Baker Goes for Student Loans and Sponsorship', *The Times*, 24 September 1986.

Chapter Twelve

EDUCATION AND THE THIRD WORLD

No-one with access to a television set can now be
unmindful of the problems of Third World countries.
Film of starving children with parched lips and
emaciated bodies, of whole families clustered
around dried-up water-holes, or of cattle trying to
nibble at the ground in dustbowl conditions where no
vegetation will grow, have become almost commonplace.
Pictures of such extreme conditions, whether in
Ethiopia, the Sudan, or Bangladesh, have perhaps
served to alert the conscience of the world as never
before to the bleakest living conditions to be found
on our planet.
      The reality of life in the Third World has to
include such terrible conditions, but it also has to
include very much more: there are well over 100
Third World countries throughout Africa, Asia and
South America and not surprisingly they vary widely
from every point of view. So much so that some
writers now suggest that a single collective term -
whether *The Third World* or *The South* - must be
seen as inadequate to encapture the heterogeneity of
these countries or of their few thousand million
inhabitants. Whilst there would be little point in
spending much time on semantics, it is worth noting
that these terms came into use because of the
allegedly pejorative connotations of such expressions
as *the poor countries*, *the underdeveloped
countries*, or even *the developing countries* (and
the last of these can be shown to be inaccurate since
at least some of the countries in question cannot be
said to be experiencing positive development in any
meaningful sense). Whatever language is used cannot
hide the fact that a wide, and ever-increasing, gap
exists between the standards of living enjoyed by the
more fortunate one-third of the world's population
and the less fortunate two-thirds. For the purposes

254

of this chapter we need initially to consider two
basic questions, firstly, what is meant by underdevelopment, and, secondly, what is the place of
education in the development process?

UNDERDEVELOPMENT

Underdevelopment is such a complex phenomenon, with
so many different but interconnecting facets, that
in attempting to describe it it is difficult to know
where to begin and any comments made are bound not
to apply to all of the countries all of the time.
Perhaps the major underlying element is the demographic, which occurs *passim*: Third World countries
have always had high birth-rates, high death-rates
and short expectancy of life. Over the last 50
years or so death-rates have been falling, especially
for infant mortality, and life expectancy lengthening
(albeit very unevenly); the inevitable result has
been the rapid population growth, often reaching 2
or 3 per cent per annum, which many commentators,
both within and without Third World countries, see
as their number one problem. In recent years, rates
of growth of population have been gradually falling
(again very unevenly) but still remain much higher
than those in developed countries and, some would
say, higher than the developing countries can cope
with.
       This demographic situation is closely related to
the question of health and hygiene: often basic
water supply and sanitation are lacking or do not
reach enough people or, for example, require water
(which is extremely heavy) to be carried by hand or
head, and medical facilities are not available or
are some long distance away or are too expensive,
although progress has been made in many countries
in respect of all of these. The hot and often humid
conditions in many Third World countries are ideal
for the growth of germs and bacteria of all kinds
and make high standards of cleanliness and hygiene
all the more desirable: cholera, typhus, hepatitis,
tuberculosis, diphtheria, yellow fever and malaria,
are just some of the killer diseases that abound in
many Third World countries and are remarkably resistant to attempts by the World Health Organisation
to control them, although here again there are some
success stories: smallpox, for example, has effectively been eradicated.
       Health and hygiene have major effects on life.
So, too, does food intake. In many Third World

countries this is inadequate, in terms of both quality and quantity: what food is available is often
lacking in adequate sustenance or in variety or is
so expensive that it is beyond the reach of many
people or it may carry with it some of the bacteria
referred to above: fruit, for example, frequently
carries hepatitis whilst dishes or other receptacles
may well hold cholera germs. Much the major effort
of each developing country is expended on trying to
feed its population: agriculture predominates in
the local economy and is usually the major form of
employment for the population, who often have to cope
with low crop yields, poor farming conditions and
much soil depletion. Local agricultural systems are
typically resistant to change but in many countries
crop yields have gradually increased with the advent
of some, usually fairly small, degree of modernis-
ation and increased efficiency.

Per capita incomes are low and a high percentage of income has to be spent on food. Women and
children typically have low status: apart from
child-rearing, feeding the family and generally running the household, women are frequently expected to
do much manual labour, including, for example, carry-
ing water and working in the fields, whilst children
will be expected to work and earn or contribute to
their keep from an early age, often five or six.
Parents will seek to have large families, for a number of reasons, one of which is often the question of
supporting the parents in their old age. In many
societies monogamy is the exception rather than a
rule and each home may include a complex extended
family network with two or three, or more, wives,
numerous children, and various other relatives.

The country's economy will depend heavily on
agriculture and on products which derive from agriculture and is therefore very susceptible to changes
in climate or in world market conditions and prices
(in so far as it is able to export some of its
produce or products). Most developing countries
have endeavoured, with varying degrees of success,
to diversify their economies so as to be less dependent on agriculture, to develop more of an industrial
base, and to lessen exports of raw materials. In so
doing, often a prime aim is to lessen the huge import
bills and balance-of-payments deficits and thus the
accumulation of external debts, which have usually
led to currency instability, frequent devaluations,
and high rates of inflation. Attracted by the
possibilities of work, population tends to drift
towards urban centres where some do find work but

256

many are unable to do so: high unemployment and high inflation co-existed in developing countries long before the developed countries found that their economic policies had to be framed with reference not to a choice or a trade-off between unemployment and inflation but to the two increasing simultaneously. Social and economic infrastructure is lacking but savings are negligible and investment is low, interest rates are typically high, credit facilities poor and the local banking system usually poorly developed; much economic activity may not be in monetary terms at all, with barter still being important. Many Third World countries have extreme inequalities with a small number of very rich families: all too often, however, the latter seek not to use their funds to aid the development of the country but to divert their savings to safer havens overseas.

It must again be emphasised that such broad brush descriptions cannot do justice to the wide varieties of conditions to be found in the poorer countries of the world and are really inadequate for an understanding of the many different ways in which development may take place (or may not: India, for example, persistently has economic growth less than population growth so that her income per head, and therefore average standard of living, decline each year). An obvious division would be between that minority of Third World countries who have found oil, and are in varying degrees reaping the benefits from it, and the majority who have not. Again, wherever wealth comes from, everything depends on how it is spent: a recent annual report from the Central Bank of Nigeria castigated the growing tendency for large sums of money to be spent nationally on imported radios, cassette players, records, televisions and other entertainment-related products, at a time when the country was desperately short of adequate water supply, sanitation, roads, pavements, power stations and other such infrastructure. Much attention has been paid in recent years to the disadvantageous effects on the developing countries of intensive advertising and marketing of consumer-related products from the world's giant multi-national companies, tinned milk powder for babies and bottles of soft drinks being two which have often been cited. But who is to say whether these countries would be better off or worse off without such products?

EDUCATION

Where does education fit into all this?   The characteristics of developing countries, as cited above,
could of course have included the high rates of
illiteracy, poor rates of enrolment in school,
dearth of higher education and lack of training in
the skills such countries desperately need, and we
shall have to revert to all of these.   It is necessary to start, however, with the widespread view
of education as a panacea which would in time lead
to the solution of most of the poor countries' problem.   This view, which found wide acceptance
throughout the developed and developing worlds, saw
the development of the poorer countries' educational
systems as one of the key instruments, perhaps even
the key instrument, for introducing the kind of
long-term change that would alleviate the misery of
the poverty and destitution that have become all too
familiar:

> *Many leaders and intellectuals in the develop-*
> *ing countries of the world have high expect-*
> *ations concerning formal education as an*
> *important lever in uplifting and transforming*
> *their societies.* [1]

The same authors quote, in similar vein, from a
resolution by the Indian Government inaugurating a
major educational reform:

> *Education, especially in science and technology,*
> *is the most powerful instrument of social trans-*
> *formation and economic progress, and the attempt*
> *to create a new social order based on freedom,*
> *equality, and justice can succeed only if the*
> *traditional educational system was revolution-*
> *ized both in content and extent.* [2]

This universal view saw education as not only the
means of changing and raising political and social
consciousness but also of more directly increasing
the number of skilled workers and raising the level
of trained manpower. [3]   It was a view spelled out at
some length by Mr Robert McNamara in his address to
the 1977 Annual Meetings of the World Bank and the
International Monetary Fund, [4] in the following terms:

> *(i)   Education is a basic human need: it gives*
> *people knowledge, attitudes, values,*
> *skills, and above all, the potential to*

>   *learn.   It enables them to respond to new opportunities, to adjust to social and cultural changes, and to participate in political, cultural, and social activities.*
>
> *(ii)   Education is a means of influencing access to other basic needs, which in turn influence the education process itself, obvious examples being adequate nutrition, safe drinking water, basic health services, and shelter. Improved nutrition, for example, directly affects children's learning capacities and therefore their potential to benefit from education, and thus eventually their future productivity and income.*
>
> *(iii)   Education is an activity that sustains and accelerates overall development. The education system, taking the term in its widest sense to include advanced and technical training regardless of the agency through which such training may be organised, provides the skilled workers at all levels to manage the country's developing technology, capital, services and administration. Such personnel will in turn contribute to the further development or local applicability of newly-arrived technology, will participate in the longer-term planning, of whatever form, which is essential if the available natural resources and local environment are to be used and conserved in the most optimal way, and will play a fundamental role in that transformation of society which is the inevitable concomitant of economic development.*

Those arguments are undeniable and they echo those enunciated by other international bodies concerned with world development issues. The General Conference of UNESCO,[5] for example, has emphasised that in the development context education must be seen not as one 'sector' of the country on the lines of, for example, industry or agriculture but as a pervasive element permeating every aspect of multi-dimensional development.

At this point it is necessary to inject a note of realism. For the broad mass of the population, of course, education will not mean advanced level study or training or the acquisition of sophisticated technical skills, nor, in many countries, will it include even *secondary* education for the majority of the population. Indeed, there are still some 14 or 15 countries in the world where only a minority of children go to *primary* school. Small wonder, then, that in such countries the rate of illiteracy is falling only slowly. The relevant statistics for selected Third World countries are shown in Table 12.1.[6]

The countries included in this table are essentially those designated by the World Bank as *low-income countries*, i.e. the poorest countries in the world, for whom complete statistics are available. Although there are some problems in the definition and interpretation of these statistics - for example, the school enrolment ratios are all liable to be overstated since they express the numbers of actual pupils, including older ones, as a percentage of the number of children deemed to be of primary school age - these do not seriously impinge on our use of this evidence, which may be said to be the most reliable available. As the table makes clear, over the period of years included, 1965-82, there was definite educational progress and expansion in these countries but at varying rates and starting from different levels. In most of the world's poorest countries the main emphasis has been on increasing the percentage of children receiving at least some primary school education and the table shows that of these countries only Pakistan had in 1982 a figure of less than 50 per cent (in contrast, for example, to Niger and Bhutan, not shown in the table, which had only 23 per cent each); still, however, in each of the countries shown large numbers of children do not receive any primary education at all, and significantly fewer girls than boys go to primary school - in Nepal less than half as many. The percentages of children enrolled in secondary schools are very much smaller, exceeding 50 per cent only in the case of Sri Lanka and around 20 per cent being a more typical figure. The overwhelming majority of children have therefore left school by around age 11 and are already at work, or may be unemployed. The percentages eventually going on to higher education are minimal, never exceeding 4 per cent except in the case of India.

It is apparent that these countries, which are among the poorest in the world, have a very long way to go before they could catch up on the educational levels achieved by those Third World countries whose somewhat higher incomes and resources have enabled them to make quite dramatic progress in their

Table 12.1: Education Statistics for Selected Third World Countries

	Number enrolled in primary school as percentage of age group						Number enrolled in secondary school as percentage of age group		Number enrolled in higher education as percentage of population aged 20-24	
	Total		Male		Female					
	1965	1982	1965	1982	1965	1982	1965	1982	1965	1982
Bangladesh	49	60	67	68	31	51	13	15	1	4
Nepal	20	73	36	102	4	42	5	21	1	3
Burma	71	84	76	87	65	81	15	20	1	4
India	74	79	89	93	57	64	27	30	5	9
Ghana	69	76	82	85	57	66	13	34	1	1
Sri Lanka	93	103	98	106	86	101	35	54	2	4
Pakistan	40	44	59	57	20	31	12	14	2	2
Sudan	29	52	37	61	21	43	4	18	1	2

Source: *World Bank, World Development Report 1985 (Oxford University Press).*

The countries included are those 'low-income countries' for which complete data were available.

educational achievements in recent years: such
countries as Kenya, Zambia, Peru or The Phillipines,
for example, now manage to give close to 100 per
cent of their children a primary school education.
It is therefore not difficult to understand why the
'panacea' view of education should have had, and
still does have, such wide appeal, particularly for
the poorest countries.

PROBLEMS ARISING

Doubts about this view have grown in recent years,
due to a number of factors. Firstly it has become
increasingly obvious that the world's poorest
countries cannot afford the huge *cost* of the education systems that would be required if they were
to endeavour to educate all their children. It is
now nearly 20 years since Professor Coombs, in his
path-breaking book, *The World Education Crisis*,[7]
showed that the cost of universal primary and secondary education would be far beyond their reach and
for them to attempt to copy the educational systems
of advanced countries would be futile. Secondly
the *content* of education came under increasing attack
for being not well suited to predominantly agricultural societies with their own distinct cultures,
customs and languages: the education offered came
to be seen as too 'bookish', too orientated towards
the humanities and a liberal education, at the
expense of neglecting those agricultural and technical skills which seemed more directly relevant to
local needs.[8] As we shall see below, this argument
did not and does not find universal acceptance but
it did achieve wide currency throughout the Third
World and it did lead to some re-orientation of
educational systems. Thirdly, at about the same
time it was sometimes difficult to avoid the
impression that as education systems were being
developed in various Third World countries they were
acquiring certain features which were being criticised in or discarded from education systems in
developed countries, such as school uniform, academic
selection for secondary schooling, social and racial
differentiation, and divorce from local communities.
Children in poorer countries were starting to study
Latin when children in richer countries were largely
ceasing to do so.

COLONIALISM

Perhaps more important than any of the factors cited above was the relationship of education to the colonial era. With the intriguing exception of Thailand, every one of the 100-plus countries that comprise the Third World formerly underwent a prolonged period of experience as a colony of at least one of the Great Power states. It was during those periods that such educational systems as there were started to develop, often with a strong impetus from Christian or Islamic missionary societies; but that development has later been seen as quite inadequate, in quantity, and as being qualitatively dominated by the colonial culture and being inimical to many facets of the indigenous society. In the words of Coleman,

> *one of the major indictments made by critics*
> *of Western colonialism has been its alleged*
> *neglect of education.*[9]

It is possible, of course, to argue that the administrators of colonial regimes just did not realise how necessary it would be for educational systems to expand sufficiently so that all children would be able to receive some schooling and at least learn to read and write. It is also possible to understand why regimes which would, at some centuries' remove, name their newly-acquired lands *The Philippines*, after King Philip, or *Rhodesia* after Cecil Rhodes, would also see it quite normal that the children in the local schools should study, as they frequently still do, *Tom Brown's Schooldays*, *A Tale of Two Cities*, the geography of Scotland, or the economics of the City of London. In other words, perhaps

> *many colonial administrators, in many different*
> *parts of the world, acted from the highest*
> *motives according to their own educational*
> *experience and upbringing and acted according*
> *to the conventional educational wisdom of the*
> *time. Colonial administrators may have been*
> *patronising but many of them had to develop an*
> *ad hoc policy on the spot with the best of*
> *intentions and without any guidance from the*
> *colonial government back at home.*[10]

If this were generally agreed to be so, it is doubtful whether critiques of educational develop-

ment, or some would say the lack of it, under
colonial regimes, would be so strongly expressed.
Or is the view quoted above too simplistic?   A widespread perception throughout many developing countries today would be quite the reverse of the above,
i.e. that colonial regimes deliberately sought to use
education locally as a means of continuing the sub-
jugation of the indigenous people or of transforming
the latter into replicas of their European masters.
Thus,

> *The French ... had a strong sense of 'mission
> civilisatrice', initially and intellectually
> believing that they could create black, brown
> and yellow Frenchmen with the same views and
> outlooks as the metropolitan Frenchman ...
> The French politicians and administrators
> believed in the superiority of French culture,
> the French language, literature and adminis-
> trative structures;   and the French language
> was used as a means of colonial domination and
> control while the indigenous languages were
> scorned.*[11]

Similarly, as the educational systems in the
Great Power states developed, aspects of them were,
not surprisingly, copied directly into their colonies.   Thus restricted entry academic secondary
schools developed in England after the Education Act
of 1902 and the same concept was subsequently translated to the colonies, whilst France's insistence at
home on centralised bureaucratic control, high
academic standards, and the secularisation of education was replicated in her colonial territories,
where it flourishes to this day.   With such
approaches, the indigenous people had little hope of
reaching the same educational standards attained by
the children of their colonial administrators and
this was explicitly recognised by the provision of
separate schools for the latter.   This view of the
educational experience under colonial rule is quite
Marxist: even more serious and more Marxist is the
view that still, many years after the granting of
independence, most aspects of the lives of developing
countries continue to be dominated by the developed
countries which dictate the terms of trade and have
the negotiating power and which can dictate the shape
of educational developments through their control of
the purse strings:

> *Far from being a dead issue, therefore,*

> *colonialism is active and well in a more subtle*
> *form - what Altbach has called 'the highest*
> *form of colonialism' - namely that of neo-*
> *colonialism.*[12]

A crucial notion here is that of *dependency*, i.e. a situation in which what happens internally in a dependent country cannot be fully explained without taking into account the external influences, a good example being the way in which the culture of Latin America is dominated by control from the United States.[13] Dependency is often seen in economic or general societal terms but that it is crucially affected by education is argued by a number of writers, including Mende:

> *The continuation of the educational system*
> *erected by the colonial regime is by far the*
> *most powerful instrument for perpetuating the*
> *concepts, the outlook, and the value on which*
> *the privileged classes' power is built,*[14]

or Myrdal:

> *The monopoly of education is the most funda-*
> *mental basis of inequality and it retains its*
> *hold more strongly in the poorer countries.*[15]

Far, then, from education being seen as the route through which children from the poorest homes may rise to the highest positions in society (which can still happen in isolated, highly-publicised, cases, but is statistically very improbable), education is here being seen as an agency of oppression, which serves to widen the gulf between the more fortunate and the less fortunate members of society. It may also convey certain values, such as contempt for menial work or for living in remote rural areas, or racist or sexist norms, which may be inimical to a country's successful and equitable development. Access to the best schools, with the most well-qualified teachers and the highest levels of educational resources, is effectively confined to children from the more privileged classes, either because of location or because the schools are fee-paying, or some other reason. Small wonder then that the most successful products of such educational systems continue to come largely from the children of the existing privileged classes.

A graphic example of the effect that education may have was given recently in an article with the dramatic headline '*How education may harm the Third World*'[16] about the views of Professor Kazim Bacchus, who was formerly Head of Planning at the Ministry of Education in Guyana: in one Carribean country aid agencies noticed that the local carpenters were unable to read blueprints and they embarked on ambitious technical training programmes for carpenters and similar groups; later these skilled craftsmen were found to form the largest group of unemployed: their aspirations had risen with their education such that they now scorned the menial work which their predecessors had been content to do for minimal rewards and they sought the kinds of highly-paid jobs which would be commensurate with their skills and their training but which were not available. As a further example of inappropriate, Western-imported, education he cited the training of motor mechanics on the parts-cheap, labour-expensive model (which works well in the West), i.e. to throw away expensive, imported components when they become faulty, rather than to patch and mend and fabricate local replacements.

VOCATIONAL EDUCATION

We must now consider more fully what has been cited as '*perhaps the most controversial of all the curriculum issues*',[17] namely the role of vocational education, which was referred to in passing above. Perhaps the major attack mounted against the bookish, academic-oriented, education that many systems sought to provide related to its inappropriateness in terms of the broad mass of the young people in developing countries, whether in urban or rural areas; in either case the typical aspirations towards white-collar type jobs in offices and the demeaning of more menial work which were likely to be the concomitants of such an education did not match with the possible job opportunities that would be open to 99 per cent of young people. The lack of training in vocationally-relevant skills, which often did not need to be at very high levels, was seen as the major single drawback to the eduation given.[18] This view has in turn been challenged by those who argue that to inject training in agricultural and industrial skills into the curricula of the *primary* education which is, still, all that the majority of children in many Third World countries receive is neither practical nor possible, that much of what is already included under general education is very relevant to employment and to development,[19] and that whatever specific skills were taught might not in the end be those that were required. Lillis[20] gives a detailed description of various vocationally-orientated innovations in developing countries' education systems and shows how unsuccessful they all were for one reason or another, including that

> *many schemes have been designed to provide training for jobs which, in practice, often failed to materialise*

before going on to consider '*Why do vocationalised curricula fail?*' Particularly important, he argues are '*the concept of education held by the target audience*', '*the set of mutually supportive assumptions about what counts as valid knowledge*' and '*built-in resistance to any form of vocational schooling*'; in other words,

> *Africans and other colonised groups aspiring to jobs and positions like those held by Europeans in colonial society sought an education similar to that enjoyed by members of the elite.*[21]

This situation was, and still is, widespread throughout Third World countries: often the indigenous people, perhaps particularly in countries in Africa, were deeply suspicious of attempts to relate education directly to local traditional or rural environments since they saw such attempts as ways of perpetuating their inferior status. Lillis comments that this historical expectation '*has proved the major barrier to vocational education and has been hard to break*': 'education' is seen as almost wholly restricted to reading and writing, plus some other 'academic' education.

Such reactions do, however, depend on the perceived status and context of the vocational skills in question: for girls to learn secretarial skills, for example, is entirely acceptable because even highly aspirant families will see this as a very acceptable career for their daughters, with a connotation of status which is out of all proportion to the work's financial rewards, social importance, or length of training required. With regard to other production- or trade-related skills, however, often poorly-qualified instructors, lack of equipment, and unattractive premises would combine to strengthen the students' feelings of being trained to become second-class citizens.

Many families have seen the route out of the traditional primitive village economy for their children as being via full-time schooling; they have sought for their children a better future than the farming to which most would be destined in rural areas and would therefore resist attempts to vocationalise the school curriculum. The steady drift of population from rural to urban areas and the growth of urban unemployment, both of which have reached alarming proportions in many Third World countries, have been seen as inevitable side-effects of such attitudes, although it can also be argued that their roots go much deeper.

There are two reasons for suggesting that this question of vocationalisation may cease to be the problem that it has been regarded as for much of this century. Firstly in virtually all developing countries the labour statistics show that jobs are growing more rapidly in the modern sector of the economy than elsewhere; many of these jobs are directly or indirectly in the government sector or in other white-collar type (although the term seems singularly appropriate in hot climates) occupations, for all of which the more bookish education is the more appropriate. Further, these jobs carry the higher rewards. Therefore,

> *African students, far from being irrational in insisting on bookish education, correctly appraised the actual job opportunities that were available; paradoxically enough, the teaching of the three 'R's provided a 'vocational' education in the best sense of the word, allowing entry to the most pres- tigious and better-paid occupations in the economy.* [22]

And, secondly, as these countries have developed industrial skills it has gradually become apparent to the local population that a variety of technically- based skills are required and do lead on to worth- while, secure, jobs, and a way of escaping from the syndrome of mass unemployment; evidence has become available of the successful technical re-orientation of at least some parts of advanced education and training, in a number of countries. [23] Hopefully, this might at least lessen the problem summarised by Robert McNamara:

> *While millions of people from among the*

> *educated are unemployed, millions of jobs are*
> *waiting to be done because people with the*
> *right education, training and skills cannot be*
> *found ...   (This is) one of the most disturb-*
> *ing paradoxes of our time.*[24]

THE OBSTACLE THEORY

Whatever the orientation of the curriculum or the
seriousness of the other problems outlined above,
there could be little doubt that the participants in
the various debates accepted the notion of education
as investment in the future, as adding to the stock
of, and enhancing the quality of, the country's
Human Capital.   Calculations of social rates of
return showed good results and ordinary village
parents, too, usually regarded any necessary educational expenditure (the most significant of which
would often be income foregone) as clearly worthwhile if it could possibly be afforded.   This
'functionalist' perspective of the education system
saw it as serving the cause of national economic and
social development and was usually satisfied that
the system would be capable of adapting to such
change as might be required.   However, in a number
of countries doubts grew when educational expansion
did not lead on to economic growth on the scale
expected, and when there were uncertainties over such
basic questions as whether education should concentrate on the use of local languages or on a national
language, often English.   In Zambia, for example,
by 1976 aspects of the educational system had come
to be seen as so dysfunctional that the Ministry of
Education proposed a series of major reforms on
egalitarian lines, including the abolition of private
schools.[25]   According to the Ministry, the system
'favours a small minority at the expense of the
majority of others ...   It breeds individualism,
elitism and class consciousness'.   So great was the
opposition to the proposed reforms that they were
effectively dropped, a move which *'seems like an act*
of irrationality ... from a functionalist point of
view the reversal is inexplicable'.[26]   Clarke saw
this opposition as ideologically-based and as
focusing on:

> *the continued allocation of a disproportionately*
> *large part of the national income to the middle*
> *class*

and the fact that,

> *the continued profitability and productivity*
> *of the modern sector is premised largely on*
> *the continuing surplus of cheap labour.*

For Clarke, the rejection of the egalitarian reforms

> *demonstrates the extent to which the school*
> *system is part of the overall structure of*
> *dependency and underdevelopment*

and shows

> *the extent to which the school system in Zambia*
> *remains an intractable obstacle to development.*

This rather Marxist view would, however, have to be
reconciled with the fact that many of the aspects of
the Zambia education system which the proposed
reforms were designed to remedy, including academic
selection and private schools, do exist, in various
forms, in most countries which have undergone
successful economic and social development.

EDUCATION AND EMPLOYMENT

The relationship between the educational system and
employment in a developing country is complex.   The
local economy will require a range of number and
types of skills on the basis of the production processes in use, whether these relate to the simplest
of agricultural work, street vending or market
trading or, for the minority, to relatively modern
and complex factory-based automated installations.
Total labour supply will usually embrace a relatively
small number of highly-qualified and highly-skilled
people at one extreme and a large number of unskilled
manual workers, many of them without even the basics
of any education of any kind and certainly unable to
read or write, at the other.   Those young people who
have had no schooling will be the most likely recruits
to the ranks of the unemployed;   where they are still
able to get some kind of a job it will be one with
poor prospects, low security and a minimal rate of
pay.   Often agricultural work has low status -
partly because living in rural areas often implies
lack of basic amenities such as adequate water supply
or sanitation - and young people will often prefer to

work in towns if such work is available.   With local
labour markets lacking in organisation, information
about possible job opportunities is hard to come by
and contact often has to be via a friend or relative.
    Rates of unemployment have always been higher
in developing countries than in the developed world
and any published statistics on unemployment for
developing countries always grossly understate the
extent of the problem;   unemployment tends to be
concentrated disproportionately amongst the youth,
first-time job seekers, women and certain disadvantaged groups such as members of particular castes or
tribes.   A common estimate is that in many developing countries 50 per cent of young people or even
more may be unable to find work[27] and that in all
developing countries the proportions are likely to
continue to increase for the foreseeable future.
    Those young people who have had some education
will tend to seek jobs in the modern sector of the
economy but such jobs may not be available in
sufficient numbers, especially as the effects of
world recession and the financial consequences for
many governments have led to the curtailment of the
growth of jobs in the public sector where a high
proportion of educated people found work.   Acquiring
and keeping a job may also involve attitudinal problems, including those relating to:

> *social relations and experiences to which*
> *workers are exposed, such as the pattern of*
> *subordination and hierarchy, labor-management*
> *relations, fulfilling work schedules, and*
> *sheer physical and mental strain.*[28]

There has particularly been sweeping criticism of the
effects of formal schools on children in rural areas:

> *They divorce the children from their rural*
> *communities, ignore their culture, inculcate*
> *unsuitable attitudes related to urban life and*
> *fail to encourage an understanding of the*
> *environment in which they will grow up and*
> *live.   As far as rural development is con-*
> *cerned they often do more harm than good.*[29]

For the children thus affected, even if they take
with them newly-acquired skills of literacy and
numeracy, it may be particularly difficult to secure
and keep any job from which they would derive any
satisfaction, but many do not even reach that basic
standard:

> *A recent estimate indicates that in poor rural
> areas less than one child in four, sometimes
> as few as one in ten or even less, attains a
> functional mastery of reading and writing;
> and this soon fades away if it is not kept in
> use, for which rural life gives little
> opportunity.*

Some children, therefore, are liable to experience
the worst of all combinations since their brief
schooling may lead them towards 'wrong' attitudinal
changes but not leave them with the abilities to
read and write which are the essential prerequisites
for an increasingly wide range of jobs - even agricultural workers are now often required to be able
to read the quite complex instructions on packets of
seeds or fertilisers.

Much has been written about the distinction
between traditional sector work, especially that
related to agriculture, and work in the modern sector
of the economy, usually characterised by larger size
units and mass production methods.   In recent years,
however, a number of writers[30] have drawn attention
to the continuing importance of 'in-between' work at
the fringe of the modern manufacturing and service
sector: this work is rooted in traditional urban
labour and typically provides only a meagre income.
As an example one might perhaps cite the internal
cleaning of office buildings in the newer town
centres: in developed countries this work would
almost invariably be done by women, often as the
second source of income in a family whose main
support was provided elsewhere, but in developing
countries such work is largely done by men and,
poorly-paid though it is, often constitutes the main
and only source of income for a (typically much
larger) family.

Professor Blaug[31] lists a number of assumptions
that are commonly made regarding the links between
education and employment in developing countries and
for each of these shows that, whilst there may be
some truth in the proposition, it may equally well be
false in different circumstances.   Thus, education
is often seen as increasing the volume of employment
either by providing children with previously unavailable skills or by imparting 'developmental' values
and attitudes: clearly neither of these may necessarily be the case since schools may simply be fulfilling a filtering or screening function, as
already discussed.   Similarly the notion that education works to eliminate poverty, especially

because of its effect in reducing the birth-rate, may not always be true or may not be the cheapest or most effective means of attaining the same end, e.g. in some circumstances sanitation or nutrition programmes may have more immediate effects. Likewise the notion that education causes unemployment, in the sense that the aspirations of educated people may be raised beyond all hope of satisfying them, may be true in some instances - such as the one indicated earlier in this chapter - but clearly cannot be true for most of the educated people most of the time, since most educated people do succeed in finding jobs.

Curle has argued forcefully that attention must focus on the twin facts that perhaps 85 per cent of a developing country's gross national product may relate to, and perhaps 95 per cent of the working population may be employed in, agriculture. But as part of the process of education young people become opposed to agricultural work, particularly on account of its low status:

> *They scorn agriculture because, as things are, there is no opportunity for them to do other than work in the manual, menial manner of their illiterate brethren.*[32]

Curle went on to propose a series of measures designed to demonstrate the practical application of scientific and other skills to agriculture, and the direct effect on national well-being that should result from an increase in the quality and quantity of agricultural production, or, in a word, to *'glamorise'* agriculture. Over 20 years later one has to note with regret that his call went largely unheeded.

By contrast, the growing industries in developing countries require effective methods of selection and training of workers, many of whom will have come direct from tribal village life, and also, ideally, of dealing with the social dislocation which often ensues. A report from the International Labour Office[33] described in graphic terms the probable hiatus:

> *Frequently the worker leaves his family behind in the village and retains close ties with them and a feeling of belonging to the land ... There is a continual drifting back and forth between countryside and city by an unskilled, unstable labour force, which brings no lasting benefit to industry, to agriculture, or to the*

273

> *worker himself: not to industry, because of*
> *the instability and high rate of absenteeism*
> *and labour turnover.*

These and other attendant factors result in inefficient working, poor productivity and a labour force
that remains permanently unskilled.   Nor is there
any incentive for industry to spend money on training
workers in these circumstances.   Only in relatively
rare cases is it possible to break out of this
vicious circle.

EDUCATIONAL PLANNING

Enough has been said above to indicate why there are
now grave doubts regarding the view of education as
a general panacea for national development and
regarding the blanket expansion and extension of
educational systems.   The planning of those systems
was until recently primarily a matter of allocating
additional resources - admittedly not easy to come
by - to those aspects of the system most in need of
development, usually some combination of moving towards eventual universal primary education, a relatively small increase in entry to secondary education
and a very expensive and prestigious expansion of
higher education, together with such other key
priorities as the balance between urban and rural
education and between male and female students.
This was no easy task but it was facilitated by the
fact that all such decisions are less problematic in
a climate of expansion;   it was also a task that
carried high status and prestige.
     By the 1980s, however, education was often
absorbing more national resources than any other
publicly financed activity, economic systems in
developing countries were suffering badly from the
world recession and increasingly misgivings were
being voiced about some of the benefits claimed for
continued educational expansion.   At the same time
no government could publicly abandon its previously-
stated commitment to provide more and more education
for more and more of its citizens.   Educational
planners have therefore increasingly found themsleves
in the invidious position of having to seek greater
managerial efficiency and cost savings from an education 'system' which has sometimes seemed to be out
of control: it is this complexity that has often
seemed to bedevil the process of educational planning:

> *Even in the least developed postcolonial*
> *nations, education already exists in such*
> *myriad forms that level, type, location, and*
> *a number of other characteristics must be*
> *known before student or resource flows can be*
> *interpreted relative to social or economic*
> *goals.*[34]

It also has to be remembered that educational planners have increasingly found themselves in a 'man-
in-the-middle' situation with educational outcomes
ultimately being determined by school principals,
teachers, parents and the students themselves, but
many of the most crucial decisions relating to
educational policy, and particularly decisions
relating to the granting of resources or the determination of overall priorities, being decided at the
level of central government, very often with the
direct personal involvement of the prime minister or
president. Another way of expressing the latter
point would be to say that each country's economic
and social development, and its educational development, are increasingly seen to be closely inter-
connected and that planning decisions should be taken
in that light. It hardly needs saying that this has
often not been the case in the past and regrettably
may not always be so now. Also it has often been
the case that an inadequate flow of information to
and from educational decision-makers makes their task
doubly difficult.

The Financing of Education

Increased attention has been given in recent years to
the methods of financing education systems in Third
World countries and the search for possible ways of
achieving economies. Studies have identified that
there is much wastage and misallocation of the scarce
funds available and international bodies such as
UNESCO and The World Bank are now initiating programmes to try to achieve education more cheaply and
more effectively. Third World countries currently
have a wide variety of systems of fees and/or sub-
sidies for education and The World Bank has recently
suggested[35] that judicious alterations to such
schemes, combined with a closer integration of the
role of private schools, may have considerable impact
on future educational expansion. At the time of
writing, the International Institute of Educational
Planning, a part of UNESCO, has nearly completed a
large-scale research project into educational costing

and financing in developing countries.   Further
reference was made to the financing of education in
developing countries in Chapter Eight.

THIRD WORLD HETEROGENEITY

It would be wrong to imply that the pattern of educational development has been homogeneous across the
100-plus countries that constitute the Third World;
almost everything written above would require some
qualification or amplification to refer to specific
local conditions in any one country.   The educational systems of most countries in Africa formerly under British colonial rule, for example, continue to be strongly influenced by the combination
of schools founded by missionary societies and
gradually increasing government control.   Whether
or not colonial schooling provided *'education for
subordination and exploitation'*,[36] it was often the
only schooling available and thus provided the basis
for future educational growth.   As commercial and
economic activity developed, education both played
its part in that development and was affected by it,
often in unexpected ways: Garvey recounts how in
North Eastern Zambia mission teachers of one Roman
Catholic order found at one time that young men were
abandoning their schools to attend the Livingstonia
mission across the border in Malawi, because the
teaching there was in the economic language,
English.[37]   Within Nigeria, economic and social
conditions in the largely Moslem north contrast
sharply with those in the Christian and more developed south where education has developed much more
rapidly and successfully.   In the south, probably
close to 100 per cent of children now receive at
least some primary schooling in the major towns such
as Lagos, Ibadan and Benin;   in contrast much of the
north can still be described as feudal and even
allowing for the prevalence of Koranic schools,
D'Aeth in 1975 quoted an estimate that less than 10
per cent of children go to primary school.[38]   On the
Indian sub-continent, religious divisions are still
of crucial importance within each of India and Pakistan and any planned educational development has to
take full account of this fact if it is to have any
chance of success.   Still many children do not
receive any schooling at all and most educational
growth has taken place in urban areas, on which the
population's aspirations are centred:

> *Education designed for a 'back to simple life*
> *in the countryside' movement has no chance of*
> *success, for that is what the young are*
> *struggling desperately through the school*
> *system to get away from, and they will go on*
> *struggling even when the odds are hopelessly*
> *against them.*[39]

South American countries have often had military
dictatorships which have made use of nascent educational systems to instil such virtues as discipline
and obedience to the law.   Curricula have generally
been narrow and conservative[40] and education has
often served to enhance the pronounced urban-rural
divide.   In countries in south-east Asia such as
Thailand, Malaysia and Singapore, Christian missionary schools have existed for over 400 years and
eventually paved the way for public sector education;
a common accusation has been that schooling was too
academic in focus and too focused towards turning out
acceptable government employees, i.e. civil servants.
Only in relatively recent years have schools re-
oriented themselves towards the positions and needs
of the children, with, for example, schools in Malaya
adopting teaching through the national language,
Bahasa Malaysia.   Earlier as a result of colonial
government policy being to exclude missionaries from
the rural areas, Malays were *'largely excluded from*
economic and social development'.   In Thailand the
missionaries *'were often arrogant and intolerant'* and
provided an intensive education remote from daily
life which led to many failures.[41]   Such brief
comments as these cannot, of course, do more than
serve as indicators of the many points of contrast
that could be elaborated if space permitted.   The
interested reader may wish to pursue these through
some of the references cited at the end of this
chapter.
     Enough has been said above to make clear the
many linkages between educational and economic development.   The latter must imply diversification of
local economies, adaptation to new and more efficient
methods and the development of monetary-based
activities, all of which necessitate the availability
of a more educated workforce, particularly in terms
of the achievement of a basic standard of literacy,
and it is the aim of any education system to provide
these.   This is undeniable.   Yet at the same time
education stands accused, as we have seen, of
impeding development: not, of course, that this is
ever a stated objective of education, but this is

allegedly an implicit effect.   This must be the fundamental paradox of education in developing countries.

NOTES

1.   D. Adams and R. Bjork, *Education in Developing Areas* (McKay, 1972).
2.   Quoted in *The Times of India*, Delhi, 17 July 1964.
3.   *Education-Sector Policy Paper*, 3rd edition (The World Bank, 1980).
4.   As quoted in *ibid*.
5.   *Ibid*.
6.   Source: *World Development Report 1985* (The World Bank, Oxford University Press, 1985).
7.   P. Coombs, *The World Educational Crisis* (Oxford University Press, 1968).
8.   R. D'Aeth, *Education and Development in the Third World* (Saxon House, 1975).
9.   J.S. Coleman, *Education and Political Development* (Princeton University Press, 1965).
10.   K. Watson, 'Colonialism and Education Development', in K. Watson (ed.), *Education in the Third World* (Croom Helm, 1982).
11.   *Ibid*.
12.   *Ibid*., quoting P. Altbach, 'Education and Neocolonialism', *Teachers College Record*, Vol.72, No.4 (1971).
13.   B. Avalos, 'Neocolonialism and Education in Latin America', in Watson (ed.), *Education in the Third World*.
14.   T. Mende, *From Aid to Recolonisation: Lessons of a Failure* (Harrap, 1973).
15.   G. Myrdal, *The Challenge of World Poverty* (Pantheon, 1970).
16.   H. Wilce, 'How Education May Harm the Third World', *The Times Educational Supplement*, 8 November 1985.
17.   Adams and Bjork, *Education in Developing Areas*.
18.   See, for example, T. Balogh, 'Education and Economic Growth', *Kyklos*, Vol.15 (1964).
19.   Adams and Bjork, *Education in Developing Areas*.
20.   K. Lillis, 'Problems Associated with Vocational Education in Less Developed Countries', in R. Garrett (ed.), *Education and Development* (Croom Helm, 1984).
21.   *Ibid*.

22.   M. Blaug, *An Introduction to the Economics of Education* (Penguin, 1972).

23.   Lillis, 'Problems Associated with Vocational Education in Less Developed Countries'.

24.   R. McNamara, in *Education-Sector Policy Paper*.

25.   R. Clark, 'Schooling as an Obstacle to Development in Zambia', in Garrett (ed.), *Education and Development*.

26.   *Ibid.*

27.   World Bank, *Education-Sector Policy Paper*.

28.   *Ibid.*

29.   D'Aeth, *Education and Development in the Third World*.

30.   e.g. M. Carnoy, *Education and Employment, A Critical Appraisal* (UNESCO, IIEP, Paris, 1977).

31.   M. Blaug, 'Common Assumptions about Education and Employment', in J. Simmons (ed.), *The Education Dilemma* (Pergamon, 1980).

32.   A. Curle, *Educational Strategy for Developing Societies* (Tavistock, 1963).

33.   International Labour Office, *Report No.1 of the Director General*, International Labour Conference, 39th Session (ILO, Geneva, 1956).

34.   D. Windham, 'The Dilemma of Educational Planning', in L. Anderson and D. Windham (eds), *Education and Development* (Lexington Books, 1982).

35.   G. Psacharopoulos and others, *Financing Education in Developing Countries* (World Bank, 1986).

36.   W. Rodney, *How Europe Underdeveloped Africa* (East African Publishing House, Dar-es-Salaam, 1972).

37.   B. Garvey, 'Education and Underdevelopment in Africa, The Historical Perspective', in Watson (ed.), *Education in the Third World*.

38.   D'Aeth, *Education and Development in the Third World*.

39.   *Ibid.*

40.   G. Howells, 'Ideology and Reform: The Effect of Military Government on Education in Brazil', in Garrett (ed.), *Education and Development*.

41.   K. Watson, 'The Contribution of Mission Schools to Educational Development in South East Asia', in Watson (ed.), *Education in the Third World*.

Chapter Thirteen

CONCLUSIONS AND FORECASTS

This book has raised many questions regarding the
relationships between the education system and the
national economy, to not all of which firm answers
can be given; this is due partly to the nature of
the material and data available, partly to the lack
of hard evidence, still, relating to various aspects
of the links between education and economic performance, and partly to the difficulty of forecasting
what the economic future holds for this country.
The connections between education and the economy,
and vice versa, have been given increased attention
in recent years and it seems likely that this trend
will continue in the years to come. Future research
is likely to seek to identify and quantify such links
in a variety of ways in which economic considerations
will feature predominantly but will not be the only
dimension and in some instances not the major ones.
This may be in considerable contrast to some of the
material, often highly technical and understandable
only to a rather limited audience, which has hither-
to comprised the subject area of the Economics of
Education.

THE ECONOMICS OF EDUCATION

> The economics of education makes an interest-
> ing case study of the development of scientific
> knowledge. In the mid-1950s it did not exist
> as an academic subject: by the mid-1960s it
> was being described by Professor Harry Johnson
> as one of the major new developments in think-
> ing about economics since the war. By the
> mid-1980s it has all but died out in Britain
> as a subject for serious academic research.[1]

Thus did Professor Williams summarise in 1985 the
rise and fall of this very technical subject area in
this country. We may note in passing that there
has since been some revival of interest in the UK
and that the subject has always been much more highly
developed in the USA where there are a number of
specialist centres on university campuses and elsewhere, including at Illinois State, Wisconsin, Stan-
ford, Berkeley, Columbia, Denver and Yale, and three
specialist journals, the *Economics of Education
Review*, the *Journal of Human Resources* and the
Journal of Education Finance. For our present
purposes it is more germane to consider implications
for the subject's development and content. These
were analysed by Professor Blaug in a review
article[2] which has attracted wide international
attention.

Blaug outlined the change of mood from the
optimism of the 1960s, when the expansion of education was seen as effectively equalising life
chances in industrial societies, to the scepticism
of the 1970s when the enrolment explosion had begun
to slow down and educational systems became the focus
of increasing criticism and much attention turned to
qualitative reform. Each of the three main traditional approaches to quantitative educational planning, the social demand approach, manpower forecasting and rate-of-return analysis, was increasingly
criticised. Sociologists had for some years been
developing the '*screening hypothesis*' and showing
how increased quantities of schooling could actually
increase observed inequalities in society rather than
decrease them and these questions, together with the
reform of education finance, especially in the USA,
became of increasing concern to economists operating
in this area.

Then came the year 1976 and the publication of
a book that was to arouse fierce controversy and
that has been hotly debated ever since, *Schooling in
Capitalist America* by Bowles and Gintis.[3] This work
argued that the traditional view that the observed
association between personal earnings and schooling
was attributable to the influence of education on
levels of cognitive knowledge was wrong or at least
inadequate. Rather, argued the authors, success at
work depended on certain non-cognitive personality
traits, the same traits that were encouraged and
rewarded in schools. These included punctuality,
docility and compliance with orders, largely required
in the mass of lower-level occupations to which
poorly-qualified school-leavers tended to be confined.

281

Only in the higher-level occupations to which graduates from higher education aspired were such
qualities as self-esteem, self-reliance and versa-
tility required. Therefore schools were to be seen
as mini-factories serving the purposes of capitalist
society: they focused on obedience and subservience,
were hierarchically organised and bred alienation,
and they fostered competition and self-interest, in
summary '*the social relations of schools reproduce
the social division of labour under capitalism*'.[4]
In Professor Blaug's words, '*most employers, whether
public or private, care less about what potential
workers know than about how they will behave*'. Nor,
Bowles and Gintis argued, was this emphasis on
effective behaviour rather than mental attainments
unintended: both teachers and employers knew that
'*educational qualities act as surrogates for qualities which employers regard as important*' and in
that sense education acted as a filter or '*screening*'
device.

If the *screening hypothesis*, with its implication that the gaining of knowledge is of rather
little significance, were to be fully accepted it
would change much of what currently passes for educational policy. Bowles's and Gintis's views have
been the subject of much criticism and most commentators, whilst accepting that there is something in
what they say, reject their conclusions: it is not
difficult to point to the many ways in which schools
do respond to the needs of society. Bowles's and
Gintis's pejorative use of the term '*capitalism*' has
particularly been attacked on the grounds that
school/society/employment relationships seem to be
much the same under socialism as under capitalism.
Amongst other criticisms, Demaine has pointed out
that Bowles and Gintis fail to make adequate allowance for social change and the ways in which this
may alter existing economic relationships.[5]

Blaug continues his review by relating the
expansion at all levels of education, and especially
higher education, in recent years to the pattern of
employers adjusting upwards their customary hiring
standards for jobs as more highly educated young
people become available. He then goes on to link
these trends to the massive rise in youth unemployment. He admits that the latter may be due partly
to changing employment requirements and partly to
increased job security for adults following recent
legislation but goes on to suggest that part of the
blame must lie with the educational expansion and
upward revision of employers' entry requirements:

> *A final element in the explanation of rising*
> *youth unemployment must be the phenomenon*
> *referred to earlier, namely, that of edu-*
> *cational inflation in which the educational*
> *hiring standards of jobs are continually raised*
> *to absorb the ever-growing number of educated*
> *entrants into the labour force ...   In other*
> *words, the problem of youth unemployment is to*
> *a considerable extent the product of the post-*
> *war explosion in post-compulsory education.*

This argument seems unconvincing. Whilst it may be
true that the trends in question will be liable to
mean that such unemployment as exists will be more
concentrated than previously on those young people
who leave school without educational qualifications -
indeed this may even be seen to have some benefit in
terms of the increased incentive it provides - they
cannot account for the incidence, in every industrialised country, of fewer workers being required in
total and mass unemployment rising.

Further, within that mass unemployment, any
explanation of why such a large percentage, as much
as 50 per cent, is concentrated on young people, must
surely include some reference to the fact that for
employers to hire young people has become, in
relation to the latter's lack of experience and
skills, considerably more expensive than previously:
those young people who do have a job are often earning more-or-less adult wage rates and are demonstr-
ably quite well-off.   Potential employers, therefore,
might just as well employ adults instead, and this
they seem increasingly to prefer to do.   If the res-
idue of this process is that large numbers of young
people are left without jobs, it seems inevitable
that the ones so affected will be those with little
in the way of educational qualifications.

Considerable space has been devoted to the
penetrating and highly-skilled analysis contained in
Professor Blaug's review article in the light of its
evident importance.   If there was a significant
omission from it, this was any reference to the quite
different problems arising in Third World countries.

THE FUTURE OF THE BRITISH ECONOMY

The immediate, short-term, economic situation in
Britain appears at the time of writing relatively
hopeful in that, save for the figure of mass unemployment, economic indicators have recently been moving

in the directions desired: inflation is low, the balance of payments situation better than had been feared, and economic growth recovering. As is typically the case in the period leading up to a general election, the next year or so may be a time of relative prosperity and, again for those fortunate enough to have a job, reasonably rising living standards.

With regard to the fundamentally more crucial long-term trends, however, it is difficult to find grounds for optimism. The UK must always depend heavily on its overseas trade and there is over- whelming evidence that, over a wide range of products, the country has been and still is losing its export markets and is also seeing large-scale penetration of imports into what were previously thought to be relatively safe home markets. (The latest scare story to have erupted, in the late summer of 1986, being that the manufacture of trucks and lorries, once a major export, seems likely to cease altogether in Britain in the near future.) This has played a major part in the story that has been told in this book. What we have seen is that there have been increasing attempts to link this secular deterior- ation in economic performance with educational trends and that in turn the worsening of the country's economic base has played a major part in the develop- ment of the financial stringency with which the edu- cation system has increasingly had to grapple.

EMPLOYMENT AND UNEMPLOYMENT PREDICTIONS

Anyone who asks young people how they see the future, in terms of their plans for education and work, can- not but be struck by the fact that their replies now almost raise the question of unemployment. Regret- tably, mass unemployment seems to be here to stay. The results have recently been published of an inten- sive investigation of trends in the use of automation in production processes in the USA over the remaining years of the twentieth century:[6] the study was based on quite conservative forecasts of future developments relating to technological change which even now, just a few months after publication, seem underestimates - e.g. it was assumed that the future increase in the use of robots and numerically-controlled machine tools in factories would be relatively slow. Even so, how- ever, the study found that capital-labour substitution would lead to significant savings in labour require- ments, of the order of 11 million fewer workers by

1990 and 20 million by the year 2000 (equivalent
figures for the UK would be 2.2 million and 4 million
respectively).

Further, within the total labour force required
there would be significant relative switches, with
much the largest decrease being for clerical workers
due to office automation: about one-third fewer
clerical workers would be needed by the year 2000.
Workers in the professional category, on the other
hand, are predicted to increase by around one-third.
Contrary to what might have been expected, the demand
for manual workers (skilled, semi-skilled and unskilled) was projected not to fall so markedly: the
number of skilled workers required would stay approximately constant in total but with switching away
from metal-working and towards construction, the number of semi-skilled and unskilled would fall by 2
million (UK equivalent = 400,000) by 1990. The
explanation apparently related to the off-setting
effects of increased production of capital goods.

This study is much the most important to have
taken place in any country regarding such future
capital-labour trends and since the research team was
headed by Professor Wassily Leontief, one of the
first Nobel prize laureates in economics, it carried
the highest credentials. The results - and particularly that relating to unemployment - clearly have
profound significance for the future of the education
system not only in terms of future work requirements
but also in terms of the increased use of leisure
time. In the absence of parallel findings for the
UK, we can only assume that similar trends will also
apply in this country. Within education, the study
projected much greater use of computers and television, both in schools and in the home, with life-
long education becoming the norm and considerable
retraining of teachers being required, probably
continuously.

It seems clear that the acquisition of educational qualifications will have more and more
importance for young people. From the point of view
both of the individual and of the national economy,
investment in education should have increased priority, especially when it is borne in mind that the
UK lags well behind its competitors in this respect.
Because skills may change and become out-of-date so
rapidly, educational emphasis should be on general
academic skills rather than specific vocational
training. If taken to heart, this would change
much current educational thinking.

EDUCATION AND VOCATIONAL RELEVANCE

Reference was made earlier to the various new
initiatives that have been taken in recent years with
a view to making the education curriculum more
directly relevant to the world of work, the two most
significant of which have been the Certificate of
Pre-Vocational Education (CPVE) and the Technical
and Vocational Training Initiative (TVEI). The
CPVE is aimed, in the words of the DES, at:

> *Young people of widely varying ability, but*
> *usually with modest examination achievement*
> *at 16+ who have set their sights on employment*
> *rather than higher education, but have not yet*
> *formed a clear idea of the kind of job they*
> *might tackle successfully, or are not yet*
> *ready to embark on a specific course of*
> *vocational education or training.*[7]

The target group is therefore rather a conglomerate
mixture but comprises essentially young people who
have not previously been very successful in their
path through the education system and who are
uncertain as to their futures; probably many of them
would not choose to remain in education at all but
for the incidence of large-scale youth unemployment
which minimises their chances of finding a job.
CPVE courses provide for such young people a common
core with major components of English Language,
Mathematics and some Science and Technology, and a
range of vocationally-oriented option courses suited
to the student's interests. Some CPVE courses
started in 1985 on a pilot or experimental basis but
the major launch of the scheme did not take place
until 1986. Although the courses will incorporate
some practical work experience, they will be mainly
school or college based; the DES expects some
80,000 students a year to enrol on these courses but
this seems an ambitious figure. What will be the
status and social esteem accorded to this new qualification must at present remain a matter for conjecture.
    The Technical and Vocational Education
Initiative has established itself quickly and has
already been greeted with some enthusiasm. TVEI
programmes began in selected secondary schools in 14
LEAs in 1983 and subsequently spread to some schools
in many, although not all, of the remaining LEAs;
colleges of further education are also involved in
the schemes in some areas, via various forms of

linking arrangements. An attraction for the
institutions is that funding for TVEI is provided,
on quite a generous scale, by the Manpower Services
Commission. The courses vary widely and much
depends on the nature and relevance of the vocational
content. Subjects such as craft, design and technology, computer familiarisation and business studies
play a significant part, as also do studies in mathematics and English language; it is noteworthy that
all new schemes of this nature have always embraced
the need to raise standards in these latter two areas.

Early indications are that both young people and
employers are responding positively to TVEI courses
and there are real hopes that the young people emerging from these courses will be successful in acquiring and retaining jobs. Needless to say, cynical
observers were not slow to point out that in the
absence of a fall in the total level of unemployment
the end result would simply be to shift the inability
to find work on to other, less fortunate, young
people. Nevertheless it seems clear that, in these
and other ways, endeavours to achieve greater
vocational relevance in education, particularly for
young people of ages 15 and 16, are finding considerable favour and will continue.

The much greater attention paid in recent years
to industrial and vocational training is part of the
same general trend. With the two-year YTS now
successfully established, large numbers of young
people are being attracted to the training offered,
and this seems likely to continue to grow. The two
major questions now at issue must be, firstly, will
the young people emerging from such training be any
more successful in securing jobs and, secondly, will
the government continue to provide funding to the
Manpower Services Commission at such generous (by
comparison with the plight of the education system
itself) levels? By the autumn of 1986 there were
grounds for pessimism regarding both of these
questions.

In the aftermath of the 1985 Green Paper *The
Development of Higher Education into the 1990s*, the
government was increasingly endeavouring to apply a
similar theme to higher education in both universities and public sector institutions. Despite widespread criticism that higher education should not
become too narrowly focused, there was little sign
of the government altering its mind on this issue.
It remains to be seen whether the expected White
Paper will indicate some change of attitude and seek
to achieve a wider consensus.

WOMEN

The position of women in society and therefore in employment and in the education system changes only slowly. Examples of outstanding individuals tend to attract media attention, from the handful of women prime ministers in the world to a woman candidate for the office of Vice-President of the United States of America; nearer home, we may cite the eminent female educationist who has recently moved from being Chief Education Officer of the Inner London Education Authority to become Master (Mistress?) of Birkbeck College, both unique appointments for a woman.

Of greater significance in the long term are the gradually increasing percentages of doctors, dentists, engineers and a range of other professions, who are women; but the overwhelming majority of women in employment are still consigned to the lowest-status and worst-paid jobs with the poorest prospects of future advancement. The position of the great majority of women in the appropriate age range to be wives and mothers means that largely they are, or feel themselves to be, geographically immobile, tied as regards hours and availability, often able to work only part-time or discontinuously, and, if they want to work at all, obliged to take such relatively unattractive jobs as are available. The return of mass unemployment in the 1980s was felt particularly severely in the kinds of jobs that are typically open to women and if the predictions of the USA study quoted above are proved correct, the changing work patterns to the year 2000 will affect most harshly clerical employment in offices, where many women with some educational qualifications have been employed. Perhaps this rather dreary picture of the working lives of the majority of women is gradually changing and improving, but only slowly: it is difficult to end this section on an optimistic note.

EFFICIENCY AND COST-EFFECTIVENESS IN EDUCATION

The search for efficiency and cost-effectiveness in education has a long history but has become the subject of renewed interest in recent years. At school level attention has focused on the research into finance and cost questions outlined in Chapters Seven and Eight and the investigations into Input-Output links detailed in Chapter Nine. Such work seems bound to continue and develop in the future. At

post-school level two developments that attracted
considerable media attention were the Audit
Commission's rather contentiously entitled report
on *Obtaining Better Value from Further Education*,[8]
and the report of the Jarratt inquiry into *Efficiency
Studies in Universities*,[9] both published within a few
months of each other in 1985.

The Audit Commission, an official body operating
under the umbrella of the Department of the Environment, has in recent years taken an increasing, and
increasingly-critical, interest in certain aspects
of education and especially public sector colleges
offering further and higher education. Its 1985
report set out in detail the reasons underlying its
view that in the management and administration of
colleges there was considerable room for improvement:
it felt that, with increased efforts and at little
cost, colleges could relatively easily recruit more
students to those courses which were not fully sub-
scribed, could make better use of college facilities
during vacation periods, could tighten their methods
of financial control and recovery of funds from
outside agencies, and save money on the costs of
each of teaching staff, non-teaching staff, energy,
purchasing and the use of space. The colleges
naturally gave the report a hostile reception but
many observers felt that the points raised by the
Commission were basically true and had been known to
those within the system for many years.

The Jarratt Report, by contrast, found relatively little to criticise within most of the six universities that it studied in detail but it did
recommend that greater cost-consciousness and more
efficient allocation of resources would be achieved
if more aspects of university administration were
costed to individual departments or courses -
examples being building space, energy costs or staff
overheads. Departments should also be given greater
powers of virement or freedom to switch expenditure
between different cost headings - e.g. to economise
on materials and supplies in order to be able to
employ an additional secretary, or vice versa.
Universities are still considering how, and to what
extent, they can implement Jarratt's proposals,
particularly regarding such devolution of financial
control. Since, as we saw in Chapter Ten, all
higher education institutions are now being required
to manage with fewer resources than previously but
with approximately the same number of students, they
have a strong incentive to take seriously the
recommendations set out by the Audit Commission and

Conclusions and Forecasts

Jarratt respectively.   It cannot be doubted that the
search for greater efficiency and cost-effectiveness
will continue.   Allied to this will be the search
for new forms of finance, very possibly including
student loans and/or education vouchers.   Lively
debate about such issues will doubtless continue
before any major changes are introduced.
     It also seems likely that in future efficiency
studies will be applied more seriously to schools,
which do after all consume the major part of the
education budget.   As we have seen, various aspects
of the financing of schools, and the connections
between what goes into schools and what comes out in
the form of the educational outcomes achieved, have
only started to be studied seriously in the last few
years.   Much greater research endeavour in this
field seems likely in the foreseeable future.

EDUCATION AND THE NATIONAL ECONOMY

The problems of the various connections between the
education system and the national economy are not
going to go away;   rather, as technological change
escalates they will become more acute.   With regard
to each of the issues mentioned above major questions
of principle arise and future policy decisions will
certainly be difficult.   By the autumn of 1986 it
was being predicted that public concern over education had become so great that this would be the
major area occupying the collective mind of the
government over the period of the run-up to the next
general election.   It would probably be little con-
solation to those concerned to say that however
serious such problems might seem in a country such
as the UK, they do not bear comparison with the quite
massive scale of the similar problems confronting the
developing countries in the Third World.
     Pressures on the educational budget will con-
tinue to be severe, increasingly so unless there is
a marked improvement in economic productivity which
must always be the basis of the country's earning
power.   It will therefore be difficult to escape
from the vicious circle in which economic retrenchment leads to cuts in expenditure on education which
in turn, imperceptibly and in the longer run, lead
to further deterioration in economic performance.
Much is expected of the new Secretary of State who
took up office in 1986 and in his few months in that
position to date Mr Baker has certainly given the
impression of understanding the need for change and

290

for bringing additional resources into the education system.

To achieve the correct balance between vocational orientation and those other wider goals which any education system ought to try to achieve will not be easy. It may be fitting to end this book with the following salutory words taken from the 1985 Green Paper:

> *The economic performance of the United Kingdom since 1945 has been disappointing compared to the achievements of others. The Government believes that it is vital for our higher education to contribute more effectively to the improvement of the performance of the economy. This is not because the Government places a low value on the general cultural benefits of education and research. Nor does it place a low value on the study of the humanities which, provided that high academic standards are applied, enriches the lives of students, helps to set the moral and social framework of our society, and prepares students well for many types of employment. The reason is simply that, unless the country's economic performance improves, we shall be even less able than now to afford many of the things that we value most - including education for pleasure and general culture and the financing of scholarship and research as an end in itself.*

NOTES

1. G.L. Williams, 'Rates of Return' (review article), *The Times Higher Education Supplement*, 21 June 1985.

2. M. Blaug, 'Where Are We Now in the Economics of Education?', *Economics of Education Review*, Vol.4, No.1 (1985).

3. S. Bowles and H. Gintis, *Schooling in Capitalist America* (Basic Books, New York, 1976).

4. *Ibid.*

5. J. Demaine, *Contemporary Theories in the Sociology of Education* (Macmillan, 1981).

6. W. Leontief and F. Duchin, *The Future Impact of Automation on Workers* (Oxford University Press, 1986).

7. Department of Education and Science, *17+, A New Qualification* (DES, 1982).

8. Audit Commission: *Obtaining Better Value*

from Further Education (Department of the Environment, 1985).

9. Committee of Vice-Chancellors and Principals: *Report of the Steering Committee for Efficiency Studies in Universities* (Jarratt Report) (CVCP, 1985).

BIBLIOGRAPHY

Adams, C. and Laurikietis, R. (1976) *The Gender
    Trap*, Virago, Quartet Books
Adams, D. and Bjork, R. (1972) *Education in Develop-
    ing Areas*, McKay
Alcock, J.A. (1979) 'A Case-History of the Merger
    Between Battersea College of Education and the
    Polytechnic of the South Bank', unpublished
    MA thesis, University of London
Amsden, A.H. (ed.) (1980) *The Economics of Women
    and Work*, Penguin
Anderson, C.A. (1965) 'Literacy and Schooling in the
    Development Threshold: Some Historical Cases'
    in C.A. Anderson and M.J. Bowman (eds) *Education
    and Economic Development*, Aldine Press
Anderson, L. and Windham, D. (eds) (1982) *Education
    and Development*, Lexington Books
Atkinson, J. (1982) *Evaluation of Apprentice Support
    Awards*, Institute of Manpower Studies
Avalos, B. (1982) 'Neocolonialism and Education in
    Latin America' in E. Watson (ed.) *Education in
    the Third World*, Croom Helm
Averch, H. and others (1972) *A Critical Review and
    Synthesis of Research Findings: A Report to the
    President's Commission on School Finance*, Rand
Barker, D. and Allen, S. (eds) (1972) *Dependence and
    Exploitation in Marriage and Work*, Longman
Barnow, B. (1975) *The Productivity of Primary Edu-
    cation in Pennsylvania*, Working Paper No.14,
    University of Pittsburgh
Barron, R.D. and Norris, D.M. (1976) 'Sexual Divisions
    and the Dual Labour Market' in D. Barker and
    S. Allen (eds) *Dependence and Exploitation in
    Work and Marriage*, Longman
Bates, I. and others (1984) *Schooling for the Dole*,
    Macmillan
Baxter, C. and others (eds) (1977) *Economics and*

Economic Policy, Longman
Becker, G.S. (1974) *Human Capital: A Theoretical and Empirical Analysis, with special reference to Education*, Princeton University Press
Birley, D. (1970) *The Education Officer and His World*, Routledge and Kegan Paul
Blaug, M. (ed.) (1968) *Economics of Education*, Vols 1 and 2, Penguin
—— (1970) *An Introduction to the Economics of Education*, Penguin
—— (1980) 'Common Assumptions About Education and Employment' in J. Simmons (ed.) *The Education Dilemma*, Pergamon
Boaden, N. (1971) *Urban Policy-Making: Influences on County Boroughs in England and Wales*, Cambridge University Press
Bosworth, D. (1981) 'Technological Manpower' in R. Lindley (ed.) *Higher Education and the Labour Market*, SRHE, Leverhulme
—— and Wilson, R. (1980) 'The Labour Market for Scientists and Technologists' in R.M. Lindley (ed.) *Economic Change and Employment Policy*, Macmillan
Bowles, S. and Gintis, H. (1976) *Schooling in Capitalist America*, Basic Books, New York
Bowman, M.J. and Anderson, C.A. (1963) 'Concerning the Role of Education in Development' in C. Geertz (ed.) *Old Societies and New States*, Free Press
Burkhead, J., Fox, T. and Holland, J. (1967) *Input and Output in Large-City High Schools*, Syracuse University Press
Burton, R. (ed.) (1970) 'Education Finance at Local Level' in *The Teacher as Manager*, National Council for Educational Technology
Bush, T. and others (eds) (1980) *Approaches to School Management*, Harper and Row
Byrne, D., Williamson, B. and Fletcher, B. (1975) *The Poverty of Education*, Martin Robertson
Byrne, E. (1971) *Planning and Educational Inequalities*, NFER
Cantor, L.M. and Roberts, I.F. (1983) *Further Education Today: A Critical Review*, 2nd edn, Routledge and Kegan Paul, and 3rd edn (1986)
Carnoy, M. (1977) *Education and Employment: A Critical Appraisal*, UNESCO, IIEP, Paris
Carroll, S. and Park, R. (1983) *The Search for Equity in School Finance*, Ballinger
Carter, M. (1966) *Into Work*, Pelican
Cavendish, R. (1982) *Women on the Line*, Routledge and Kegan Paul

Caves, R. (ed.) (1968) *Britain's Economic Prospects*,
    Brookings Institute, Allen and Unwin
Clarke, R. (1984) 'Schooling as an Obstacle to
    Development in Zambia' in R. Garrett (ed.)
    Education and Development, Croom Helm
Cohen, C.D. (ed.) (1982) *Agenda for Britain 2: Macro
    Policy Choices for the 80's*, Philip Allan
Cohen, P. (1984) 'Against the New Vocationalism' in
    I. Bates and others *Schooling for the Dole*,
    Macmillan
Cohn, E. (1975), *Input-Output Analysis in Public
    Education*, Ballinger
Coleman, J.S. (1965) *Education and Political Develop-
    ment*, Princeton University Press
—— and others (1966) *Equality of Opportunity:
    Summary*, Government Printing Office, Washington
    D.C.
Committee of Vice-Chancellors and Principals (1985)
    *Report of the Steering Committee for Efficiency
    Studies in Universities* (Jarratt Report), CVCP
Coombs, P. (1968) *The World Educational Crisis*,
    Oxford University Press
—— and Hallak, J. (1972) *Managing Educational
    Costs*, Oxford University Press
Crowther Report (1959) *Central Advisory Council for
    Education in 15-18*, HMSO
Cumming, C. (1971) *Studies in Educational Costs*,
    Scottish Academic Press
Curle, A. (1963) *Educational Strategy for Developing
    Countries*, Tavistock
D'Aeth, R. (1975) *Education and Development in the
    Third World*, Saxon House
Dainton Report: Great Britain, Command Papers (1968)
    *Enquiry into the Flow of Candidates in Science
    and Technology into Higher Education*, Cmnd 3451,
    HMSO
Daniel, W.W. and others (1980) *Maternity Rights:
    the Experience of Women*, Policy Studies
    Institute
Demaine, J. (1981) *Contemporary Theories in the
    Sociology of Education*, Macmillan
Denison, E.F. (1962) *The Sources of Economic Growth
    in the United States*, Committee for Economic
    Development, New York
—— (1964) 'Proportion of Income Differentials
    Among Education Groups due to Additional
    Education' in J. Vaizey (ed.) *The Residual
    Factor and Economic Growth*, OECD
Dennison, W.F. (1984) *Educational Finance and
    Resources*, Croom Helm
Dex, S. (1975) *The Sexual Division of Work*,

Harvester Press

Edwards, T. (1984) *The Youth Training Scheme: A New Curriculum. Episode One*, Falmer Press

Elias, P. and Main, B. (1982) *Women's Working Lives: Evidence from the National Training Survey*, Institute for Employment Research, University of Warwick

Finniston Report: Great Britain, Command Papers (1980) *Engineering Our Future*, Cmnd 7794, HMSO

Fowler, G. and others (eds) (1973) *Decision-Making in British Education*, Heinemann

Freeman, C. (1982) 'The Economic Implications of Microelectronics' in C.D. Cohen (ed.) *Agenda for Britain 1: Micro Policy Choices for the 80's*, Philip Allan

Gaines, A. and Turner, N. (1985) *Student Loans: the Costs and Consequences*, National Union of Students

Galbraith, J. K. (1958) *The Affluent Society*, Pelican

Gannicott, K. and Blaug, M. (1977) 'Scientists and Engineers in Britain' in C. Baxter and others (eds) *Economics and Education Policy*, Longman

Garrett, R. (ed.) (1984) *Education and Development*, Croom Helm

Garvey, B. (1982) 'Education and Underdevelopment in Africa: the Historical Perspective' in K. Watson (ed.) *Education in the Third World*, Croom Helm

Geertz, C. (ed.) (1963) *Old Societies and New States*, Free Press

Glennerster, H. and Wilson, G. (1970) *Paying for Private Schools*, Allan Lane

Gray, J. and others (1983) *Reconstructions of Secondary Education: Theory, Myth and Practice since the War*, Routledge and Kegan Paul

Great Britain, Command Papers (1977) *University Grants Committee: Annual Review for 1975-6*, Cmnd 6750, HMSO

——— (1977) *Education in Schools*, Cmnd 6869, HMSO

——— (1985) *Better Schools*, Cmnd 9469, HMSO

——— (1985) *The Development of Higher Education into the 1990s*, Cmnd 9524, HMSO

Great Britain, Department of Education and Science (annually) *Statistics of Education*, Vols 1 to 5, HMSO

——— (1963) *A Plan for Polytechnics and Other Colleges: Higher Education in the Further Education System*, HMSO

——— (1972) *Education: A Framework for Expansion*, HMSO

——— (1982) *17+: A New Qualification*, HMSO

Great Britain, Department of the Environment
(annually) *Local Government Financial
Statistics*, HMSO
—— (1985) Audit Commission, *Obtaining Better Value
from Further Education*, HMSO
Hannon, V. (1979) 'Education for Sex Equality:
What's the Problem?' in D. Rubinstein (ed.)
Education and Equality, Penguin
Harbison, F. and Myers, G. (1964) *Education, Man-
power and Economic Growth*, McGraw-Hill
Hartman, R.W. (1977) 'The Distribution of Benefits
of Student Loans' in C. Baxter and others (eds)
Economics and Education Policy, Longman
Hencke, D. (1978) *Colleges in Crisis*, Penguin
Henderson, P.D. (1968) 'Investment Criteria for
Public Enterprises' in R. Turvey (ed.) *Public
Enterprise*, Penguin
Hill, S. (1981) *Competition and Control at Work*,
Heinemann
Hirszowicz, M. (1981) *Industrial Sociology*, Martin
Robertson
Hough, J.R. (1981) *A Study of School Costs*, NFER,
Nelson
—— (1982) *Educational Policy: An International
Survey*, Croom Helm
—— (1982) *The French Economy*, Croom Helm
Howells, G. (1982) 'Ideology and Reform: the Effect
of Military Government on Education in Brazil'
in R.M. Garrett (ed.) *Education and Development*,
Croom Helm
Hunt, A. (1975) *Management Attitudes and Practices
Towards Women at Work*, OPCS, HMSO
Hurstfield, J. (1978) *The Part-Time Trap: Part-Time
Workers in Britain Today*, Low Pay Unit
Institute of Manpower Studies (1984) *Competence and
Competition: Training and Education in the
Federal Republic of Germany, the United States
and Japan*, NECD, Manpower Services Commission
Institution of Electrical Engineers (1984) *Evidence
to House of Lords Select Commission on Science
and Technology*, IEE
Institution of Production Engineers (1984) *Press
Release No.6852*, IPE
International Labour Office (1956) *Report No.1 of
the Director General, International Labour
Conference, 39th Session*, ILO, Geneva
Jackson Report: Great Britain, Command Papers (1965)
Committee on Manpower Resources for Science and
Technology, *A Review of the Scope and Problems
of Scientific and Technological Manpower Policy*,
Cmnd 2800, HMSO

James Report: Great Britain, Department of Education
and Science (1972) *Teacher Education and Train-
ing*, HMSO
James, H., Kelly, J. and Garms, W. (1966) *Determin-
ants of Educational Expenditures in Large Cities
of the United States*, US Office of Education
Joseph, G. (1983) *Women at Work: the British
Experience*, Philip Allan
Knight, B. (1977) *The Cost of Running a School*,
Occasional Paper No.6, Scottish Centre for
Studies in School Administration
────── (1983) *Managing School Finance*, Heinemann
Lawyers Committee for Civil Rights under the Law
(1977) *Summary of State-Wide School Finance
Cases since 1973*, Lawyers Committee for Civil
Rights under the Law, Washington D.C.
Layard, R. (ed.) (1972) *Cost-Benefit Analysis*,
Penguin
Leontief, W. and Duchin, F. (1986) *The Future Impact
of Automation on Workers*, Oxford University
Press
Lewis, A., Sanford, C. and Thomson, N. (1980)
Grants or Loans?, Research Monograph No.34,
Institute of Economic Affairs
Lewis, A.M. (1983) *Descriptions of the Vocational
Training Systems - United Kingdom*, European
Centre for the Development of Vocational
Training, Berlin
Lillis, K. (1984) 'Problems Associated with
Vocational Education in Less Developed
Countries' in R. Garrett (ed.) *Education and
Development*, Croom Helm
Lindley, R. (ed.) (1980) *Economic Change and Employ-
ment Policy*, Macmillan
────── (ed.) (1981) *Higher Education and the Labour
Market*, SRHE, Leverhulme
Lonsdale, S. (1985) *Work and Inequality*, Longman
Lord, R. (1984) *Value for Money in Education*, CIPFA
McNally, F. (1979) *Women for Hire*, Macmillan
Machlup, F. (1962) *The Production and Distribution
of Knowledge in the United States*, Princeton
University Press
Mahoney, P. (1985) *Schools for Boys?*, Hutchinson
Marks, J. and others (1983) *Standards in English
Schools*, National Council for Educational
Standards
Martin, J. and Roberts, C. (1984) *Women and Employ-
ment: A Lifetime Perspective*, OPCS and Depart-
ment of Employment, HMSO
Maynard, A. (1975) *Experiment with Choices in
Education*, Hobart Paper No.64, Institute of

Economic Affairs

Mende, T. (1973) *From Aid to Recolonisation: Lessons of a Failure*, Harrap

Mincher, J. and Polachek, S. (1980) 'Family Investments in Human Capital', in A.H. Amsden (ed.) *The Economics of Women and Work*, Penguin

Morris, V. (1973) 'Investment in Higher Education in England and Wales' in G. Fowler and others (eds) *Decision-Making in British Education*, Heinemann

Moser, C. and Layard, R. (1968) 'Estimating the Need for Highly Qualified Manpower in Britain' in M. Blaug (ed.) *Economics of Education*, Vol.1, Penguin

Mumford, E. and Banks, O. (1982) *The Computer and the Clerk*, Routledge and Kegan Paul

Myrdal, G. (1970) *The Challenge of World Poverty*, Pantheon

National Council for Civil Liberties (1973) *Women's Rights*, NCCL

National Economic Development Council (1982) *Education and Industry: Memorandum by the Director General*, NEDC (82) 55, NEDO

Newsom Report: Central Advisory Council for Education in England (1963) *Half Our Future*, HMSO

Parker, S.R. and others (1981) *The Sociology of Industry*, Allen and Unwin

Parnes, H.S. (1977) 'Planning Education for Economic and Social Development' in C. Baxter and others (eds) *Economics and Education Policy*, Longman

Pearson, R., Hutt, R. and Parsons, D. (1984) *Education Training and Employment*, Series No.4, Institute of Manpower Studies, Gower

Peschek, D. and Brand, J. (1966) *Policies and Politics in Secondary Education: Case Studies in West Ham and Reading*, Greater London Papers 11, London School of Economics

Pollert, A. (1981) *Girls, Wives, Factory Lives*, Macmillan

Pratt, J. and others (1973) *Your Local Education*, Penguin

Psacharopoulos, G. (1973) *Returns to Education*, Elsevier

—— and others (1986) *Financing Education in Developing Countries*, World Bank

Rice, L.D. (ed.) (1977) *Student Loans: Problems and Policy Alternatives*, New York College Entrance Examinations Board

Robbins, Lord (1979) *The Taming of Governments*,

Readings 21, Institute of Economic Affairs
Robbins Report: Great Britain, Command Papers (1953)
Higher Education, Cmnd 2154, HMSO
Rodney, W. (1972) *How Europe Underdeveloped Africa*,
East African Publishing House, Dar-es-Salaam
Routh, G. (1980) *Occupation and Pay in Great Britain
1906-79*, Macmillan
Rubinstein, D. (ed.) (1979) *Education and Equality*,
Penguin
Russell Report: Great Britain, Department of
Education and Science (1973), Committee of
Enquiry on Adult Education, *Adult Education: A
Plan for Development*, HMSO
Rutter, M. and others (1979) *Fifteen Thousand Hours:
Secondary Schools and Their Effects on Children*,
Open Books
Sanders, D. and Reed, J. (1982) *Kitchen Sink or Swim?*,
Penguin
Seear, B.N. (1971) *Re-Entry of Women to the Labour
Market after an Interruption in Employment*, OECD
Sharpe, S. (1976) *Just Like a Girl*, Pelican
Simmons, J. (ed.) (1980) *The Education Dilemma*,
Pergamon
Smith, R. (1984) *Access and Recruitment to Engineer-
ing*, Kingston Polytechnic (mimeo.)
Steedman, J. (1983) *Examination Results in Selective
and Non-Selective Schools*, National Children's
Bureau
Stillman, A. and Meychell, K. (1986), *Choosing
Schools - Parents, LEAs, and the 1980 Act*,
NFER, Nelson
Stone, J. and Taylor, F. (1976) *The Parent's School-
book*, Penguin
Taylor, G. (ed.) (1970) *The Teacher as Manager*,
National Council for Educational Technology
Thomas, J. (1971) *The Productive School*, Wiley
Tizard, B. and others (1980) *Fifteen Thousand Hours:
A Discussion*, University of London Institute of
Education
Turvey, R. (ed.) (1968) *Public Enterprise*, Penguin
University Grants Committee (1981) 'Procedure Lead-
ing to the 1981-82 Grant Distribution',
Appendix to Chairman's letter to Select
Committee for Education, Science and the Arts,
2 November
Vaizey, J. (1958) *The Costs of Education*, Allen and
Unwin
—— (1962) *The Economics of Education*, Faber
—— (ed.) (1964) *The Residual Factor and Economic
Growth*, OECD
—— and Sheehan, J. (1968) *Resources for Education*,

Allen and Unwin
—— and others (1972) *The Political Economy of
Education*, Duckworth
Watson, K. (1982) 'Colonialism and Education Develop-
ment' in K. Watson (ed.) *Education in the Third
World*, Croom Helm
—— (1982) 'The Contribution of Mission Schools to
Educational Development in South East Asia' in
K. Watson (ed.) *Education in the Third World*,
Croom Helm
—— (ed.) (1982) *Education in the Third World*,
Croom Helm
Weiler, D. and others (1977) 'The First Year at Alum
Rock' in C. Baxter and others (eds) *Economics
and Education Policy*, Longman
West, J. (ed.) (1982) *Work, Women and the Labour
Market*, Routledge and Kegan Paul
Williams, G.L. (1977) 'The Events of 1973-4 in a
Long-Term Planning Perspective' in C. Baxter
and others (eds) *Economics and Education Policy*,
Longman
Windham, D. (1982) 'The Dilemma of Educational Plan-
ning' in L. Anderson and D. Windham (eds)
Education and Development, Lexington Books
Woodhall, M. (1972) *Economic Aspects of Education*,
NFER
—— (1977) 'The Economic Returns to Investment in
Women's Education' in C. Baxter and others
(eds) *Economics and Education Policy*, Longman
—— (1982) *Student Loans: Lessons from Recent Inter-
national Experience*, Paper No.605, Policy Studies
Studies Institute
World Bank (1980) *Education-Sector Policy Paper*,
3rd edn, World Bank
—— (1985) *World Development Report 1985*, OUP
Wragg, E. and others (1980) *The Rutter Research*,
University of Exeter School of Education
Young, M. (1971) *Knowledge and Control: New Directions
for the Sociology of Education*, Collier
Macmillan
Ziderman, A. (1977) 'Does It Pay To Take A Degree?
The Profitability of Private Investment in
University Education in Britain', in C. Baxter
and others (eds) *Economics and Education Policy*,
Longman